The Great European Stage Directors

Volume 4

The Great European Stage Directors
Series Editor: Simon Shepherd

The Great European Stage Directors

Volume 4

Reinhardt, Jessner, Barker

Edited by Michael Patterson
Series Editor: Simon Shepherd

methuen | drama
LONDON · NEW YORK · OXFORD · NEW DELHI · SYDNEY

METHUEN DRAMA
Bloomsbury Publishing Plc
50 Bedford Square, London, WC1B 3DP, UK
1385 Broadway, New York, NY 10018, USA
29 Earlsfort Terrace, Dublin 2, Ireland

BLOOMSBURY, METHUEN DRAMA and the Methuen Drama logo are trademarks of
Bloomsbury Publishing Plc

First published in hardback in Great Britain 2019
Reprinted 2019
This paperback edition 2024

Cover design: Adriana Brioso
Cover image: Deutsches Theatre. (© imageBROKER/Alamy Stock Photo)

A catalogue record for this book is available from the British Library.

A catalog record for this book is available from the Library of Congress.

ISBN: HB: 978-1-4742-5397-0
          HB Pack: 978-1-4742-5411-3
              PB: 978-1-3504-4580-2
          PB Set: 978-1-3504-4598-7
            ePDF: 978-1-4742-5991-0
           eBook: 978-1-3504-6191-8

Series: Great Stage Directors

Typeset by Integra Software Services Pvt. Ltd.
Printed and bound in Great Britain

To find out more about our authors and books visit www.bloomsbury.com and sign up for
our newsletters.

To Natasa

CONTENTS

LIST OF ILLUSTRATIONS

NOTES ON CONTRIBUTORS

Philippa Burt is Lecturer in Theatre and Performance Theory at Goldsmiths College, University of London. Her research interests include the sociology of the theatre; directorial processes, focusing on the work of ensemble companies; twentieth-century British theatre; the performer–spectator relationship; immersive theatre; installation art; and the problematics of social and architectural space. She has published three articles, including one on Harley Granville Barker and Fabian Theatre (2012).

Colin Chambers, formerly a journalist, theatre critic and Literary Manager of the Royal Shakespeare Company (1981–97), is Professor of Drama at Kingston University. His books include *Other Spaces: New Theatre and the RSC* (1980), *The Story of Unity Theatre* (1989) and the award-winning *Peggy: the Life of Margaret Ramsay, Play Agent* (1997). He has also edited *The Continuum Companion to Twentieth Century Theatre* (2002) and *Granville Barker on Theatre* (Bloomsbury, 2017).

Sascha Förster is Research Associate and Junior Lecturer at the University of Cologne. His research interests include Fundus and repertoire; material conditions of performance; theatre historiography; interplay of memory, history and theatre; theatre architecture; performance and game studies; queer performance historiography; theatre merchandizing; post-dramatic theatre. He is the author of *Versprechungen, Gemeinschaften und Identitäten bei den Thomas-Münzer-Festspielen 1931 in Bad Frankenhausen* (Promises, Communities and Identities at the Thomas Münzer Festival 1931 in Bad Frankenhausen, 2014) and of several articles and chapters in edited volumes.

Matthias Heilmann is Dramaturg at the Municipal Theatre of Fürth in Bavaria. His research interests include *Regietheater* (Director's Theatre) and Leopold Jessner. He is author of *Leopold Jessner: Intendant der Republik* (2005) and editor of Andras Batta, *Opera: Composers, Works, Performers* (2010).

Michael Patterson was Emeritus Professor of Theatre and taught at five universities in the UK. His publications include *The Revolution in German Theatre 1900–1933* (1981); *Peter Stein* (1981); *Strategies of Political Theatre* (2003); *The Oxford Dictionary of Plays* (2005); and *The Oxford Guide* *to Plays* (2007); for Bloomsbury he edited *Büchner: the Complete Plays* (1987); and he wrote over twenty articles and chapters in edited volumes.

Ann-Christine Simke Lecturer in Performance at University of the West of Scotland. She gained a PhD for her thesis on 'Berlinische Dramaturgie, Dramaturgical Practices in the German Metropolis in the 20th and 21st Centuries'. She has read papers at several international conferences, written book reviews and co-authored one article on 'Theatre as Community Art' (2014).

ACKNOWLEDGEMENTS

Grateful acknowledgement is due to the following for the use of copyright material: Cambridge University Press, Deutsches Theater Berlin, Duke University Press, Felix Bloch Erben/Desch Verlag, Fischer/Krüger Verlag, Harper Collins, Harvard University Press, Henschelverlag, Kovač Verlag, Manchester University Press, Max Niemeyer Verlag, Midwest Modern Language Association, *Modern Language Review*, Orell Füssli/Atlantis Verlag, Oxford University Press, Peter Lang Verlag, Professor Klaus Völker, Suhrkamp Verlag, Residenzverlag, Routledge, Rowman & Littlefield, The Society of Authors as the Literary Representative of the Estate of Harley Granville Barker, *Theater heute, Theatre Research International,* Ullstein/Propyläen Verlag, University of Minnesota Press, *Die Zeit.*

Philippa Burt wishes to thank for their support the Andrew W. Mellon Foundation Research Fellowship Endowment at the Harry Ransom Center, University of Texas at Austin.

We also wish to thank the following for supplying and granting permission for the use of illustrations: The British Library; Getty Images; Theaterwissenschaftliche Sammlung, Schloss Wahn, University of Cologne; ArenaPAL/University of Bristol; Yale University.

Every effort has been made to trace copyright holders and to obtain their permission for the use of copyright material. The publisher apologizes for any errors or omissions in the above list and would be grateful if notified of any corrections that should be incorporated in future reprints or editions of this book.

Introduction to the Series

Simon Shepherd

The beginnings of directing

Directors have become some of the celebrities of contemporary theatre. Yet for most of its life, and across a range of practices, theatre has managed perfectly well without directors, celebrated or otherwise.

This is not to say that it has lacked direction, so to speak. Some form of directing, by actors, prompters, stage managers, designers, has always featured as an activity within theatre's processes. What was new was the concept that directing should be done by a role specifically dedicated to that purpose. Emerging around the 1890s after many centuries of theatre, it was both a historical novelty and geographically limited, to Europe and North America.

What these cultures had in common, at the start of the twentieth century, were the ideas and practices which we now call Modernism. In the arts it is associated with particular sorts of innovation made by short-lived movements such as Constructivism, Dada, Expressionism and Surrealism. But modernist thinking also influenced industrial innovation. This is seen in the creation of what F.W. Taylor called 'scientific' management, the systematization and hence separation of the role of a manager who bears responsibility for planning and oversight of the production process. As I have argued before,[1] the concept of director comes to be formulated at the same time as a managerial class is becoming defined. The value put upon the activity of management might be said to create the conditions for, and justify, the creation of a separable role of director.

This was apparent to Barker in 1911 when he observed that in Germany it was precisely the proliferation of management duties that made it impossible to combine the role of manager with that of actor. But German practice was perhaps in advance of the rest of Europe. Many of those now regarded as the founders of directing appeared to work in very similar ways to those who are not categorized as directors. Antoine ran his own company, selected the repertoire, took acting roles and directed plays, as did Stanislavski and Copeau. In this respect their practice differed little from, say, Henry Irving or Herbert Beerbohm Tree, both regarded as actor-managers.

Where the practice of the early directors seems consistently distinct throughout Europe is in its cultural, and sometimes political, positioning. Antoine, Copeau, Barker, Piscator, among others, positioned themselves against a dominant theatrical culture which they aimed to challenge and change. This positioning was an ideological project and hence brought with it an assumption of, or claim to, enlightened vision, artistic mission, the spirit of innovation. Adopting this rhetoric Antoine declared that directors had never existed before – that he was the first of a kind. When P.P. Howe wrote his 1910 book on that new organizational phenomenon the repertory theatre he distinguished the new director from the old stage manager on the grounds that, while the stage manager was adept at controlling the 'mechanical' aspects of the stage, the director was the guardian of the 'vision'.[2] This aesthetic formulation is, though, wholly cognate with management as industrially understood, as Alexander Dean makes clear. In 1926 he recommended that each company should have one person in the role of overall director because the director is not only responsible for each production but also, crucially, is 'the great connecting link between all parts of the organization'. Furthermore: 'Every organization needs a leader who has a vision; who sees a great achievement ahead.'[3] The non-mechanical visionary is also the Taylorist planner.

But some, it seems, were more visionary than others. You will have noted that none of the directors so far mentioned is North American. Yet while Antoine, Copeau and others were founding their theatres outside the mainstream, the same was happening in the United States. The Little Theatres of Chicago and New York started in 1912, the Neighbourhood Playhouse (New York), Portmanteau Theatre and Washington Square Players followed in 1915–16. Contemporary commentators such as Constance D'Arcy Mackay (1917) saw both the European and the American experiments as part of the same 'little theatre' movement.[4] Their practices look similar: founding theatres, against the dominant; culturally selecting audiences, possibly by a membership scheme; working with amateurs; performing explicitly naturalist dramatists, such as Ibsen. But while Antoine and Copeau have entered the canon of great directors, Winthrop Ames and Alice and Irene Lewisohn have not.

Reflecting on the contrast between North American and European practices, William Lyon Phelps suggested in 1920 that the United States lacked a public discourse that would take theatre as seriously as cars. His argument built on Moderwell (1914) and was taken up by Dean (1926).[5] Both saw little theatres as the mechanism for developing a larger theatre-going public, and hence were primarily interested in their success as organizational and economic entities, being much less interested in directors as artists. In Britain similar arguments proposed repertory theatre and the amateur movement as the mechanisms for building both democracy and a dramatic renaissance. Theatre, Barker argued in 1910, is a 'sociable' art. Thus North American and British discussions proposed that theatre could develop the cultural accomplishments of civil society. European discourses, meanwhile, were more interested in, and driven by, avant-gardist movements and experiment. For instance, Antoine positioned himself within an already existing public discourse about art, allying himself with the naturalist, and anti-racist, Zola; staging censored playwrights; distributing Strindberg's polemical preface to *Fröken Julie* (*Miss Julie*) – and making sure to invite reviewers to his theatre. For Piscator and Brecht the energizing link was to activists and ideas within both the political and the artistic avant-garde. The European director thus acquired the status of artistic activist, linked to and recognizable by existing networks of activists and makers, with their own mechanisms for dissemination and publicity. The European avant-garde, long celebrated as the supposed origins of performance art, was perhaps more clearly the originating moment of the theatre director.

The discursive position of European directors was consolidated by their own pronouncements and publications. Each of the early directors was adept in an established theatre craft, as were actor-managers. But when Barker, Meyerhold or Saint-Denis lectured on and wrote about the crafts of theatre, and even more when directors established regimes of training, they were showing themselves to be not just practitioners but theorists of a craft, not so much mechanics as visionaries. The early directors, and indeed directors since, claimed to understand how theatre works as an art form, and to have proposals for its future developments. In this sense they show themselves to be not only guardians of the vision of the play but also guardians of a vision of how theatre itself can and should work. The success of the claim to be visionary is evidence that what the director manages is not just the company or production but also the discourse about them.

Taken together new ideas about management, avant-garde practices and theories of theatre enabled the formulation of, and justified, a separated role of director. The role could then be seen as providing a specialism, missing hitherto, which is necessary to ensure the artistic seriousness and importance of theatre.

While the mechanism that formulated the role of director may have been discursive, its consequences were much more than that. Properly to carry out the guardianship of the vision meant taking responsibility for ensuring the aims and coherence of the processes of theatre-making. The artistic visionary slides into place as Dean's industrial manager. The discursive formulation results in actual power over other theatre workers. The director's control can determine not just that which is staged but also the hiring, if not firing, of those who stage it.

With the invention of directors a new power structure emerges. Yet it had been, and is, perfectly possible to make theatre without that role and its power structure. So there is a potential tension between the effectiveness and productivity of the crafts necessary for theatre and the new, but not demonstrably necessary, power structure that came to claim organizational authority over those crafts. This tension has made the role of director important and yet unstable, treated as celebrity and yet, after only a century, subject to questions as to whether it is actually necessary.

Those questions have been asked not least by directors themselves. Tangled up with the other issues summarized above they run through the volumes of this series. For the directors here have been selected not only because they are generally taken to be important, indeed 'great', but also because they reflect in interesting ways on the role of directing itself. Of course there are other important names, and interesting reflections, which have not made it into the selection list. Decisions such as these are usually difficult and almost always never satisfactory to everybody. But more stories are told than those of big names. The featured directors are not important because they possess some solitary essence of greatness but because they offer ways into, and are symptomatic of, a range of different practices and ideas. The discussion of each featured director frequently involves other directors, as well as designers, writers and actors with whom they worked and by whom they were influenced. For example, the authors of Volume 3 insist that we move our focus outwards from the featured male directors to attend to the women with whom they collaborated and on whom they depended.

The series begins with some of the earliest examples of the practice, but the only other chronological principle governing the distribution of directors is the decision to create two groups of volumes falling roughly either side of the midpoint of the twentieth century. What this arrangement highlights is the extent to which the practice of directing generates a system of self-reference as it rapidly developed an extensive discourse of its own very new art. Thus, for example, Volume 6 features directors who engage with, and perpetuate, the practices and legacy of Brecht.

Rather than suggesting a chronologically seamless evolution of practices the distribution of the directors across the series seeks to call attention to debate. Volume 1 deals with Naturalism, Volume 2 with critiques of Naturalism. The aim is to provoke thinking not so much about the director as an individual as about the art of directing in its different approaches and concerns. The vision of which the director is guardian and the assumptions as to what constitutes the art of directing are revealed as diverse and provisional. For some directors their creative work mainly involves the staging of their ideas about the world, for others creativity comes in the design of processes and the management of people, for yet others creativity has to do with the design and management of theatres. While Brook's philosophy of life may have constructed powerful and influential stagings, Guthrie's philosophy of life more or less invented the equally powerful, and perhaps more influential, concept of the role of artistic director.

If Volumes 1 and 2 display contrasted aesthetic approaches, Volume 3 has us focus on directors as founders and managers of companies and theatres. That topic of company formation and management returns again, in the context of the latter part of the twentieth century, in Volume 7. In a similar way Volume 4 brings together directors who may be seen as auteurs working within a modernist climate while Volume 5 gives us auteurs emerging from a post-Second World War Europe. In Volume 8, the directors are also auteurs, perhaps most powerfully so in that there is often no dramatist's text. But at the same time here the role of director begins to wobble, blurring into that of choreographer or visual artist.

In exploring the various directors, it becomes clear that, as noted above, some directors are major contributors to the discourses about directing, both reflecting on practices in general and foregrounding their own work in particular. This has an effect on their apparent status within the field. The existence of texts authored by directors often facilitates the study of those directors by others, which in turn generates more texts and elevates their apparent status, as a sort of greatness-construction machine. But there are other directors who are less textually established, perhaps because the director actively refuses to document their work, as did Planchon, or perhaps because there are cultural or geographical boundaries that English-speaking academics tend not to cross, as is the case of Strehler. Or it may be that directors have simply fallen out of theatrical or academic fashion, as, say, for Saint-Denis. That they are no longer, or ever were, serviced by the contemporary greatness-construction machine does not make these directors any less significant. Celebrity is not in itself necessarily relevant to being important.

Introduction to Volume 4

Michael Patterson

Reconstructing past performance

Of all the arts performing arts are unquestionably the most ephemeral. Architecture, sculpture and literature can be admired and enjoyed for millennia, painting and music for centuries, but when the curtain closes after a performance of theatre or dance, what is there left? The theatre historian who wishes to explore productions dating from more than two-thirds of a century ago can piece things together only from fragments: playwright's stage directions; manifestos and theoretical writings by writers and theatre practitioners; still photographs; actors', directors', set designers' and dramaturgs' memoirs; contemporary reviews; critical studies; programmes, and, if lucky, set designs; sketches made during performance; and prompt books. Each of these sources is beset with problems.

Playwright's stage directions: While these are a good guide to the intentions of the author with regard to the staging of his or her play, they do not necessarily coincide with the actual execution of the piece. As we shall see, the three directors in this volume all staged Ibsen in ways unintended by the dramatist. Indeed, with the onward march of Modernism, playwright's stage directions have tended to revert to the simplicity of those of the Elizabethan stage, thereby entrusting the realization of the text to the director and designer.

Manifestos and theoretical writings by writers and theatre practitioners: One such source, *Die Blätter des Deutschen Theaters* (The Journal of the Deutsches Theater), is discussed at length by Ann-Christine Simke in her chapter on Reinhardt, where she shows how such a document can throw valuable light on Reinhardt's work. However, such material may reveal a search for innovation without actually achieving it in practice. So, Edward Gordon Craig and Antonin Artaud, both well known for their theoretical pronouncements, actually achieved little in practice.

Still photographs: While these should supposedly offer an authentic record of the visual quality of the staging, their value is severely restricted in terms of the directors we are considering here. Not only could the photographs not record colour, but, until 1926, it was not possible to take a photograph during a performance; all pictures were taken with the performers posed under full lighting (one of the special exhibits at the Magdeburg Theatre Exhibition of 1927 was 'Photographs taken during performance' with the new Ermanox camera).[1] The resulting images therefore almost assuredly failed to capture the nuance and the excitement of the actual performance.

Memoirs: These may suffer from the gap in time between event and recollection, as Simke points out with regard to the reminiscences of Reinhardt's dramaturg, Arthur Kahane, published over a quarter of a century after his first meeting with Reinhardt.[2] While sometimes providing useful descriptions of earlier productions, all too often the analytical is replaced by the anecdotal.

Contemporary reviews: These are clearly an essential source of information. They suffer, however, from the journalistic pressure of providing a response to a new theatrical event; the play itself will usually be discussed in some detail, the reaction of the audience will be recorded, but often little space remains for an analysis of the theatrical style of the performance. Moreover, the contemporary reviewer may lack perspective; a set design may appear startlingly innovative, when in fact, in the light of later developments, it may be regarded as a minor modification to an existing style.

Critical studies: Here the critic possesses the perspective lacked by the journalistic reviewer. However, the tendency in critical works, certainly in the first half of the twentieth century, tended to remain on the sure ground of textual criticism, and theatrical style was seldom discussed.

Programmes: While recording the names of the performers and resolving questions about the doubling of roles, programmes usually offer little further information. They can also be notoriously unreliable (one recalls that Lotte Lenya's name was missing in the programme for the premiere of *Die Dreigroschenoper* (The Threepenny Opera, 1928)). In the more recent past, especially in Germany, theatre programmes have developed into discursive commentaries on the production, containing contributions by the director and designers, background historical material and relevant essays.

Set and costume designs: These express the intention of the designer, but often the theatrical realization resulted in a compromise owing to limited resources or the conservatism of the performers or theatre management. A comparison between designs and photographs of the same production will frequently bear this out.

Sketches made during performance: Unfortunately these are rare, for while they are inevitably a rapid and subjective impression by one artist, they provide probably the most authentic record of the visual impact of a production, as could be seen in the interesting sketches made on his visit to Germany in 1921 by the American set designer Robert Edmond Jones, who had studied under Reinhardt at the Deutsches Theater in 1913/14.

Prompt books: Where these are available, they offer an invaluable record of a production, although, while giving details of the staging, they will seldom offer an analysis as to why certain directorial decisions were taken.

Today the problems faced by the theatre historian have been considerably ameliorated with video and DVDs, and once hologram technology is perfected we may be able to store an authentic three-dimensional record of a performance. But even this could not replace the experience of sitting in an audience in the presence of a live actor creating his or her art in the here and now. It would be similar to the disappointment we feel on discovering that a beautiful-looking flower is in fact made from plastic.

Because theatre is so ephemeral and therefore so hard to recreate, it is all too easy to judge wrongly who contributed most to this popular art form in the past. Theatre students today will be familiar with the names of Stanislavski, Craig, Artaud, and Brecht, possibly with Piscator. Yet Max Reinhardt, arguably the most important theatre director of German-speaking countries, and Leopold Jessner, a remarkably innovative director during the Weimar Republic, will hardly be known to the typical student and are unlikely to appear on any syllabuses. Look up Reinhardt in a modest encyclopaedia, and you are more likely to find an entry on Django Reinhardt the guitarist than on Max Reinhardt. As for Harley Granville Barker, he will be better remembered for his plays than for his work as a practical man of theatre.

The reason for this is soon found. Stanislavski, Craig, Artaud, Brecht and Piscator all wrote extensively about the kind of theatre they were trying to create. The fact that Craig and Artaud actually achieved little in practice and that Piscator failed after struggling for years to create his political theatre seems less important than the fact that they wrote provocatively about performance. The three directors considered in this volume were all too engaged in working on the theatre they sought to create to find time to write at length about their intentions. Reinhardt seldom stated what he wished to achieve with his theatre. As the prominent critic Hermann Bahr recorded: 'No one could be a better listener, but he himself was a silent man.'[3] Barker did write retrospectively about the theatre he envisioned in works like *The Exemplary Theatre* (1922) and *The Use of Drama* (1944), but despite his contribution to transforming the theatre of his day, his engagement with British theatre is probably best remembered through his failed attempt to set up a British national theatre, a topic he addressed in *The National Theatre* (1930) or for his influential *Prefaces to Shakespeare* (1927–46), rightly described by Dennis Kennedy as 'the first major Shakespeare study to attend to practical matters of staging'.[4]

This volume hopes to rectify this. By focusing on three very different but important theatre directors of the previous century the attempt will be made to establish their importance for the development of modern theatre and to acknowledge their significance alongside the better known names of Stanislavski and Brecht.

The context in which these directors worked

In 1908 a book appeared, entitled *Abstraktion und Einfühlung* (Abstraction and Empathy), written by an art critic, Wilhelm Worringer. Despite its unappealing title it ran to seven editions by 1919. Worringer's central thesis is suspiciously simple and yet remarkably persuasive: that civilizations which have felt at home in the world have produced 'empathetic' art, that is to say, a realistic art which celebrates the world about them. A prime example is classical Greece with its lifelike statues realistically celebrating the human form. On the other hand, civilizations which have regarded existence as a terrible burden, such as the ancient Egyptians, have turned to abstract art to express their response to the world: 'While the impulse towards empathy depends on a happy pantheistic relationship of trust between man and the world of external appearances,' wrote Worringer, 'the impulse towards abstraction is the consequence of a great inward disturbance in man through the same world of appearances ... We should like to call this state a colossal spiritual agoraphobia.'[5]

In the late nineteenth century European civilization was at its height. Industrialization had provided goods and employment for the growing populations, and even though many were obliged to live in insanitary conditions, nearly everyone had shelter and food. Raw materials flooded in from exploited colonies in Africa and Asia. Technological inventions, such as steam-powered iron-hulled ships (1838), the commercial telegraph (1838), the printing telegraph (1855), the internal combustion engine (1859) and the radio (1896), promised to transform travel and communication.

As Europe entered the new millennium, the old certainties were being undermined. Most obviously, within less than two decades political tensions led to the First World War, which cost the lives of some 10 million, mainly young men, and left 20 million suffering from wounds. Sigmund Freud was asserting that much of human behaviour was dictated not by the rational brain but by the unconscious. The influential philosopher Friedrich Nietzsche had argued that beneath the Apollonian reason of the ancient Greeks lay the celebration of the Dionysian ecstasy. Einstein's Theory of Relativity (1905) and Max Planck's Theory of Radiation (1906) spelt the end of Newtonian physics. The artist Wassily Kandinsky in his widely read *Über das Geistige in der Kunst* (On the Spiritual in Art, 1912) praised scientists 'who repeatedly examine matter, unafraid of any question, and who finally place in doubt the very existence of matter, on which only yesterday everything was founded and the whole universe reposed'.[6]

For the young European intellectual the recognition of the limits of rational thought, the discovery that this world is not as stable or as solid as once believed, and eventually the nightmare of a war that devoured so many, all served to intensify the sense of spiritual agoraphobia of which Worringer had spoken. The Swiss artist Paul Klee, writing in his diary in the trenches, summed it up: 'The more terrible this world (as it is today), the more abstract our art, while a happy world produces art of the here-and-now.'[7] Add to this sense of alienation the fact that two of the directors here discussed were Jews (note the difficulties which Jessner in particular experienced in becoming assimilated into German society, as described by Matthias Heilmann in his chapter.)[8] It is therefore very understandable why Reinhardt, Jessner and Barker turned their backs on the realistic theatre that had been at the forefront of theatrical innovation to discover more challenging and immediate forms of communicating with an audience under the admittedly very wide umbrella of Modernism.

While for Klee and Picasso, whose revolutionary *Demoiselles d'Avignon* had appeared in 1907, and for Arnold Schönberg, whose first atonal compositions were heard the following year, painting and music could more easily embrace abstraction, the theatre has only been able to achieve this in scattered examples such as Samuel Beckett's *Breath* (1969). So long as theatre involves living performers, it cannot in the same way abandon the sure ground of reality, and much of the interest in considering the work of our three theatrical innovators is to see how they could turn their backs on realistic theatre to embrace Modernism in ways that would continue to attract audiences and offer their own brand of reality in place of the foregoing Realism.

The eminent theatre critic Michael Billington, admittedly writing from an Anglo-Saxon perspective, observed in 1986: 'if you look at drama over the past 100 years you will find that most of the greatest writers have, in spite of constant digressions, worked inside the naturalistic mode'.[9] In this volume we shall be looking at three directors who pursued these 'digressions' in what Brecht was to call theatre 'for the scientific age', using the memorable image: 'If you hit a car with a coachman's whip, it won't get it going.'[10] Our three directors would all have agreed with Fredric Jameson's statement: 'Realism, by suggesting that representation is possible, and by encouraging an aesthetic of mimesis or imitation, tends to perpetuate a preconceived notion of some external reality to be imitated, and indeed to foster a belief in the existence of some common-sense, everyday, ordinary shared secular reality in the first place.'[11]

However true this statement may be in a philosophical sense, it did not generally accord with the expectations of the average theatregoer. It was Max Reinhardt who most successfully negotiated a rejection of Realism while nevertheless managing to fill his auditoria and run a very profitable business empire. Indeed, his very success has perhaps led to the received impression that he is somehow not as significant a force in the theatre as other less financially successful innovators. He has too easily been dismissed as the grand showman seeking and finding spectacular effects rather than creating new forms of theatre. As Allan S. Jackson observed: 'His reputation is for spectacle when it should be for innovation and experimentation.'[12]

In what ways then was Reinhardt an innovator and experimenter? His many achievements may be briefly summarized as follows:

- He created new theatre spaces by staging plays in a circus, in exhibition halls, in front of a cathedral.

- He built a huge theatre, the Theatre of Five Thousand, seating over 3,000 in a horse-shoe arrangement like ancient Greek amphitheatres.

- He also transformed the traditional proscenium arch stage, employing flights of steps, a semi-circular cyclorama and walkways borrowed from the oriental stage.

- He embraced new technology, affording lighting an almost autonomous role in the theatre, and installing a revolving stage not just for scene changes but as an integral part of the production.

- He employed painters to design his sets and helped to transform the traditional 'scene painter' into the modern indispensable role of 'set designer'.

- He directed a huge range of plays from Ibsen to oriental mime pieces, from Aeschylus to the latest modernist works.

- He confronted each theatrical challenge with the same care and intelligence, from close-up work with actors to colossal spectacles such as *The Miracle*.

- He encouraged lesser-known writers including Sorge and Sternheim and helped to secure the reputation of more established writers such as Strindberg, Maeterlinck and Wedekind.

- He developed the talents of actors and actresses, allowing them freedom to experiment while maintaining a firm directorial role.

- He made Berlin one of the most important theatre capital cities of Europe.

This extraordinary record did not bring immediate success in its wake. As Ann-Christine Simke shows in her chapter, Reinhardt's dramaturgs not only helped him to his supremacy in the Berlin theatre but also found it necessary to publish an in-house journal which set out to explain the new directions Reinhardt had taken and to convert their audiences to embrace Reinhardt's innovations. However, when it came to the challenge of Modernism, Reinhardt, while decisively turning his back on Realism, stood to one side with regard to the major development of modernist theatre in Germany, Expressionism. As I discuss in my chapter, although Reinhardt in many ways anticipated Expressionism, he himself was never truly in sympathy with the movement. Nor did he embrace the new political theatre of the Weimar

Republic, not even combating the rising tide of anti-Semitism. In the last analysis, even though he is to be acknowledged for his many innovations, his view of theatre as an autonomous aesthetic experience did not accord well with the progressive nature of Modernism and so did not create a road map for modernist developments in theatre.

With Leopold Jessner we encounter a very different and arguably a more significant force in the development of theatre. This is an irony, since, while most educated Germans will be at least familiar with the name of Max Reinhardt, many will have never heard of Jessner, and in British and American writing about him he is almost completely ignored; for example, J.L. Styan's book on Reinhardt gives Jessner only two passing mentions.[13] His name may have been obscured by the caesura of Nazi barbarism, but, as the chapters by Matthias Heilmann and Sascha Förster clearly demonstrate, he was a very significant force in the development of theatre.

Where he is known to theatre historians, Jessner is most likely best remembered for his frequent use of steps onstage, the so-called 'Jessner-Treppe'. The imaginative use of monumental steps had many advantages. On a practical level it became easy to prevent actors masking one another, and the director could compose stage pictures which employed vertical as well as horizontal relationships. An actor's move from step to step was magnified by the addition of this new dimension, and so the performer was inhibited from making the trivial and unmotivated moves characteristic of the worst naturalist acting. A flight of steps can also reinforce the meaning of a scene. So in Jessner's 1922 staging of Schiller's *Don Carlos* the Spanish court entered over the top of the steps, slowly increasing in magnificent array as it descended towards the waiting Carlos, the figure of youthful freedom, who seemed swamped by this surge of splendour from above.

The major innovation that Jessner brought to the theatre, so persuasively argued by Heilmann and so well illustrated by Förster, was what came to be known as *Aneignung*, the appropriation of texts to provide a commentary on contemporary society. Brecht, who attended Jessner's rehearsals in the 1920s, learned from him how to take a play, whether by Schiller, Grabbe or Shakespeare, and to reinterpret it freely, so that theatre could no longer be considered a living museum but a forum for discussing the here and now. The whole concept of *Regietheater*, theatre that embodies above all the vision of an individual director, began – for Western Europe at least – with Jessner. It was as though this approach was, like an underground river, forced beneath the theatre landscape but bubbled up vigorously after the defeat of Nazism.

It is now a commonplace of contemporary theatre that a director will seek social relevance for his or her audience in the staging of a play, and this 'appropriation' encouraged by Brecht and practised by post-Second World War directors like Fritz Kortner, who had worked with Jessner, can be traced back to Jessner's revolutionary approach. Furthermore, in order to focus on the play's meaning and to rid the stage of the clutter of traditional images,

Jessner worked repeatedly with a bare stage, often with ramps or steps, establishing the specific location of a scene with a simple scenic addition, like a banner or a throne. No wonder a large section of the audience who came to see his premiere of *William Tell* at the former theatre of the Kaiser himself experienced such outrage. Not only was a more than 100-year-old classic play of German theatre being served up as a cry for freedom of the newly founded Weimar Republic, but the audience was also deprived of the pretty Alpine scenery, which had always accompanied the play.

So, while one could not create such a long list of achievements for Jessner as was possible with Reinhardt, it is arguable that he in fact gave more to the future of theatre than did his more overtly successful rival. And we must note that *Regietheater* together with the use of an essentially bare stage – which of course anyway harks back at least to the Elizabethans – would now be described as 'Brechtian' but actually began with Leopold Jessner.

When we come to Harley Granville Barker, we see both differences and similarities with his German contemporaries. First, the context in which he was working was quite different from that of Germany. Reinhardt could depend on a reasonably cultured theatre-going audience at least prepared to experience even if not always to approve his innovative style; Jessner worked in a subsidized theatre at a time of experimentation; while Barker had constantly to contend with the traditional conservatism of British audiences and suffered financially as a consequence. After the First World War and into the 1920s, when Reinhardt became established as the great Berlin theatre impresario, and Jessner was making his mark on the theatre of the capital, Barker almost entirely gave up directing. Indeed, his repeated appeal for state subsidies for theatre would eventually lead to the support for theatres from the Arts Council, founded in the year of Barker's death, 1946, and to the establishment of the Royal National Theatre.

In the 1920s, then, when Reinhardt and Jessner were going from strength to strength, Barker withdrew from directing to write his theoretical books on theatre, his *Prefaces to Shakespeare* and to write two more plays, for which, as I said, he is now better remembered than for his directing. By writing plays himself he also distinguished himself from Reinhardt and Jessner. Despite these differences, the similarities between the three men are greater. All three began their careers as actors, although Barker alone continued to perform major roles, notably in premieres of George Bernard Shaw's plays, even after beginning his career as director. Having seen Reinhardt at work in Germany, Barker also went outside the confines of the proscenium arch theatre in 1915 to stage Euripides' plays in vast amphitheatres in the United States, attracting huge audiences. Like Jessner, Barker was a socialist and believed that even the tragedies of Euripides had a relevance to his contemporary audience.

All three directors were also true theatre people. Since each had a background as an actor, when it came to directing a play they understood well how to work with actors while maintaining a balance between directorial control and encouragement to the performer to develop his or her own role – always a director, never a dictator. As Barker put it: 'A director may direct the preparation, certainly. But if he only knows how to give orders, he has mistaken his vocation; he had better be a drill-sergeant.'[14]

Most significantly, though, all three directors discussed in this volume represent Modernism, turning away from both the stale declamatory style and the more progressive realistic modes of nineteenth-century theatre and establishing theatre not just as a means of transferring a written text to the stage but as an art form in its own right.

If the reader of this volume can develop some sense of the excitement engendered by the innovations of Reinhardt, Jessner and Barker, and the way that they, while largely unacknowledged, helped to create the theatre of today, then this book will have served its purpose.

Note. In Britain 'director' can refer both to the head of a theatre (in German *Intendant*) and to the individual who is responsible for staging a piece (in German *Regisseur*). In this volume 'Director' is used to refer to the managerial role and 'director' to the artistic one.

Max Reinhardt

1

Max Reinhardt and the Theatre of his Time

Michael Patterson

Max Reinhardt's life and career

Max Reinhardt, born Max Goldmann near Vienna, dominated the theatre of Germany and Austria for much of the first half of the twentieth century. The critic Herbert Ihering, no fan of Reinhardt, described him as 'the most colourful theatre talent of all time'.[1] He was certainly extremely prolific, having been responsible for well over 500 new productions, hitting a high point with forty-eight in the 1916/17 season. His work embraced many different styles, ranging from ancient Greek tragedies, performed in a huge arena, to the latest plays, mounted on the small stage of his Kammerspiele with an auditorium of less than 300 seats. Despite this huge output and wide range, Reinhardt's direction was always characterized by care and, where appropriate, innovation. He may justifiably lay claim to being the greatest twentieth-century theatre director of German-speaking nations, raising the quality of the theatre in Berlin to rival that of Paris and Vienna. Giorgio Strehler, the major Italian theatre director, named Reinhardt as one of his two theatrical god-fathers (the other was Brecht): 'He was a "man of the theatre" and he endeavoured to interpret the dramatic text in the best possible alliance of movement and sound.'[2] Small wonder that the playwright Arthur Schnitzler could write: 'If God ever came to Berlin, he'd make sure that he got tickets to see Reinhardt.'[3]

Not only was Reinhardt a brilliant artistic director, he was also a shrewd entrepreneur, who built up his own theatre empire first in Berlin and then in Austria. His father had been a businessman who was badly affected by the economic crisis of 1873, and it is possible that this was one reason why his eldest son Max was determined to succeed not just artistically but also financially. He built or rebuilt thirteen theatres, and at one time was simultaneously managing ten theatres in Berlin and Vienna. In the course of his career he managed a total of thirty theatres and companies.

Starting out in Vienna as a young actor specializing in playing old men, he was engaged in 1894 by the leading Berlin theatre director, Otto Brahm. In 1901 Reinhardt opened his own cabaret, Schall und Rauch (Noise and Smoke), later the Kleines Theater (Little Theatre), where alongside the usual satirical sketches he staged short pieces by Strindberg, and it was here in 1902 that he produced Frank Wedekind's highly controversial 'Lulu' play, *Erdgeist* (Earth Spirit). In 1906 he acquired the Deutsches Theater, a building that dated from 1850 and had once offered popular entertainment, but which in 1883 was taken over by Adolphe L'Arronge in an attempt to set up a kind of German national theatre with a serious repertoire. Once installed in the Deutsches Theater, Reinhardt soon extended it to include a small intimate theatre on the lines demanded (but never realized) by Strindberg in his preface to *Fröken Julie* (Miss Julie, 1888). This new theatre was named by Reinhardt as the Kammerspiele on an analogy with *Kammermusik* (chamber music). Later, in 1915, he was appointed director of the Volksbühne, saving it from bankruptcy during the difficult years of the First World War. He went on to become director of the Kleines Schauspielhaus, and then in 1919 opened his Grosses Schauspielhaus, the so-called 'Theatre of Five Thousand'. It in fact seated just over 3,000, the seats arranged in an arc on the lines of ancient Greek amphitheatres. Unfortunately, it opened in a period of economic collapse in Germany and could not pay its way, eventually being taken over to present popular revues.

In the early 1920s, no doubt aware that the Berlin theatre had moved on in a way that was not conducive to his own style, Reinhardt shifted the epicentre of his theatrical activity back to his homeland, Austria. In 1920, together with Richard Strauss, Bruno Walter and Hugo von Hofmannsthal, he founded the annual Salzburg Festival. He renovated the Theater in der Josefstadt, turned the Redoutensaal of the Imperial Palace in Vienna into a performance space, staged productions at Schloss Leopoldskron and opened the Salzburg Festspielhaus (Festival Theatre) in 1925. In 1933, while directing *A Midsummer Night's Dream* in Oxford, he wrote an open letter to Goering and Goebbels, reluctantly abandoning his Berlin theatres to Nazi control. In 1937, a year before the Nazi takeover of Austria, the *Anschluss*, Reinhardt directed for the last time in Vienna and then emigrated to the United States, where in Hollywood he opened the Max Reinhardt Workshop for Stage, Screen and Radio and directed a sugary film version of *A Midsummer Night's Dream* with Mickey Rooney as Puck and James Cagney as Bottom.

Reinhardt's relationship to Expressionism

What is truly remarkable is that this colossus of the German-speaking stage had so little engagement with the two major theatre innovations of the German theatre of his day, Expressionism and the political theatre of the Weimar Republic. It is even more remarkable when one considers the many ways in which Reinhardt helped to make expressionist theatre a possibility, but he was never truly in sympathy with this new movement. First, Reinhardt decisively turned away from Naturalism, from theatre which frequently took place in one room and depended primarily on dialogue. As the critic Hermann Bahr rightly asserted, it was Reinhardt who 'ended for this generation the sway of the literary play'.[4] His rejection of Naturalism, however, never led him to embrace the excesses of Expressionism.

He was one of the first German directors to embrace Strindberg, directing five of his plays between 1902 and 1907. Later, his productions of *Todestanz* (Dance of Death) and *Gespenstersonate* (Ghost Sonata) toured throughout Europe, and his *Traumspiel* (Dream Play) was actually first performed in Stockholm in 1921. He also staged plays by Wedekind, battling with the censor over *Frühlings Erwachen* (Spring's Awakening, 1907), a play which, like Strindberg's dramas, is an obvious forerunner of Expressionism in its social theme, its depiction of the teachers as grotesque stereotypical figures rather than real people and in the symbolic figure of the Man in the Mask in the final scene. As J.L. Styan records: 'In his first sixteen years as director, Reinhardt put on 1,171 performances of no less than twelve different plays by this controversial satirist.'[5] Six hundred and fifty-seven of these were of *Spring's Awakening*. However, while Reinhardt has traditionally been regarded as the great promoter of Wedekind, Matthias Heilmann persuasively argues that this accolade should belong to Leopold Jessner.[6]

While some distance separates expressionist theatre from the symbolist and neo-romantic works that preceded it, nevertheless writers such as Maeterlinck, Verhaeren, Hofmannsthal and Eulenberg, all of whom featured in Reinhardt's early repertoire, showed how theatre could be created with poetic diction and with representative figures in the place of rounded naturalistic characters. Even when he directed a realist play, Reinhardt often sought poetic and symbolic elements in the text rather than pursuing the attempt to bring credible daily life on to the stage. For his 1906 production of Ibsen's *Gespenster* (Ghosts), for example, he invited the expressionist painter Edvard Munch to design the set. Munch created a claustrophobic room with heavy furniture and with walls, as Reinhardt himself described them, 'the colour of decaying gums'.[7] The critic Siegfried Jacobsohn had been to Berlin productions by both the arch-naturalist Otto Brahm and by Reinhardt and concluded that while Brahm's staging had been overwhelmed by realistic detail, Reinhardt's penetrated to the core of the play, 'from the heart to the heart'.[8]

Reinhardt's rejection of Naturalism also led him to open up the stage space in ways that would offer considerable opportunities to the Expressionists. Not only did he perform plays in unexpected venues, most famously his 1910 *Oedipus* in a circus, thus opening up new possibilities to move beyond the peepshow stage of traditional theatre, but he also explored ways of using the conventional end-on arrangement. Stanislavski had spoken of the 'fourth wall removed', but Reinhardt went beyond that. He removed the second wall as well.

Curiously, even naturalist German productions of the day still used a painted backdrop at the rear of the stage. Ever the innovator, Reinhardt challenged this too. Not only did he make use of the *Rundhorizont* (semi-circular cyclorama), and the more recent Fortuny 'Kuppelhorizont' (sky dome); but he went further still: in his 1908 productions of *Lysistrata* and *King Lear* he opened up the back of the stage, replacing the backcloth with a flight of steps, thus anticipating Jessner's famous use of steps by over a decade. This was not merely a new way of using stage space; it often contributed to the meaning of the piece. So, for example, at the end of the second part of *The Oresteia* (1911) Orestes, having committed the matricide, slowly mounted the steps at the rear towards darkness and an unknown future.

Reinhardt's use of stage space was also characterized by selectivity in his choice of sets. As he stated in his autobiographical notes: 'Introduce furniture, tables, chairs, walls as means of expression. Nothing arbitrary. No furniture that does not play a part, that is only used as decoration.'[9] Naturalistic clutter was to be replaced by sets that were 'a means of expression'.

A further significant contribution to the future of the theatre by Reinhardt was in his handling of crowd scenes. Except in the productions by the innovative Duke of Saxe-Meiningen and his director Ludwig Chronegk in the nineteenth century, extras on the German stage had been treated as a necessary evil. They were often enough drafted in from the local barracks or recruited from the unemployed or those wishing to add to their meagre income, happy enough to be offered warmth and a small wage for an evening's easy work. The director could at best hope that they got on and off stage without bumping into the scenery or otherwise drawing attention to themselves.

The care taken by Reinhardt in directing crowd scenes is evidenced by contemporary photographs: Thebans strain their hands in supplication before Oedipus, the band of the Robber-Baron in *Das Mirakel* (The Miracle), some lying, some crouching, reach threateningly towards the nun. It is hard to imagine that the crowd scenes of Georg Kaiser's plays, *Die Bürger von Calais* (The Burghers of Calais), *Von morgens bis mitternachts* (From Morning to Midnight) and *Gas*, or indeed Fritz Lang's film *Metropolis*, could have been contemplated without Reinhardt's pioneering work in this area.

FIGURE 1.1 *Rehearsal for* Oedipus Rex, *Covent Garden Opera House, London, 1912 (Ullstein Bild, Getty Images).*

In addition to his work on crowd scenes, Reinhardt also worked imaginatively with individuals, ushering in a new style of acting. He encouraged often quite inexperienced actors to become expressive, responding well to impulses coming from his actors while maintaining a firm directorial role. He decisively turned from the so-called 'hands in the pocket' style of Naturalism and encouraged his performers to commit themselves entirely to the role in a way that anticipated the 'ecstatic' style of expressionist acting and Paul Kornfeld's injunction to the actor in 1916 to 'dare to spread his arms out wide and with a sense of soaring speak as he [*sic*] had never spoken before in his life ... Let him not be ashamed that he is acting, let him not deny the theatre.'[10]

So Tilla Durieux, who in 1910 played Jocasta in Reinhardt's *Oedipus Rex* and the title role in Friedrich Hebbel's *Judith*, was praised for her 'mixture of the bestial and demonic'.[11]

Two years previously Paul Wegener, whom Brecht declared in 1920 to be one of the two delights of Berlin (the other was the underground railway) had performed the leading role of Franz Moor in Reinhardt's production of Schiller's *Die Räuber* (The Robbers) with disturbing intensity, described by Jacobsohn as 'a raving fanatic with a shock of red hair, broad mouth and a complexion sallow enough to give you jaundice. Wegener believes that Franz Moor ... cannot be explained in human terms and so thrusts him into the

FIGURE 1.2 *Paul Wegener as Franz Moor in Schiller's* The Robbers, *1908.*

realms of mental imbalance.'[12] Under Reinhardt's tutelage actors felt free, encouraged even, to throw themselves fully into their role. Small wonder then that, despite his frequently paying his actors less than the norm, leading actors of the day were keen to work with him and bear the honoured title of 'Reinhardtschauspieler' ('Reinhardt actor').

One possible contribution to Expressionism was made by Reinhardt's first Berlin venture, the Schall und Rauch Cabaret. One of his close friends, Christian Morgenstern, the translator of Ibsen and Strindberg but better known as a satirist, provided short dramatic pieces to the Cabaret. One of these, *Epigo und Decadentia: Ein satirisches Märchen* (Epigo and Decadentia: A Satirical Tale, written 1894, performed 1901) contained lines that directly anticipate the *Telegrammstil* (telegram style) of the Expressionists:

I.
You.
He!
She ... ?
It –
We?
You?
They! ...[13]

However different the intentions of the satirist and of the serious writer, the similarity with dialogue from August Stramm's expressionist piece *Geschehen* (Happening, 1915) is striking:

Who?
Man?
Woman?
Sweetheart?
Shout.
I?
You.
Her?! You![14]

However great Reinhardt's contribution to the creation of expressionist theatre was, he could never, though, become part of the movement. As Günther Rühle observed: 'Expressionism in Reinhardt's theatre went only half way, that is to say, it was always overshadowed by the artistic subtlety of Reinhardt.'[15] Indeed, Reinhardt was impelled towards Expressionism without real inner conviction. Witnessing the regional theatres of Frankfurt, Mannheim, Munich and Dresden take the lead in the performance of avant-garde works under the slogan 'Los von Reinhardt!' ('Freedom from Reinhardt!'), the king of Berlin theatres saw his regime threatened in a way not dissimilar from his own dethronement of Otto Brahm a decade previously. With characteristic resilience and eclecticism, therefore, Reinhardt tried his hand at the new expressionist style and gave personal encouragement to young playwrights such as Reinhard Johannes Sorge, Walter Hasenclever and Fritz von Unruh.

The major step that Reinhardt took in this direction was the establishment at the Deutsches Theater in Berlin in 1917 of 'Das Junge Deutschland' ('Young Germany'), a programme of expressionist pieces under the overall direction of Heinz Herald. It opened on 23 December 1917 with Reinhardt's own production of Sorge's Der Bettler (The Beggar). The clearest statement of the intentions of the production was given by Herald in the journal, also entitled Das Junge Deutschland, published in conjunction with the new experimental season:

> The action takes place on an empty stage. There is nothing out of place, no construction which constricts or confines. From this large black space, which possesses something untouched, unfulfilled, unbounded, the light tears a hole: this is where the action takes place. Or a man stands on his own, a lighted figure in front of a black background. A room in this twilight space is formed by a few pieces of furniture, a door, a window frame, pictures hanging in space. A birch illuminated in blue creates a garden. One is far removed from reality, but the eerie, secret effect is achieved through a fine, exquisitely fine portrayal of reality with its thousand different nuances.[16]

While this passage might suggest that Reinhardt had after all embraced the avant-garde style of theatrical Expressionism, one must first remember that Sorge had specified directional spotlights in his script. Moreover, much of the visual quality described above owes as much to Reinhardt's own earlier productions of symbolist pieces, like those of Maeterlinck, as it did to contemporary trends. One may become even more suspicious of the conviction with which he pursued an expressionist style when one learns from Jacobsohn that Reinhardt encouraged his actors to perform Sorge's text in the same way one would Shakespeare.[17]

Significantly, most of the subsequent productions of Das Junge Deutschland were farmed out to other directors. Georg Kaiser's Koralle (The Coral, 1918), Walter Hasenclever's Der Sohn (The Son, 1918) and Georg Kaiser's From Morning to Midnight (1919) were given to Felix Hollaender; Fritz von Unruh's Ein Geschlecht (A Generation, 1918) and Else Lasker-Schüler's Die Wupper (The Wupper, 1919) were directed by Heinz Herald; Paul Kornfeld's Himmel und Hölle (Heaven and Hell, 1920) by Ludwig Berger; and Oskar Kokoschka's Hiob (Job, 1919) and Der brennende Dornbusch (The Burning Thorn Bush, 1919) and Kaiser's Der Brand im Opernhaus (The Fire in the Opera, 1919) by the authors themselves.

Only twice more did Reinhardt return to his own staging of expressionist drama. First, in March 1918 he produced Reinhard Goering's *Seeschlacht* (Naval Encounter). A month previously this impassioned dramatic poem set in the gun turret of a warship had been premiered in Dresden with inappropriate realism (a naval expert had even been called in to advise on authentic sound effects). The same realism was adopted by the designer Ernst Stern in his set for Reinhardt's production, which, in Emil Faktor's words swung 'between reflections of reality and their symbolic meaning'. This was seen above all in the contradiction between the realistic set and Paul Wegener's intense acting style:

> The action all takes place in the armoured arch of the gun-turret, which Stern's skill in imitation had mounted on stage with almost life-like accuracy ... The performer [Paul Wegener] held the audience in his thrall. He began with a mysterious enigmatic whispering, then defiance broke through until a miracle occurred and flaming roses burst forth from this mighty charismatic heroic figure.[18]

Reinhardt's final essay into Expressionism was the one-act piece by August Stramm, *Kräfte* (Forces), which opened on 12 April 1921. Jacobsohn remained unimpressed: 'Reinhardt, who just once wanted to prove that he can do Expressionism too and how easy Expressionism is, proved it emphatically: the master-Impressionist simply turned Expressionism into Impressionism.'[19] Alfred Kerr expressed himself more concisely: 'Reinhardt provided flesh – where Stramm would have wanted lines.'[20]

The unavoidable conclusion is that Reinhardt was not in sympathy with the Expressionists. Their revolutionary idealism affronted his own gentle humanism. While he himself was undeniably something of a showman, their blatant aesthetic contrasted with his own love of subtlety. He rejected the '*Schrei*' (scream) in favour of the gently modulated voice. Above all, while Reinhardt celebrated the special quality of individuals and their relationships, the Expressionists were committed to the portrayal of 'universal Man'.

Reinhardt and political theatre

It is perhaps even more predictable that Reinhardt also turned his back on the political theatre of the Weimar Republic, the agitprop performances, the technically adventurous work of Piscator and the socialist playwriting of Brecht. When he was appointed Director of the Berlin Volksbühne (People's Theatre) in 1915, incidentally in favour of the socialist candidate, Leopold Jessner, the news was greeted by many with a cry of dismay. The influential critic Herbert Ihering even wrote a pamphlet entitled *Der Volksbühnenverrat* (The Betrayal of the Volksbühne). The Freie Volksbühne, as the name indicates, was founded in 1890 to offer theatre to the working classes in return for a modest subscription. Despite early political differences between those who regarded the Volksbühne as a purely cultural institution and those who wished to use it as a means of specifically socialist education, the organization went from strength to strength. By 1913 it had 70,000 members, and in the following year its own theatre building, the Neue Freie Volksbühne, was opened on the Bülowplatz in Berlin. However, there remained the tension between those, like Ihering, who wished this theatre of the people to be truly that, a popular institution embracing socialist principles, and those who, while accepting the subscription system, did not feel themselves constrained to perform only for workers or to commit themselves to a diet of left-wing pieces. Reinhardt clearly belonged to the second group, and opened on 1 September 1915 with a classical piece, albeit one depicting revolutionary anarchy, Friedrich Schiller's *The Robbers* (1781), a very different production from Piscator's 1926 controversial socialist version, in which one of the characters was made up to look like Trotsky. Reinhardt followed this with even less challenging pieces, predominantly by Shakespeare.

In fact, the initial ideals of the Volksbühne had already been compromised. Quite soon, not only in Berlin but by 1930 also in the 305 Volksbühne clubs across Germany the middle classes began to take up the subscriptions regularly to attend their local municipal theatre – as indeed they still do today. So, just as the Workers' Educational Association in Britain now offers courses in yoga and flower arranging, the original concept of offering a worker's theatre had been abandoned. Besides, in the difficult economic climate of the First World War, the Volksbühne would have collapsed entirely if it had not been for Reinhardt's skilful financial management. For as Piscator ruefully commented when his own attempt to set up a political theatre failed: 'Like a thread running through ... the story of my ventures is the recognition that the proletariat, for whatever reason, is too weak to maintain its own theatre.'[21]

It is not that Reinhardt had no political sensitivity. A letter of 1917 at the height of the slaughter of the First World War, written to his friend Siegfried Jacobsohn, attests to this:

Light will not penetrate into the heads of the dozen sad men who at present rule the world. So the slaughter continues, blood continues to flow, and people starve, while the leaders of nations tirelessly and with great seriousness hurl at one another the dung reported in the press. But what for me is the most terrible is to recognize that it makes no difference whether we are ruled by autocrats or democrats. Republicans are just the same as monarchists. Tyranny is not imposed from above; it is the result of a deep-seated and unshakeable need of the masses. Whether the dictator is called Rickelt or Napoleon, Kerenski or Marat, Venizelos, His Majesty [presumably Kaiser Wilhelm II] or Erzberger, in the final analysis the elementary fact remains the same: that the mob wishes to be dominated, enslaved, ruled by something they cannot comprehend. If they begin a revolution, they do so only because someone has exploited them and forced them to rebel, not for liberty, equality and fraternity. Liberty and fraternity are mutually opposed and cannot be achieved in this world, and equality? There are not two identical creatures in nature, and would we want them to exist? These ideas are just a different kind of murder weapon for tyrants but no less dangerous than 'emperor', 'nation', 'fatherland', etc. Nothing was more bloody than the 'Committee of Public Safety' of the French Revolution ... There is nothing terrible that human beings would not undertake if someone encourages or orders them to do it.[22]

But while he clearly held impassioned political views, Reinhardt never used his theatre to express them. Karl Kraus, a fellow Austrian, who wrote satirical articles in his journal *Die Fackel* (The Torch) was prominent in his attack on Reinhardt for his failure to address contemporary issues. So when two war veterans starved to death, Kraus commented: 'If you can imagine such a thing without becoming mad, while Herr Reinhardt displays the flesh of three hundred dancing girls in front of three thousand three hundred spivs, ... '[23] The attack was somewhat unfair, since Reinhardt was only partly responsible for the erotic revues staged in his Theatre of Five Thousand in an attempt to keep it financially viable. But the essence of Kraus's critique remains, and is reminiscent of Erwin Piscator's decision to take up political theatre:

We came out of the filth of war, we saw a people that was half-starved and tormented to death. We saw how their leaders were ruthlessly murdered, we saw, wherever we looked, injustice, exploitation, torture, blood. Were we to go home and sit at our desks, drawing-boards or director's tables to dream about 'fantastic fictions' or listen to the tinkle of sleigh bells? Our art was created from a knowledge of reality and a desire to replace this reality. We founded political theatre.[24]

Brecht was equally disparaging about Reinhardt's theatre. Learning of his death in 1943, Brecht wrote in his diary:

Max Reinhardt died in New York. In the early twenties I saw nearly all the rehearsals for *A Dream Play* at the Deutsches Theater. The stylistic elements he used were as obsolete as with anyone in our age who has a yawning gap between life and art, so that there is little art in life and little life in art. Art cannot be natural when life is artificial.[25]

Needless to say, Piscator's concept of 'reality' and Brecht's of 'life' would have differed radically from Reinhardt's understanding of these terms. While Piscator and soon Brecht were committed to theatre that might help to change the world, Reinhardt would have argued that it is ridiculous and impractical to insist that all works of art should contain a political message. Picasso may have done so in his *Guernica*, but does it mean that all his other works are worthless? Should the writing of symphonies or of lyric poetry be banned because they do not provide a comment on armies slaughtering each other? Reinhardt stood aside not only from the crude reductionist thinking of Expressionism but also from the didacticism of much political theatre and could argue that by providing beauty and by exploring human relationships in his theatre, he was exploring his own 'reality', was depicting his own perception of 'life' and, above all, offering an antidote to the horrors of his age.

Reinhardt and anti-Semitism

However, one may fairly question why he never addressed a growing and frightening horror, and one that touched him personally as a Jew, that of anti-Semitism. With the colossal influence that he wielded in Germany in the early 1920s, it might have been expected that, without descending to performing agit-prop pieces in 'halls with their smell of stale beer and gentlemen's toilets',[26] he could have used this influence to attempt to stem the tide of racism that was washing over Germany and which led to such a horrific outcome.

Anti-Semitism was rife in Germany at the time and was certainly not invented by Hitler. For example, in 1925 the deposed Kaiser living in exile in the Netherlands, one of many strongly influenced by the writings of the British-born Houston Stewart Chamberlain,[27] blamed his forced abdication on the Jews: the 'deepest, most disgusting shame ever perpetrated by a person in history, the Germans have done to themselves ... egged on and misled by the tribe of Judah ... Let no German ever forget this, nor rest until these parasites have been destroyed and exterminated from German soil!' He added, in a frighteningly accurate prediction, that Jews were like mosquitoes, 'a nuisance that humankind must get rid of some way or other ... I believe the best thing would be gas!'[28]

Although Reinhardt directed Lessing many times, including no less than eleven productions of his comedy *Minna von Barnhelm*, he staged Lessing's great plea for religious tolerance, *Nathan der Weise* (Nathan the Wise), only once, and that was as early as 1911. As for Lessing's comedy *Die Juden* (The Jews), in which two villains pretend to be Jews, whereas the noble hero of the piece really is Jewish and gains the hand of the local baron's daughter, it appears nowhere in the long list of Reinhardt's productions. Of contemporary pieces he might have staged a play dealing with anti-Semitism by his fellow countryman Arthur Schnitzler, *Professor Bernhardi*, first staged in 1912. Even though Reinhardt directed many pieces by Schnitzler, he failed to present this drama depicting a humane Jewish doctor, Bernhardi, who prevents a priest from administering the last rites to a dying patient to save her from the knowledge that her end is near. In the resulting conflict with the Catholic Church the Professor is eventually stripped of his title and his licence to practise medicine. Yet again Reinhardt apparently ignored this disturbing and topical analysis of anti-Semitism.

On the contrary, with pieces such as *The Miracle*, for which each venue was transformed into a cathedral, and *Jedermann* (Everyman), performed on the steps of Salzburg Cathedral, he sympathetically portrayed icons of Roman Catholicism. In one of his most favourite plays, *The Merchant of Venice* which he directed in 1905, 1906, 1908, 1910 (twice), 1913, 1915, 1918 and 1924, he did at least have a Jew on stage. But when Portia, with her legalistic sleight of hand insists that Shylock may not shed a drop of blood when claiming his pound of flesh, and thereby totally humiliates the Jew, there was jubilation in the courtroom and almost certainly in the auditorium as well. In 1935 Reinhardt rounded this off by performing the play on a canal bridge in Venice, which must have been aesthetically very pleasing but cannot have lent sympathetic focus to the Jew at the centre of the piece.

It is true that Reinhardt to his credit rejected Goebbels' offer of becoming an 'honorary Aryan' in return for the possibility of continuing to work in Germany, but then Goebbels would have hardly made the offer if Reinhardt had been more closely identified with his co-religionists. Indeed, in 1933, when he rather naively made over his Berlin theatres 'to the German people', he belatedly discovered that the Nazis then introduced strict censorship and used his theatres as part of their propaganda machine. It is also true that in 1937 Reinhardt directed in New York the premiere in English of Franz Werfel's *Der Weg der Verheissung* (The Eternal Road), a drama dealing with the long history of suffering of the Jewish peoples, which Brecht referred to as 'the glorification of Jewish history for America'.[29] Indeed one wonders whether Reinhardt did this at least in part to ingratiate himself with the powerful Jewish community of America. It is very doubtful whether he would have dared to try staging the piece in Austria before the *Anschluss*.

On the other hand, as Gottfried, Reinhardt's son, demanded of Piscator and Brecht: 'Whenever did they perform for the working class as Reinhardt did?'[30] And Reinhardt himself declared to his biographer Gusti Adler: 'The so-called "good" public is in reality the worst. Dull sophisticates. Inattentive, blasé, used to being the centre of attention themselves … Only the gallery is worth anything.'[31] Since tickets for the Kammerspiele cost twenty marks each, the audience comprised the cultural elite of Berlin, attired in furs, jewels and dinner jackets. By contrast, the cheapest tickets for Reinhardt's production of *Oedipus Rex* in the arena of the Schumann Circus could be bought for fifty pfennigs, one-fortieth the price at the Kammerspiele. To afford a ticket for the former would have obliged a female manual worker to pay two weeks' wages, while going to see *Oedipus* would have cost the equivalent of five eggs.

So, can one assert that, even if Reinhardt decisively stood aside from the political theatre of his day, he championed popular culture in a way that was arguably more successful than that of the more committedly socialist theatre workers of his day?

Reinhardt and popular theatre

Reinhardt was not alone in his aspiration to make his theatre a truly popular medium again. In the early years of the twentieth century, progressive theatre practitioners repeatedly expressed a profound dissatisfaction with the state of the theatre of the day. There were the court theatres, notably the Königliches Schauspielhaus in Berlin and the Burgtheater in Vienna. Here innovation was impossible, and a diet of expensively dressed classics and historical dramas was served, in accordance with Kaiser Wilhelm II's injunction not to perform contemporary realist plays in his theatre, because one does not 'plant potatoes in a vineyard'.[32] Then there were the municipal and commercial theatres of the major cities and towns, significantly often under the jurisdiction of the *Gewerbepolizei* (police administration concerned with trading) and so regarded as businesses rather than cultural institutions. Predictably, therefore, these theatres tended to satisfy the conventional taste of the urban bourgeoisie. The only recent models of innovation in Germany had been Wagner's search for the *Gesamtkunstwerk* (the total work of art), coupled with the founding of the Festspielhaus in Bayreuth, and Otto Brahm's championing of naturalist theatre and the creation of the Freie Bühne in Berlin. But the Festspielhaus had opened in 1876, the Freie Bühne in 1889, and neither had yet succeeded in initiating the cultural renewal that was so longed for by young German-speaking intellectuals of the 1900s.

When they looked for past models of great periods of theatre, that of ancient Greece, the Middle Ages, the Spanish Golden Age or the Elizabethan period, one thing appeared common to all of them: such theatre was popular, offering a cultural experience to the whole community, reinforced in the case of the first three by a common religious belief that bound the audience together. The desire to renew the theatre became therefore not only an aesthetic striving but also a search for a spiritual reawakening, for a theatre that would be founded on a newly integrated society, for a theatre that might indeed help in the creation of this new sense of community. This is the essentially utopian vision inspired by Nietzsche's image of Dionysian fellowship in *Die Geburt der Tragödie* (The Birth of Tragedy, 1872) and is reflected in works such as Georg Fuchs' *Die Schaubühne der Zukunft* (The Theatre of the Future, 1905) and *Die Revolution des Theaters* (Revolution in the Theatre, 1909): 'This movement which is now considered revolutionary, is merely the renaissance of a sound inheritance after a period of chaos which was at variance with our best traditions.'[33]

But where was this 'renaissance' to come from? One possibility was to embrace existing popular culture. In pursuit of this, some theatre practitioners, not without a certain sentimental condescension, embraced the *Variété* (the vaudeville), a form that was lively, skilful, theatrically rich, founded on a close rapport with the audience and evidently popular with the ordinary public. As Fuchs rather sneeringly put it: 'Vaudeville offers unlimited scope to physical perfection and finds worthy recruits in the very dregs of the proletariat.'[34] The vigour and fun of the *Variété* offered the desired populist dimension, and indeed its format had been adopted by the cabaret, as in Reinhardt's own Schall und Rauch. But, with the best will in the world, the *Variété*, with its tawdry urban image, could hardly form the source of a communal spiritual renewal.

A more compelling alternative was offered by rural folk-theatre. Here Fuchs found the hope for a possible renewal. On New Year's Day 1905 he was an enthusiastic member of the audience (or should one say congregation?) at the revival, after a 300-year interval, of a Passion play in a small Bavarian town: 'The atmosphere was hushed, as in a church ... everything that was universal and essential became significant ... there was harmony throughout that was a joy to see ... everything that was done was developed according to the ways and customs of the land.'[35] Perhaps in the simple staging by peasants of a medieval piece could the way forward be found.

It was in Austria that Reinhardt hoped to be able to create the sacral theatre of which Fuchs spoke. So, Reinhardt left Berlin for Vienna in 1920. There are many reasons why the acknowledged king of the Berlin theatre abdicated. Post-war Berlin was no longer very congenial. There was fighting in the streets. And, as we have noted, the new directions in theatre seemed to be leading into the unshaded emotionalism and schematic characterization of Expressionism and into the first manifestations of the new political theatre. Moreover, the growing Berlin film industry was threatening the very future of live theatre. And besides, Reinhardt was an Austrian and was returning home.

Already in 1917 there had been proposals to invite him to direct at the Burgtheater in Vienna, but these had come to nothing because of petty squabbles in the administration. However, in the late summer of 1918, Reinhardt met Leopold Freiherr von Andrian, who had just been appointed as *Generalintendant* (General Director) of the Court Theatres in Vienna. The two men clearly established a strong rapport, and the thrust of their discussions can be gleaned from a letter from Reinhardt, dated September 1918. Significantly, Reinhardt argued for a widely accessible theatre, firmly rooted in rural Austria: 'Especially at this time it has become clear that theatre is not a luxury for a small upper class but an indispensable spiritual food for the public at large.' To this end he supported the building in Salzburg of a festival hall that would give to Austria the blend of quasi-religious devotion and theatrical spectacle enjoyed at Bayreuth and Oberammergau. In an unashamedly nationalistic reference he speaks of the ideal site for this *Festspielhaus* (Festival Theatre): 'a site on the slope of the hill of Maria Plain, which looks across the border to Bavaria like an emblem of Austria'.[36]

The collapse of the Austro-Hungarian monarchy and the resultant administrative upheavals put an end to Andrian's and Reinhardt's plans. However, thanks largely to Hugo von Hofmannsthal's good offices, Reinhardt's future in Austria was secured. It was Hofmannsthal whom Reinhardt almost a decade previously had encouraged to write an adaptation of the medieval morality play *Everyman*. The terms in which he did so were significant: writing on Reinhardt's behalf, Arthur Kahane urged Hofmannsthal to apply populist techniques to a religious piece: 'The notion of applying the circus idea to a religious mystery is so obvious that any day now someone might get in ahead of us.'[37] Hofmannsthal was duly rewarded by having his *Everyman* performed regularly as the centrepiece of the Salzburg Festival.

Already in 1911 Reinhardt had successfully staged *The Miracle*, Karl Vollmoeller's mime-piece based on a medieval legend of a nun who leaves her convent and is replaced there by the Virgin Mary. After experiencing the horrors of the outside world, the nun gladly returns to her spiritual home in the convent. The premiere took place at London's Olympia with seating for 8,000 spectators and proved to be an instant popular success, so much

FIGURE 1.3 The Miracle *in the Olympia Exhibition Centre, London, 1912 (Ullstein Bild, Getty Images).*

so that it was later performed not only at many venues in Germany but also in Vienna, Prague, Stockholm and Bucharest. In 1924 it reached New York and toured for a further six years across the United States, eliciting a cynical reference to the circus impresarios Barnum and Bailey by the *Herald Tribune's* drama critic, Percy Hammond.[38]

Hoping to repeat this bringing together of a spiritual theme and a popular audience, in the autumn of 1919 Reinhardt had gone to Salzburg to begin work on Max Mell's adaptation of the *Halleiner Weihnachtsspiel* (The Hallein Christmas Play*)*, to be performed over Christmas in the Franciscan church there, but desperate food shortages forced rehearsals to end. So, it was not until the summer of 1920 that Reinhardt began to realize his plans for a popular festival theatre by staging the Austrian premiere of Hofmannsthal's *Everyman* on the Cathedral Square in Salzburg. The simple atmospheric setting on the splendid steps of the Salzburg Cathedral assured much greater success than that enjoyed by the Berlin premiere of *Everyman* in December 1911, staged like *Oedipus* in the Zirkus Schumann. As Franz Hadamowsky commented: 'Under Reinhardt's direction ... the play has lost its theatrical character and has become an institution of higher spirituality.'[39]

The spiritual quality of the production was not a little helped by the weather. Bernhard Paumgartner, director of the Mozarteum, who sat watching the performance beside Reinhardt, reported:

FIGURE 1.4 Jedermann *(Everyman), performed before Salzburg Cathedral, 1920 (Imagno, Getty Images).*

In the western sky a storm threatened. Suddenly however, when Moissi as Everyman recited the Lord's Prayer, the sun broke through the clouds, casting a gentle evening light. The cupola and towers at the front of the cathedral shone in a transfiguring glow. For the first time a flock of doves flew upward. A deep sense of awe settled on us all. Reinhardt himself was so overcome that he was hardly able to speak.[40]

Hofmannsthal himself spoke of the awe-inspiring quality of the event:

The cries uttered by invisible spirits to warn Everyman of his approaching death sounded ... from all the church-towers of the city, as twilight deepened about the five thousand spectators. One of these criers had been placed in the highest tower of a medieval castle, built far above the city, and his voice sounded, weird and ghostly, about five seconds after the others, just as the first rays of the rising moon fell cold and strange from the high heavens on the hearts of the audience.[41]

Something of Reinhardt's longing to restore the theatre to the social and cultic significance it had enjoyed in ancient Greece and in the Middle Ages seemed to have been achieved. Already in 1911, Reinhardt, in terms reminiscent of Fuchs, had spoken of his vision: 'The audience of the great folk-theatre of the future will enter the theatre like a place of worship.'[42] Or, as he expressed it in the 1920s: 'The fundamental idea was: to let the theater become a festival again, as it was in ancient times and in the Middle Ages under the leadership of the Church, while in the great city it is in most cases rather entertainment and amusement.'[43] Even Reinhardt's major spectacles had in Berlin been only a part of the capital's entertainment; here in Salzburg, so the story goes, ordinary life came to a halt, while the fortunes of Everyman captured the attention of the whole community: 'Traffic is completely stopped, and the whole city listens and watches breathlessly.'[44]

The acting style was also geared to a simple storytelling tradition. In his published dissertation on Reinhardt's staging of *Everyman*, Stefan Janson speaks of 'stylization like the woodcuts of the late Middle Ages ... The stiff marionette-like gestures are repeatedly emphasized in the notes in the margins of the promptbook.'[45] The tone was set by the playing of the Prologue, described by Reinhardt's prompt book as 'immobile, abrupt, curt, peasant-like'.[46] And of Werner Krauss's performance as the Devil, Hadamowsky reports: 'He played a gross, stupid Devil, one from an old fairytale.'[47] One of the more significant changes made to Hofmannsthal's text was the increase of ten guests in the banquet scene to twenty. This, together with a band of musicians and servants, not only enhanced the spectacular quality of the scene but also allowed Reinhardt to involve local amateurs in the production. Thus, 'a peasant player from Reichenhall played the Peasant; a citizen of Salzburg, Curiosity'.[48] Had Reinhardt then fulfilled his ambition of creating a truly popular theatre in his homeland, one that would help to unite a disintegrating Europe in a new sense of community, and one that would restore the cultic significance of performance to its place in earlier civilizations?

While addressing these major issues concerning the nature of the theatrical experience, Reinhardt continued to offer a programme of plays to suit the tastes of the Viennese bourgeoisie, mainly at the Theater in der Josefstadt. Even more so than in Berlin, production styles were unadventurous. Photographs in Hans Böhm's *Die Wiener Reinhardt-Bühne im Lichtbild* (Reinhardt's Vienna Stage in Photographs), which proudly declares that the pictures were taken during the actual performance, reveal conventionally realistic sets and costumes, apart from a fairly outlandish striped design by Oskar Strnad for the costumes in *King Lear*. To judge by these images, the revolution in scenic design that characterized much of the theatre of the first quarter of the century, exemplified by the work of Adolphe Appia, Edward Gordon Craig, Alfred Roller, and the Expressionists, might simply have never happened. It is noteworthy, too, that none of the texts selected for performance could be considered avant-garde – no expressionist writers, no Sternheim, no Pirandello, definitely no political theatre or *Zeitstücke* (plays dealing with topical social issues). Whatever Reinhardt's attempt to create a renaissance in theatre, it certainly was not going to lie in his embrace of Modernism.

Instead, he continued to champion the audience in the gallery compared with those in the stalls: in 1932 he declared, no doubt referring to his work at the Theater in der Josefstadt: 'I once made a big mistake. I sat my audience in armchairs that were too comfortable. In armchairs the audience want to be entertained. On wooden benches they get involved.'[49] Despite the huge differences between them, this is reminiscent of Bertolt Brecht's rejection of what he called 'culinary theatre'.

So, with the audience on wooden benches, *Everyman* was revived for the 1921 Salzburg Festival. The following year a new piece by Hofmannsthal, based on Calderón, *Das Salzburger grosse Welttheater* (The Salzburg Great World Theatre), was performed in the Kollegienkirche. The climax of this piece presents the Beggar, threatening the figures of power that surround him. In Hofmannsthal's own words: 'The Beggar raises his axe against everything that opposes him ... King, Rich Man, Peasant (who over here represents the conservatism of the secure small property holder) ... the edifice of an ordered society that has lasted a thousand years.'[50] However, this act of rebellion soon fails, and after a Road-to-Damascus-like conversion, the Beggar drops his axe and resolves to withdraw to the woods to live out his life as a hermit. As in Reinhardt's much-travelled production of *The Miracle,* where the nun, chastened by her experience of normal life, returns obediently to her convent, the solution here is profoundly Catholic and conservative. And indeed, Reinhardt regarded the Beggar's initial stance as characteristic of the communists: 'The beggar [is] deeply affected by communistic ideas, which are carried ad absurdum.'[51]

Reinhardt's intentions were never political, but a public act of performance cannot avoid containing a political meaning, even if it merely reinforces the attitudes of the audience. By allying themselves to a conservative and acquiescent political philosophy, an attempt, amid the chaos of post-war Europe, to preserve 'the edifice of an ordered society that has lasted a thousand years', Reinhardt and Hofmannsthal may have been populist in the sense that they reflected the thinking of a Catholic Austrian rural populace. In the wider context of developments across the Continent, they were swimming against the tide of the popular movements of fascism, socialism and communism.

Nor were the Salzburg productions populist in the sense that they were born of the community, as in Oberammergau. True, local amateurs did participate in minor roles or as extras, and two versions of the piece were later toured by amateurs, one in dialect, the other performed by local children. But the major speaking parts of Reinhardt's production were taken by the top German-speaking actors of the day: Alexander Moissi, Johanna Terwin, Helene Thimig, Hedwig Bleibtreu, Heinrich George, Werner Krauss and Wilhelm Dieterle. Moreover, despite the strong lines of the production, Reinhardt was not prepared to sacrifice the subtleties of fine acting. As Janson records of Reinhardt's promptbook: 'It is significant how detailed is the laying down of a particular colouring or mood required by a passage of text.'[52]

Furthermore, the vast open-air public performance area of the Cathedral Square, which he chose for *Everyman*, was an effort less to make the piece accessible to the ordinary citizens of Salzburg than to enjoy the advantages of a large-scale arena that lent freedom to and exploited the strengths of his actors. As he said in an interview a decade previously: 'Those works of theatre, in which decorative detail is forced into the background, once again afford the actor the yearned for opportunity of standing in the middle of the audience, free from the illusions of set design.'[53]

The fact is that despite the initial impetus behind the Salzburg Festival productions, Reinhardt was not performing in a populist style or catering for a mass audience. He was here, merely on a larger scale, exploring the aesthetics of the theatre and playing to a wider elite. As Janson admits, 'The performances did not take place before the "people," but before an audience of the international elite, among whom there were many who regarded it as a social duty to have attended a performance.'[54]

Reinhardt's hope to restore a sacral quality to theatre, one to which audiences would respond in harmonious ecstasy, remained a dream, as it did with the utopian visions of Georg Fuchs, Edward Gordon Craig, Antonin Artaud and many others. How could it be otherwise in the complex, sophisticated and individualistic societies of the twentieth century? How indeed could a secular Jew like Reinhardt identify wholly with the Catholic world of *Everyman* or of Calderón and find here a source of renewal? It would soon become clear that Dionysian ecstasy could not be achieved by theatre, however excellently it was performed, but only by appealing to the lowest common denominator in the national psyche. So, it was left to that other Austrian showman, Adolf Hitler, to generate a sense of self-surrendering passion in his audiences. It is sobering to reflect that a well-intentioned but nationalistically coloured search for a true theatre of and for the people to some extent anticipated the blind devotion cultivated by the Nazis. Ominously, the Passion play so praised by Fuchs happened to take place in the town of Dachau, site of the first Nazi concentration camp,[55] and Reinhardt's 'Theatre of Five Thousand', in which 'a human ring of thousands ... opens the soul of the people once more to the drama',[56] was utterly overshadowed just over a decade later by the vast Nazi Party rally at Nuremberg.

Already in 1936 Karl Kraus had asserted a similarity between Reinhardt and Hitler. Commenting on Reinhardt's move from Germany to Austria, he wrote:

That Reinhardt ... more than ever dazzles and anaesthetizes, that in all the fuss surrounding this man who has nothing to say, the rumour about his genius as a '*Führer*' grows stronger and stronger, all this can be traced back to our urge here to seek the equivalent of the Germans' need to believe in something, which they find in the Hitler *mise en scène*. That people do not really want to believe what is happening in Germany, but are deeply affected by the magic of the tenth time [Offenbach's] 'Beautiful Helen' has been raped or of a piddling little drama like [Gerhart Hauptmann's] *Vor Sonnenuntergang* (Before Sunset), this is both a comedy and a tragedy at the same time. There is no doubt that by banning Reinhardt ... Germany has been deprived of more than one spectacle, deprived of the *circenses* [circuses] that are needed because there is no *panis* [bread], something he really understands how to manage but which will now benefit the tourist trade of Salzburg.[57]

One must not imply, however, that Reinhardt, or indeed Fuchs, was instrumental in furthering fascist barbarism. On the contrary, a utopian vision may operate as a progressive force in social thinking. As Mark Fortier argues in *Theory/Theatre*: 'As an alternative to questioning or subverting the status quo, cultural forms can also take on a utopian or romance function, presenting a vision of a different social order preferable to our own. As a public space, theatre functions as what the anthropologist Victor Turner calls the liminoid, a place set apart for the process of transformation.'[58]

In that 'liminoid' Reinhardt devoted his life to creating beauty as he envisioned it and to discovering truth as he understood it. If that beauty and that truth could be communicated best in the intimacy of a small auditorium, as with Ibsen's *Ghosts*, then Reinhardt fulfilled his dream of an intense, close-up theatrical experience, even if it was reserved for the few: 'Since I've been in the theatre I have been haunted and finally obsessed by a certain idea: to bring together actors and audience – squeezed together as tight as possible.'[59] If, on the other hand, as with *Everyman*, a vast public arena was more suited, then he could claim to be a populist director.

So in Reinhardt's confrontation with Modernism, one looks in vain for a commitment to the emotional intensity that characterized Expressionism, even less for a willingness to join with Piscator and Brecht in a search for a theatre that offered left-wing challenges for the working classes. Indeed, one looks in vain for any overriding political or philosophical convictions which informed his long career in the theatre. Hofmannsthal summed it up well with the simple statement: 'What fascinates him is the solution of any given problem.'[60]

Reinhardt's theatre: A summary

Thus, despite occasional pronouncements about the importance of creating theatre for the masses, Reinhardt was neither a political nor a social reformer, was neither committed to an agenda of reinventing the nature of the theatrical experience (as was Artaud, for example) nor determined to experiment in isolation free from the pressures of commerce and popular culture (as later was, for instance, Jerzy Grotowski). Max Reinhardt was wholly dedicated to his own multifaceted theatre, and it was the needs of the theatre that he constantly sought to fulfil rather than some political programme. As he said in his piece, 'On the Living Theatre', written for Oliver Sayler's volume:

> It would be a theory as barbaric as it is incompatible with the principles of theatrical art to measure with the same yard stick, to press into the same mold, the wonderful wealth of the world's literature. The mere suggestion of such an attempt is a typical example of pedantic scholasticism. There is no one form of theater which is the only true artistic form. Let good actors today play in a barn or in a theater, tomorrow at an inn or inside a church, or, in the Devil's name, even on an expressionistic stage: if the place corresponds with the play, something wonderful will be the outcome.[61]

Ignoring the modernist currents swirling around him, Reinhardt's emphasis simply remained focused on good actors and good theatre, on creating a space and an audience appropriate to the dramatic material. And if one were to compare Reinhardt's achievement with that of the other German theatrical giant of the twentieth century, Bertolt Brecht, then one has to recognize an ironical twist to their careers: Brecht, the great champion of the masses, forced into exile and having to work in elitist fashion with a select band of supporters; while Reinhardt ends up in the United States working in the most populist medium of the day, Hollywood movies.

2

Max Reinhardt and his Company

Ann-Christine Simke

The career of Max Reinhardt shows us how the emergence of the star director can be as much a result of the organization as the art produced by that director. The investigation of this proposition will take us not only into the personnel of Reinhardt's company but also into the pages of the in-house journal produced by that company; not only, therefore, into the practical organization but also into the discourse that the organization produced about itself.

Reinhardt's Deutsches Theater in context

The emergence of Reinhardt as a director on the Berlin theatre scene needs to be understood in the context of the theatre of his day. His directing style presented a fundamental contrast to the highly acclaimed aesthetic of Otto Brahm's naturalist theatre that the Deutsches Theater had previously been known for.

Author and critic Otto Brahm (1856–1912) had already been heavily involved in the promotion of contemporary naturalist playwriting in his function as the co-founder of the progressive, independent theatre society Freie Bühne (Free Stage). On 1 September 1894 he opened his first season as the artistic director of the Deutsches Theater with a production of Schiller's *Kabale und Liebe* (Intrigue and Love). This was followed two days later by the production of Henrik Ibsen's *Nora* (A Doll's House) and three weeks later by Gerhart Hauptmann's naturalist play *Die Weber* (The Weavers).

FIGURE 2.1 *Deutsches Theater, Berlin (Schloss Wahn)*.

These productions effectively announced the change in the Deutsches Theater's artistic direction. Under Brahm's directorship from 1894 until 1904, the Deutsches Theater developed into a platform for contemporary naturalist writers, among whom Ibsen and Hauptmann featured as the famous figureheads of their dramatic form. Brahm employed Cord Hachmann and Emil Lessing as his principal directors and ran his theatre by assuming the role of a versatile dramaturg.[1] His literary knowledge qualified him for this work, carefully choosing plays for his repertoire, while his analytical skills and interest in a realistic acting style enabled him to function as a proactive production dramaturg. In his comprehensive and extensively illustrated publication on the history of the Deutsches Theater, Alexander Weigel describes this specific style, which came to be known as the 'Brahm-Stil', as trying to achieve 'a complete illusion of reality: fragmented speech of everyday life, silent and detailed acting with realistic props, within interior spaces in front of muted, earthy colours, with rather dimmed lighting'.[2] The consequence of the focus on naturalist drama and realistic acting and stage design led his audience to perceive him as a director who achieved a powerfully authentic depiction of real life as well as a strong faithfulness to the playtext.[3] Brahm's directing style clearly foregrounded the dramatic text and consequently emphasized the literary bias of his theatre aesthetic.

Under the directorship of Brahm, Max Reinhardt, who had been part of Brahm's ensemble from the very beginning, soon developed into a celebrated and highly acclaimed actor who, despite his young age, came to be best known for his detailed and realistic representations of older characters and character parts. He was considered to be a cornerstone of Brahm's ensemble and when he left the Deutsches Theater in 1902 in order to pursue his 'artistic emancipation'[4] and open up his own stage,[5] he was not only fined with a contract penalty, but was also confronted by a collective outcry from the theatre press, which constructed Reinhardt's career development, from being Brahm's pupil to breaching the contract with his mentor, into a narrative of parricide. This narrative was solidified when Reinhardt took over the artistic directorship of the Deutsches Theater in 1905 from Paul Lindau, whose one-season intermezzo as the artistic director had been uneventful. Reinhardt, by contrast, who had presented several successful productions as director of the Neues Theater between 1903 and 1905, was perceived as Brahm's artistic replacement at the head of the Deutsches Theater and introduced a fundamentally new approach to staging performances.

The development of the Reinhardt style

Contributing to the successful narrative of Max Reinhardt's ascent to his status as one of Germany's and indeed Europe's most influential theatre directors are the numerous accounts by his colleagues about his work and his vision. One of these often-quoted accounts is given by Arthur Kahane, Reinhardt's long-term dramaturg, who, in his *Tagebuch eines Dramaturgen* (Diary of a Dramaturg), remembers his first professional meeting with Reinhardt in 1902 at the Café Monopol in Berlin. Kahane's diary was published in 1928, which means that he describes his meeting with Reinhardt and their discussion with the benefit of hindsight and the knowledge of how successfully Reinhardt's career developed. It is interesting how Kahane tries to present a consistent and coherent narrative of the intentionality of Reinhardt's artistic trajectory, which remained seemingly unchanged and uncorrupted over the course of nearly three decades. Everything Reinhardt had postulated in 1902 seemed to have been fully realized during his subsequent career.

Kahane presents Reinhardt's vision as diametrically opposed to the work produced under Brahm. Although Reinhardt acknowledged the qualities of the realistic acting style, he refused to focus on 'a specific literary programme, as little on Naturalism as on others'.[6] He contrasted the dark and muted atmosphere of everyday life as depicted by naturalist theatre with his bright and colourful vision of a theatre that shows an enhanced version of life.[7] The emphasis on visuals and sound ('I cannot tell you how much I long for music and colour')[8] puts forward a sensual approach to theatre with a focus on the affective qualities of performance and not on its literary value.

'As a matter of fact, the theatre is more than an auxiliary art to other art forms. There is only one purpose of the theatre: *the theatre*, and I believe in a theatre that belongs to the actor.'[9] As we shall see, a decade later there still seemed to be the need to communicate the principles of Reinhardt's artistic agenda by declaring them in the *Blätter des Deutschen Theaters* (Journal of the Deutsches Theater). This indicated the challenge that the process of familiarizing critics and audience with this new approach to theatre posed to Reinhardt's artistic team.

A look at the critical reception of Reinhardt's very first directorial work, the staging of Maurice Maeterlinck's symbolist play *Pelléas and Mélisande* at the Neues Theater[10] in March 1903, provides an impression of the paradigm shift that his aesthetic represented. Reinhardt had hired the impressionist painter Lovis Corinth, who, together with the artist Leo Impekoven, created a striking set design. Interesting is the claim by some of the approving critics that Reinhardt had started 'a reform of the stage and costume design',[11] followed by the wish that others would take his new approach as an example. Critics consistently pointed out how successfully his diverse settings affected the audience: from an enchanted birch forest to a scene at the seaside under steep rugged cliffs or a night-time setting in the park; each stage design created a new atmosphere which addressed the audience on an emotional and sensual level. In his review in the *Berliner Tageblatt*, critic Fritz Stahl approvingly stated: 'One does not need to know anything of the drama in order to enjoy this picture';[12] whereas Isidor Landau, a critic with a strong bias towards naturalist theatre, bemoaned the fact that the dramatic text was no longer positioned at the heart of the production but instead occupied an equal status to musical and visual elements.[13] Others, such as Alfred Klaar in the more conservative newspaper *Vossische Zeitung*, still focused on a lengthy discussion of the dramatic text in his review, trying to link his knowledge about dramaturgical structure, predominantly shaped by the naturalist movement, to Maeterlinck's unconventional symbolist dramaturgy.[14] These different reactions show that Reinhardt had noticeably introduced his move away from the literary-centred naturalistic theatre to a more holistic and sensual aesthetic.

The lack of guidance by a text or adherence to a conventional dramaturgy together with the wider focus on diverse elements of performance challenged the audience's perception. In lieu of a naturalistic theatre that was characterized by a distinct predominance of drama and could be predominantly accessed on a textual and intellectual level, the audience was confronted with theatre experiences that spoke to them on a more phenomenological level, attacking their visceral senses as much as challenging their intellectual understanding.

The fact that Reinhardt appeared as a first-time director at the Neues Theater, a fairly new and less historically charged theatre, gave him leeway to experiment without being scrutinized too much by the press. But, in 1905, when he started his artistic directorship of the prestigious Deutsches

Theater, Reinhardt had to win over a core audience that was used to Brahm's naturalist theatre, a theatre aesthetic biased towards the literary text and easily readable to those who were used to the 'Brahm-Stil'. Reinhardt's emphasis on the theatre as a holistic and sensual art form presented a challenge to this audience's reading of the stage, and thus his artistic team continuously worked on the communication of his theatrical agenda.

Metropolis, Parvenupolis, Theatropolis

However important the aesthetic context of the Deutsches Theater's and ultimately Reinhardt's work is, it is intricately linked to the geographical and demographical circumstances that were at play in the young metropolis of Berlin.[15] Herbert Ihering's (1888–1977) account from 1907, the year he came to live and work in Berlin, provides the reader with a vivid impression of a culturally vibrant area, which today would be situated in the larger district called Berlin Mitte:

> I was right in the middle of this young and fresh Berlin, in the vicinity of the Linden and the Friedrichstrasse, the Weidendammer Bridge and the Kupfergraben, the City Palace and the National Gallery. A few steps – and I was at the Deutsches Theater and at Hans Gregor's Komische Oper. A few steps further – and I reached the Lessing-Theater, the Kleines Theater and the Königliches Schauspielhaus.[16]

This later very successful theatre critic, director and dramaturg had rented a room in Krausnickstrasse, just off Oranienburger Strasse, and in the above-cited extract from his autobiography, Ihering poignantly merges important landmarks of the Prussian capital with the new attractions of the burgeoning metropolis. Indeed, Berlin in 1907 presented itself as a young and fresh city and this was the case for several reasons. Since the founding of the German Reich in 1871, Berlin's population, economy and, with it, its cultural assets had grown significantly. Over the course of half a century, 'between 1848 and 1905, the population of Berlin leaped from 400,000 to 2 million; huge suburbs ringing the city added another 1.5 million.'[17] With this increase in status and population emerged a new metropolitan identity: 'Berlin began to be called the *parvenu* capital of Europe; loud, pushy and ostentatious.'[18] In his monograph *Ein theatralisches Zeitalter* (A Theatrical Age), theatre scholar Peter W. Marx argues that in the narrative of Berlin's rapid ascent to a metropolis of international recognition, the parvenu – the self-made man – is the emblematic figure of a city in which identities are quickly acquired and changed. Moreover, the figure of the parvenu serves as a fundamental driving force for Berlin's metropolitan theatre culture whose inherent motto 'to see and to be seen' served as an ideal platform for the parvenu's project of self-fashioning at the visual surface of society.[19] Ihering mentions the heart of this parvenu culture, the famous Friedrichstrasse, a name iconic for Berlin's nightlife and entertainment district. During the day the nearby boulevard Unter den Linden, which had been the heart of the Prussian state's military self-staging, was now the meeting place for Berlin's upper and middle classes. In illustrious cafés and restaurants and on Sunday afternoon walks, the nouveau-riche citizens paraded the newest fashion and claimed their position at the top of Berlin's society in the same way that military parades had asserted – and continued to assert, yet not to the same degree – the presence of the Prussian state in the public sphere.

A further landmark mentioned in Ihering's description is the Weidendammer Bridge, a bridge across the river Spree emblematic of Berlin's growth and expansion, connecting the Dorotheenstadt district (including Friedrichstrasse and the boulevard Unter den Linden) and the Friedrich-Wilhelmstadt Theater (north of the river with the Lessingtheater and the Deutsches Theater). Further along the river Spree is the Kupfergraben, a street leading up to the Museumsinsel (museum island) with, among other museums, the National Gallery and ultimately the Hohenzollern City Palace, the residence of the Prussian king and German Kaiser Wilhelm II. Ihering's short description culminates in an enumeration of the most significant theatres in his vicinity among which the Deutsches Theater tried to claim its place at the top. For what seemed like a city of endless cultural experiences to the nineteen-year-old Ihering, was, however, a very competitive environment for those who were trying successfully to run a theatre. Around 1910 the city of Berlin hosted about thirty theatre institutions, most of which were privately run as economic enterprises which had to be financially viable.[20] And still investors were looking for new theatre businesses to start up, as Max Epstein describes in *Theater als Geschäft* (Theatre as a Business), published in 1911. Concerned about his observation that 'in Berlin, there are at least 20 people milling about with nothing else in mind than the launching of a theatre enterprise',[21] he methodically explains step by step what a theatre entrepreneur has to consider when starting up a new theatre business in order to avoid financial ruin. Epstein covers a range of issues, from the building regulations to an efficient ticket sale system, the renting out of facilities and the best way of handling press relations. His book is as much a guidebook for his contemporaries as it is a cultural portrait of the contemporary theatre scene in Wilhelmine Berlin. His advice on the best theatre location is very helpful for learning more about the Deutsches Theater's theatrical neighbourhood. Although the area seems to be saturated with theatres, a true theatropolis, Epstein acknowledges the district around the Friedrichstrasse with its highly frequented train station and array of shops and locales to be an ideal area. It meets the criteria of accessibility and vibrancy, which he considers to be the key factors for drawing in large audiences. According to Herbert Ihering, the issue of the district's density of theatres does not pose an obstacle since every theatre has its own specific profile; he even goes so far as to attest that Berlin enjoys a healthy balance of different theatres.[22] Concerning the demographics of the Deutsches Theater's audience, Siegfried Jacobsohn, Ihering's subsequent editor-in-chief at the theatre journal *Die Schaubühne*, differentiates between two kinds of audiences at the Deutsches Theater. He personally dislikes the loud and ostentatious crowd which, according to him, attends any kind of sensational Berlin premiere 'which are insufferable due to the vapour of impropriety of a tarted up and clamorous cohort of show-offs'.[23] Instead, he recommends attending a performance during the week where he describes the audience as consisting of 'quiet, educated and tasteful people from all of Germany's social classes and regions'.[24] Jacobsohn identifies with this kind of audience and claims that they appreciate the Deutsches Theater 'because for thirty years now, it is full of memories of celebrations of art, because it is simple and intimate and graceful in a good way'.[25] As problematic as this glorifying description of the right audience for the Deutsches Theater is, Jacobsohn is not alone in his criticism. Influential theatre critics such as Maximilian Harden (1861–1927) and Alfred Klaar (1848–1927) articulated similar concerns about the superficial attitude of some parts of Berlin's new audiences.[26] Regardless of whether one would want to join them in their critique or dismiss these accounts as heavily biased towards a glorification of the established *Bildungsbürgertum* (educated middle classes), what these accounts ultimately show is the change in the demographics the Deutsches Theater was trying to address.

Concerning its location and demographics, the Deutsches Theater therefore was both advantaged and challenged at the same time. Factors such as the easy access to the Deutsches Theater owing to the train station nearby, the highly frequented area around Friedrichstrasse and a loyal core audience were certainly considered advantageous to Reinhardt's theatre business. At the same time, these factors can be interpreted differently: located in a very popular area of Berlin with entertainment competition right around the corner, Reinhardt had to satisfy the hunger for new and flashy entertainment which the audience of parvenupolis was developing, while at the same time trying to live up to the Deutsches Theater's artistic and historical importance. Successfully bridging the gap between those seemingly contradictory demands meant to establish a continuity of artistic standard while at the same time drawing in audiences large enough to secure the theatre's profitability.

Dramaturgical practices at the Deutsches Theater

Key to the efficient functioning of Reinhardt's company, and to the production of his artworks, was the role of dramaturg. In the British theatre the dramaturg, despite now becoming more common, is still hardly known.

The position is perhaps better known as literary manager, a role that for instance Kenneth Tynan and John Russell Brown filled when Laurence Olivier and Peter Hall, respectively, were Directors of the British National Theatre. The dramaturg is a much better known figure in German theatres, dating back to Gotthold Ephraim Lessing's association with the short-lived attempt to create a national theatre in Germany at the end of the eighteenth century. The role of dramaturg has been described by Adam Versényi as follows:

> A dramaturg is a person with knowledge of the history, theory, and practice of theatre who helps a director, designer, playwright, or actor realize their intentions in a production. The dramaturg ... is an in-house artistic consultant cognizant of an institution's mission, a playwright's passion, or a director's vision, and who helps bring them all to life in a theatrically compelling manner. This goal can be accomplished in myriad ways and the dramaturg's role often shifts according to context, and is always fluid.[27]

As we shall see, Max Reinhardt, while undoubtedly controlling the artistic output of his theatres, was indebted to his two major dramaturgs: Felix Hollaender and Arthur Kahane.

Although in the nineteenth century theatres had already widely employed dramaturgs, the introduction of an institutionalized dramaturgical office, responsible for the literary management as well as the inner and, above all, outer communications of the theatre, was an important development under Reinhardt's directorship. It became a necessity and cornerstone of the administration of his growing theatre imperium. The dramaturgical practice at the Deutsches Theater was highly organized, and although Reinhardt's work was advertised under the label of the ingenious director – also referred to as 'the Professor' – his creative practice was fuelled by the artistic team with which he surrounded himself. The two heads of his dramaturgical department were Hollaender and Kahane. Joined by changing assistant dramaturgs, they consistently accompanied Reinhardt throughout his career at the Deutsches Theater.[28] In his diary, Kahane humorously describes a chaotic but typical *Regiesitzung* (directorial meeting) with Reinhardt and his artistic as well as technical staff. This description is very informative with regard to the distribution of tasks at the Deutsches Theater as well as to the way in which Kahane portrays his dramaturgical position:

> Everyone is present. Even the busiest, the administrative director ... Aside from him: both of the dramaturgs; one of them the quasi minister of the theatre's foreign affairs, the other the literary office clerk working on text, concept, casting etc.; furthermore, he has to provide for some humour in those meetings ... While [the technical team] is quickly gathering designs and models, the foreign minister, with a bold leap, is already at

the director's left ear and whispers to him – mysteriously and in a low voice, but still loud enough so that everybody has to listen – the battle report from the ten theatres of war. The poor man has to fight with the authorities, with the press, with the competitors, with the most famous and most recalcitrant authors, the most prominent members bearing down on him. He has lawsuits, appointments, peace agreements and engagement deals behind him as well as ahead of him, and so, in the theatre world, as with everywhere else, the political tune is the nastiest.[29]

In this almost allegorical description, Kahane compares the theatre with a state at war, in which both of the dramaturgs occupy central positions in the government – one of them responsible for foreign affairs, the other one assuming the role of home secretary. He effectively portrays them as being indispensable to the smooth running of the theatre and it almost seems as though he is fiercely defending the importance of the dramaturgical advisors. This does not seem surprising when looking at the contemporary satirical discourse surrounding Reinhardt's 'army of dramaturgs'[30] who figured prominently in caricatures and satirical plays such as Hermann Bahr's (1863–1934) *Die gelbe Nachtigall* (The Yellow Nightingale), which premiered in 1907 at the Lessingtheater, practically around the corner from the Deutsches Theater. The six dramaturgs in this satirical play are reduced to redundant, inarticulate bystanders who are lurking in corners, unable to make a decision without the approval of their charismatic artistic director. In this context, it does not come as a surprise that Arthur Kahane defended his seminal position in the theatre institution by emphasizing his valuable contribution to the theatre's survival in the face of constant competition, not least from the Lessingtheater.

The two fundamentally important but very different dramaturgical job profiles were split between Hollaender and Kahane, with the former fulfilling the task of the outward-facing dramaturg and the latter focusing on the literary desk job within the institution. The difference between the two dramaturgs with regard to their work but also to their personalities is a recurring theme in the account of actors and directors who worked with them. In his autobiography, actor Eduard von Winterstein (1871–1967) simply states: 'Hollaender was loud, Kahane was quiet, this characterizes the difference between those two men most aptly.'[31] According to von Winterstein's description, Hollaender was an energetic and clamorous personality, who knew how to handle the press and the public relations of his theatre, giving his dramaturgical profile the distinct edge of an advertising man who knows how to sell his product ('market crier')[32]. Kahane, by contrast, seems to have embodied the stereotype of the bookish and intellectual literary dramaturg. Von Winterstein admits his fondness for Kahane, with whom he had long, stimulating discussions in his office. However, he recalls that Kahane's popularity among the ensemble of the Deutsches Theater was adversely affected by Reinhardt's habit of delegating unpleasant tasks, like delivering bad news about the recasting of roles or the rejection of scripts.[33] With mordacity, Kahane himself describes this thankless aspect of his profession at the beginning of his diary and draws the conclusion that the dramaturg, despite serving as the artistic conscience of the theatre, will always be its sole scapegoat.[34]

Time and again, by contemporaries as well as theatre historians, Kahane has been described as no less and at the same time no more than Reinhardt's right-hand man.[35] This familiar trope can also be found in the most recent article on Kahane in 2007 in the *Journal for Studies of History and Culture of the Jews, Aschkenas*. Tracing the considerable influence of the many Jewish dramaturgs in Berlin's theatrical culture, the author, Anat Feinberg, explains Kahane's seminal position in the infrastructure of the Deutsches Theater. However, she also claims that Kahane almost vanished behind the overbearing name of the ingenious 'Professor Reinhardt'. According to Feinberg, in contrast to his dramaturgical colleague Heinz Herald (1890–1964), who managed the experimental stage *Das Junge Deutschland* (Young Germany) at the Deutsches Theater, Kahane did not have a proper project of his own, thereby simply remaining 'Reinhardt's dramaturg'.[36]

However, there was one area where the presence of the dramaturg with a strong voice in his own right becomes very noticeable, the publication of an in-house journal, *Blätter des Deutschen Theaters*. The journal might not have been Kahane's own exclusive project but he was certainly the animating force in this endeavour. And it was by means of this publication project that the dramaturg not only contributed to the operation of Reinhardt's company but also helped to construct the public image of Reinhardt the director.

Blätter des Deutschen Theaters

On the evening of Saturday, 26 August 1911, the Deutsches Theater Berlin opened its seventh season with a premiere of Friedrich Freksa's new play *Der fette Caesar* (Fat Caesar). That evening, most audience members would have noticed a change in the routine of their theatre visit. In addition to the programme informing the audience about the artistic team behind the production as well as the cast onstage, every audience member received the first issue of the new in-house theatre journal *Die Blätter des Deutschen Theaters*. Therefore, a look around the auditorium of the Deutsches Theater before the lights went down might have shown audience members thumbing through or even curiously studying this unfamiliar, sixteen-page booklet with a drawing of the recognizable Deutsches Theater façade on its cover, probably wondering about the function and purpose of this publication. Flipping it open, the curious spectator would have been addressed by the head dramaturgs of the theatre, Arthur Kahane and Felix Hollaender. In a preface to this first issue and to the project of their theatre journal in

FIGURE 2.2 *Cover of the* Blätter des Deutschen Theaters *(Schloss Wahn).*

general, they elaborated on its purpose and, on a larger scale, the purpose and aim of their theatre, the Deutsches Theater under the directorship of Max Reinhardt. The preface was followed by seven texts that differed in genres, ranging from explanatory statements by dramatists about their work to poems and short commentaries on events of the day. These contributions varied in form and content significantly, yet all of them related in some way or other to the Deutsches Theater's artistic and dramaturgical agenda.

The title of the theatre journal can be roughly translated as *The Journal of the Deutsches Theater*; however, a faithful translation of this title would have to respect the original term *Blätter* – the plural of the word *Blatt*, which either translates into a *sheet of paper* or, in a *pars pro toto* meaning, is a colloquial term that designates a newspaper or journal. This twofold meaning already hints at the ambivalent nature of the *Blätter*. They can both be considered as a loose collection of ideas and statements with a distinct experimental stance; however, they can also be seen as seeking the status of a proper journal among other legitimate print media in Wilhelmine Berlin. These *Blätter* reveal something of the mostly hidden dramaturgical work of Kahane and Hollaender which played a seminal part in the process of the branding of the label Reinhardt. In a style that was part education, part propaganda, the two leading dramaturgs described the artistic direction that the Deutsches Theater was taking:

This journal is concerned with what we think is the concern of the Deutsches Theater ...

New routes and new objectives lie ahead of us. And since it is essential to protect a work that we deem to be good and just against everything that wants to disturb, to repudiate any misinterpretation and misconception – we open up the workshop. No new idea! It is naive and wrong to think that art speaks for itself to its contemporaries, especially if there is a neat distinction drawn between success and understanding. No artist yet has conquered his time with his first assault ... Critical objection, however, which accrued from the matter itself, has never inhibited us. And yet we think that the essential idea of what we aimed for, and sometimes even achieved, was not always recognized. Therefore it seems useful to us to articulate the result of long-time experience if it is supposed to point to and have an effect on the future.

To us, the essence of this result is: the theatre belongs to the theatre. It has always been our effort to give it back to itself. Its fantastic colourfulness, the infinity of its possibilities and variabilities, the interweaving of sound, word, colour, line, rhythm create the soil from which grows its deepest impact.

The theatre is neither a moral nor a literary institution.

All the attempts of theoretical heads to alienate it from its actual destiny, to turn it into a secondary aid, a mere servant of poetry, have to ricochet off its resilient nature. Theatre and literature are separate terms ...

This was executed more methodically than any spectator would have guessed – no matter if we, informed by contemporary sensibilities, tried to transform masterpieces from the past into a lively present or risked applying our forces to an experiment; attempts which were not always successful. On a route prescribed to us, we sought to expand the frame of current theatre, to heighten its effects, to make the contact with the audience more intimate. Thus, it was not a coincidence that we moved from the small theatre to the arena. We will continue on this route. Perhaps not without cause, we are confident that new, clear views and perspectives will open up to those who follow us.

FELIX HOLLAENDER.
ARTHUR KAHANE.[37]

To a reader from the twenty-first century, this lengthy extract from the first issue's preface might first and foremost provoke criticism. Too boastful seems the tone in which the Deutsches Theater praises its project, too obvious is the clear and urgent need to regulate and control, maybe even police the audience's reception. It can be argued that this frank language ('naive and wrong', 'misconception') is simply reflecting the strongly worded criticism of the contemporary theatre press,[38] and that a contemporary reader would not have seen this as an unusual choice of words. However, the attempt almost to force the reader/spectator into a certain mode of perception remains a rather problematic aspect of the *Blätter* and points to their uncomfortable position between propaganda and educational purpose. Simply taken at face value, the preface alludes to several issues that Kahane and Hollaender are trying to address in their function as head dramaturgs of the Deutsches Theater. They establish clearly that the work of the Deutsches Theater is concerned with innovation. According to them, the innovative approach is based on a holistic concept of theatre that promotes the equality of all the different elements in performance and discards the supremacy of the written word. In allusion to Schiller's famous speech *The Stage Considered as a Moral Institution*[39] in 1784 – which featured as a prominent motto in the bourgeois theatre of the previous century – and in reference to the strong literary bias in the naturalist theatre movement at the end of the nineteenth century, they problematize the instrumentalization of the theatre for moral or literary purposes. Instead, they put forward the autonomy of theatre as art form. Their main interest lies in the specific sensual and affective qualities of performance and in creating a special, more intimate relationship with their audience. According to Kahane and Hollaender, a significant aspect of their commitment to the audience is to create new theatre spaces, one of which is the arena stage, which can facilitate a renegotiation of the stage–auditorium divide.[40] In this heavy emphasis on theatre as art form, and in the stress upon the value of innovation, Kahane and Hollaender's argument implicitly strengthens the position of the director.

However, it becomes clear throughout their manifesto-like text that there is an urgent concern to communicate the above-described agenda appropriately. The head dramaturgs of the Deutsches Theater are explicitly worried that their audience is largely oblivious or even hostile towards attempts at innovation in staging, set design or theatre architecture. ('And yet we think that the essential idea of what we aimed for, and sometimes even achieved, was not always recognized.') The emphatic purpose of the *Blätter*, therefore, is to communicate the Deutsches Theater's artistic agenda. As a result of this educational project, Kahane and Hollaender are hoping to protect their work against attacks by un- or ill-informed theatre critics and audience members. Thus, the closing lines bear a twofold meaning: 'those who follow us' refers to the audience following the work of the Deutsches Theater by attending performances and, at the same time, to the readers/ followers of their journal who Kahane and Hollaender promise to provide a deeper insight into and a more profound understanding of the Deutsches Theater's artistic work. Working towards the systematic dissemination of information about the artistic profile of the theatre seems to have been crucial in preventing the loss of a core audience owing to a lack of understanding and/or familiarity with Reinhardt's work. Apparently, the distribution of an in-house journal was considered to be an appropriate remedy for these potential problems. The journal was thus effectively introduced as a guide for the audience, an audience which in Berlin specifically was[41] by now well enculturated in the habit of reading and thus familiar with the concept of being guided by the written word.

As a guide for its audience the *Blätter* produced a discourse about theatre practice that was not bound up with performed plays, as was the discourse of theatre journalism. Before the journal's first publication, in a letter that he wrote to the author Rudolf Alexander Schröder in 1911 Kahane outlined the journal's purpose:

> we want to campaign not only for the continuance of our theatres but also for new comprehensive plans, … we wish to apply the spoken and written word as an effective instrument for the promotion of our ideas with the press and the audience … It should be multifaceted, educational and amusing, it should – in a cheerful and romantic tone – provide stimulation to the expert as well as the layperson …
>
> If the theatre is the house of unlimited possibilities, then our weekly journal will allow as much space for factual consideration and clear and conscious measuring of realities as for visionary gazing into the future. Those who have a connection to this iridescent phantom that we call theatre are invited to our table.[42]

What makes this letter interesting and very informative is Kahane's explicit wish to create a journal that addresses a wide and diverse audience with the aim to promote not simply his theatre, like any other means of advertising, but also 'new comprehensive plans'. Although in the letter itself, he does not go into detail about these plans, the content of the journal later showed that those plans comprise fundamentally new directions in writing, acting and, above all, stage design.

Moving away from a focus solely on the products of dramatists, the journal demonstrates that plans, the work of directors and dramaturgs, are as interesting and worthy of attention as plays. When the dramaturgical department of the Deutsches Theater quite consciously decided to start mediating the theatre experience through the written word, this decision allowed them not only to exploit a popular medium of its time – the journal – but also to bring the dramaturgical department to the forefront. In doing so the dramaturgical department and its journal may be said to have established a free-standing discourse of dramaturgy and directing, offered explicitly to audiences as a discourse of interest in its own right.

New spaces

The first issue of the *Blätter* spoke of moving 'from the small theatre to the arena'. The development of large arena-based productions is now regarded as one of the key features of Reinhardt's aesthetic practice as a director, and celebrated as one of his most significant innovations. It was in the pages of the *Blätter* that this innovation was not only rationalized but also, simultaneously, promoted as an important and valuable new theatrical practice. This can be seen in Kahane's article in the second issue, entitled 'Glossen zum Theater der Fünftausend' (Notes about the Theatre of Five Thousand), in which he introduces the idea of a theatre for the masses.[43] The article, from September 1911, has to be read in close connection with Max Reinhardt's earlier staging of *König Ödipus* (Oedipus Rex) in the venue Zirkus Schumann in November 1910 and the upcoming production of the play *Jedermann* (Everyman), which would premiere in the same venue on the 1 December 1911. The Zirkus Schumann, a veritable circus arena, could accommodate over 5,000 spectators, a noticeable difference to the auditorium of the Deutsches Theater with its capacity of around 600. Kahane explains the reasons behind Reinhardt's artistic decision to perform *Oedipus Rex* and *Everyman* in another venue. Arguing that theatre as an art form has a strong sensitivity to the Zeitgeist, he relates the changes in society to those in the theatre and claims to have observed a newly found appreciation for the masses, the myth and the body. According to Kahane, the simplicity forced upon the production by the different spatial layout of the arena stage showcases best the actor's physicality. Only the human presence, the voice and lighting should be used to create an impact. Kahane's reference to the bare Elizabethan stage serves as an argument for the timeless value and appeal of simplicity in stage design. Furthermore, he asserts that the vast space and musical elements should facilitate a strong bond between the audience and the performers, with individual spectators becoming part of a whole and timeless theatre community. He states: 'Here, the audience stops being an audience and instead becomes a people who feels simply and primitively but greatly and powerfully, like the people of all times.'[44]

In this instance, the *Blätter* may be said to have created a truly intertheatrical connection.[45] In doing so it helped to promote an image of Reinhardt as a director who was not confined to a particular theatre. While the Deutsches Theater may have been identified by audiences with Reinhardt's work, the *Blätter* as the official journal of the Deutsches Theater, invited the audience to take an interest in how Reinhardt tackled aesthetic challenges posed by a different venue. Therefore Zirkus Schumann was positioned as an extension of the Deutsches Theater. And it was able to be thus positioned because both theatres were linked together by the common purpose of taking forward Reinhardt's theatrical innovations. In this way the aesthetic practice comes to be associated with the creative figure of the director as an autonomous individual rather than with particular theatres. The director as it were becomes bigger than the theatre. This discourse took hold through the penetration of the *Blätter*'s ideas into journalists' writing. Issue 10 of the *Blätter*, distributed on 1 December 1911, the evening of the premiere of *Everyman* at the Zirkus Schumann, also contained an article on the theatre. This was clearly absorbed by the critic Julius Keller who, in his review in the *Berliner Lokalanzeiger*, pointed out the elucidating function and overall value of the articles dedicated to explaining the challenges of and reasons behind the arena stage.[46] This positive reaction can be read as an indicator of a general awareness of the existence of the *Blätter*. The critic has not only taken notice of the new in-house journal, but has even read it and decided to refer to it in his article, thereby directing his readership towards the journal. Keller describes the function of the journal as a legitimate source of information and acknowledges it as more than simple promotional material. This incident serves as an example of how the journal was starting to be taken seriously by the critics, which subsequently led to a dialogue between the theatre and the wider public via the theatre press. The reflection on productions was no longer a one-way street, initiated and dominated by the theatre critics, but a discourse with participants on both sides of the production–reception divide. Of course the status of the director whose theatrical innovations were the topic of the articles and reviews was discursively strengthened within this process. But there was a further element that contributed to the production of the image and status of Reinhardt the director.

New acting styles

As announced by the advertisement for the *Blätter*, not only directors and dramaturgs but playwrights and actors too contributed to the journal. Gertrud Eysoldt (1870–1955), a regular member of the Deutsches Theater ensemble, known for her eccentric acting style, explains her approach to the role of Kleist's *Penthesilea* in Felix Hollaender's production of the play and thus actively contributes to a broader discourse around new acting styles that was being introduced after a period of dominant Naturalism. Her short essay 'Penthesilea', from the third issue in late September 1911, passionately describes her work on the role and even comes close to comparing it to physical torture. Eysoldt speaks of feeling the heartbeat of Penthesilea in her chest, of her own tense body, which is being painfully subjugated to Penthesilea's temper, and of her longing to be devoured by the force of a stranger's volition.[47] This emphatic, visceral description echoes the many reviews of Eysoldt's performances, which confess to being fascinated by her 'cat-like ingenuity', her 'excesses of imagination' and her ability to 'apply the colour of the perverse as thickly as possible'.[48] Especially in contrast to the production at the Königliches Schauspielhaus, directed by Paul Lindau shortly before Hollaender's production premiered at the Deutsches Theater, Eysoldt stands out as an expressionistic actor who almost pushes past the limits of propriety on stage.

The discussion surrounding Eysoldt and her extraordinary acting style began several years before her portrayal of the character Penthesilea. Eysoldt had become instantly known as a wildly physical and extreme performer with her embodiment of the role of Elektra in Hofmannsthal's rewriting of the ancient Greek myth in 1903. The correspondence between Eysoldt and Hofmannsthal, who were intimate friends and professional colleagues, bears witness to the intensity with which Eysoldt responded to the character Hofmannsthal had created. Similarly to her strongly worded commentary on *Penthesilea*, Eysoldt paints a visceral picture of her first reading of *Elektra*: 'I suffer – I cry out from this violence – I fear my own forces – this torture that is waiting for me. I will suffer terribly from this.'[49]

Positioning Hofmannthal's play and Eysoldt's performance in its theatrical context, Sally McMullen explicates:

> Hofmannsthal's Elektra was played in 1903 by Gertrud Eysoldt. She helped to implement the changes introduced by Max Reinhardt by emphasizing the need for a fully physical kind of acting. The old static stylization gave way to a mode of representation characterized by great mobility. It was important that each new idea expressed verbally should also be expressed in a supremely visual manner, through movements capable of conveying the slightest nuance to the audience. Gertrud Eysoldt's genius lay in her ability to mime: her movements, whilst appearing spontaneous and fresh, represented a new mode of stylization, which rapidly became a hallmark of Reinhardt's theatre.[50]

Eysoldt's acting was not only a hallmark of Reinhardt's practice in her appearances on stage; it may also be said to promote that practice by being described in the official in-house journal of Reinhardt's theatre. In

FIGURE 2.3 *Gertrud Eysoldt as Elektra, 1903 (Schloss Wahn).*

the forty-fourth issue of the *Blätter* in March 1914, commenting on the character Juliane in Knut Hamsun's play *Vom Teufel geholt* (In the Grip of Life), Eysoldt describes a process of somehow ingesting or being ingested by a character. This sort of language suggests something more than simply carrying forward a programme for a new mode of acting. Going deeper than merely pursuing a conscious programme, Eysoldt allows herself to be taken over by the role. As a representative of Reinhardt's new mode of acting her statement may be taken to bear witness to the depth by which the director's project penetrates his performers. As such it contributes to the emergence of the image of a director whose control over others goes beyond organization and inhabits their being.

Consolidating the Reinhardt discourse

We have looked at how both the *Blätter* and the members of the company promoted Reinhardt's innovation and indeed his potency as a director. But the *Blätter* also did a slightly more complex job of work.

At the beginning of the 1912/13 season and in the twentieth issue of the *Blätter*, Kahane and Hollaender reflected on the development of the in-house journal so far. They arrive at the preliminary conclusion that the *Blätter* project had been fairly successful. The dramaturgs claim that their journal had been read by a considerable part of the audience, which, owing to the strong attendance at the Deutsches Theater, amounts to a large readership. Very noticeable is the change in tone compared to the preface in the first issue of the *Blätter*, where they had generally talked about trying to react to misunderstandings and avoid misconceptions and misinterpretations. A year later, they quite openly use the terms 'friend and foe' and call the summer break between the seasons the time 'between battles'. This use of language shines a light on why Kahane, in looking back at the beginning of the *Blätter*, had called the journal a '*Kampfblatt*' (combat organ). The dramaturgs, as the case of the battle for sovereignty over the interpretation had shown, considered the main function of the journal to retaliate to attacks by the press on the theatre. In their opinion, their highest achievement was that 'almost without polemics, all those legends about the theatre that were being disseminated, those buzzwords that were being spread, they had fallen silent since the existence of the *Blätter*'.[51]

From outside the inner circle of the Deutsches Theater's artistic team, this was regarded somewhat more cynically. The avid theatregoer Max Epstein suggested that publications initiated by the Deutsches Theater merely promoted its own work: 'They contained essays by well-known men and commissioned pages by the employees of the theatre, which should somehow substantiate the importance of the Deutsches Theater, its repertoire and its ensemble.'[52] For him, the articles in the journal do not possess any more analytical value than simple advertisement.

The tension between an educational project, rationalizing the innovative practices, and self-advertisement by an institution was articulated several years later by Herbert Ihering: 'The *Blätter des Deutschen Theaters* opened up a long line of far too many theatre journals; soon almost every municipal theatre had one. But the original still had interesting contributors and at times even a point of view, although back then the advertisement, sometimes hidden behind Kahane's lyrical glance, already predominated.'[53] Here, Ihering speaks with the benefit of hindsight and admits that the journal in its origins provided the reader with informed and stimulating contributions without necessarily lapsing into self-praising mode. Interestingly, he explicitly mentions Kahane as the dramaturgical figure who packaged an advertising agenda into an intellectual artistic project.

The tension that is being articulated here had its origins in the material circumstances of the director's project. The Deutsches Theater was run by Reinhardt as a private enterprise based on making a profit. The profit was necessary not only to survive but also to be able to afford the technical and artistic innovations that the theatre, and its Director, were known for. The official in-house journal had the role of negotiating the balance, or tension, between idealistic artistic endeavour and the quest for profit. The discourse generated by this negotiation can be said to be both symptomatic of and perhaps influential in perpetuating the role and image of the innovative director who seeks to work within the commercial sphere.

The company man

To an observer from outside the German theatre, with its particular traditions and values, the *Blätter* said one further crucial thing about Reinhardt the director. In 1914 the English art and theatre critic Huntly Carter (1861–1942) published a book about Reinhardt. Carter was particularly interested in innovative practices in art, cinema and theatre, producing a series of books attempting to describe what he saw as the 'new spirit' in various arts. His book on Reinhardt was one of the first books about directing in the English-speaking world. In writing that book he drew on the *Blätter*, thereby helping to disseminate the journal's discourses to a wider, and non-German, audience.

Writing about Reinhardt's innovatory attempt to develop a theatre for the masses, Carter quotes at length from Kahane's article *Das Theater der Fünftausend*. But quite apart from his interest in new artistic forms Carter was also interested in artistic institutions and their functioning. For him the *Blätter* represented a challenge to traditional ways of engaging in the arts. He attributes to the journal a 'value to those who desire to come into communication directly with the theatre, instead of through an outside medium'.[54] This statement is of interest for the reflection on dramaturgical practices at the Deutsches Theater insofar as it points to a quintessential function of any form of dramaturgical profession: the task of facilitating a discourse between the theatre and its audience, of providing enough contextual material or offering up interesting provocations in order to start a dialogue. Carter certainly perceives this attempt and values it for his own reflection on Reinhardt's theatre.

But to Carter the journal said something more. In its pages members of Reinhardt's company, whether dramaturg or actor, could be seen to be speaking for themselves, describing their own roles in a shared artistic project. The importance of this, for Carter, can be judged in the context of his views as to what was wrong with contemporary theatre: 'nothing it has done or can do in its present condition has brought it or brings it within measurable distance of producing the complete vision, the design of the poet filled in by answering minds, unified and vital in all respects'.[55] The pages of the *Blätter* seemed to show that Reinhardt the poet was surrounded by 'answering minds'. This provides the evidence which allowed Carter to discriminate between Reinhardt and other sorts of director. As Shepherd points out, Carter's book on Reinhardt takes issue with the model of directing that had been promoted by Edward Gordon Craig:

> In his book Carter celebrates the model of directing which he saw as being initiated by Reinhardt. It was a model which contrasted with the rather more public, and more polemically stated, position adopted by Edward Gordon Craig. Craig was highly critical of the number of departmental 'heads' that tended to operate in contemporary theatre processes. He suggested that these need to be replaced by a single role.[56]

By contrast with Craig's absolutist and individualistic director Reinhardt was, for Carter, a director who worked by cooperation and collaboration:

> All the talk about ruler-art and ruler-artist is drivel. If producers really desire to make an advance, let them study Reinhardt, not Nietzsche, and learn how to think in terms of a circle, not of a pyramid. Reinhardt's contribution to the problem of the theatre is co-directorship. Except to the theatre, co-directorship is not a new thing to this mighty booby world, but outside the theatre dull persons are expounding it in the form of co-management and guild-socialism as *the* idea of the century. The new and significant thing in the theatre is the expression of the Will of the Theatre by co-ordinated minds, each artist taking the keenest interest in presenting the artistic work of the theatre.[57]

Carter goes on to elaborate on what he means by 'co-directorship' and why it is important. The contemporary theatre, he says, produces bad art because it is badly organized:

the great number of units engaged in the production of a play are not properly organised as a body to give that play the widest and most complete expression. They have not a vision in common, but they interpret each in his own way. As a rule they are a spineless and disjointed crew, without the faintest concept[s] of a possible unity.

By contrast there is 'co-directorship':

The system of Max Reinhardt reminds us that what is needed is a new harmonious and intelligent body of interpreters in whose hands all the processes of interpretation are complementary and complete. Such interpreters may be briefly divided into seven classes – the artist-author, director-producer, stage-manager, musician, actor, decorator, and mechanician.[58]

The pages of the *Blätter* showed how various representatives of the different classes of interpreters were indeed working in harmony.

In Carter's analysis Reinhardt's 'co-directorship' model worked to produce both good art and harmonious organization, negotiating the balance between commerce and innovation. 'Co-directorship' provided the unity that would prevent the organization being 'spineless' and thereby make it successful. And so indeed it was. Towards the end of the 1920s the *Blätter des Deutschen Theaters* became *Die Blätter der Reinhardtbühnen* (The Journal of Reinhardt's Stages). During that decade the *Blätter* had diversified significantly. They now included not only an edition for the Grosses Schauspielhaus which, formerly known under the name of Zirkus Schumann, had re-opened after a thorough renovation in 1919, but also editions for Reinhardt's Komödie at the Kurfürstendamm and later the Kurfürstendammtheater.[59] With their diversification the *Blätter* also changed their design, appearing now in a more colourful format and including not only texts but also photographs of popular actors. The company comes to inhabit the journal even more intensively, but now not so much as banner carriers for innovation as celebrity properties. And quite literally above them all of course sits the name of Reinhardt. As both impresario and artist the director's celebrity image itself is now so powerful as to bind together and give coherence to the whole multi-company project.

Leopold Jessner

3

Leopold Jessner: Father of Modern *Regietheater* (Director's Theatre) in Germany

Matthias Heilmann

It was unquestionably Max Reinhardt's contemporary Leopold Jessner who rose to the rank of father or grandfather of modern *Regietheater* in Germany. The two great men of the theatre were absolute opposites in both nature and background. Reinhardt enjoyed a middle-class upbringing in the emancipatory world capital of Vienna, whereas Leopold Jessner, who was born to Lithuanian parents in East Prussian Königsberg on 3 March 1878, had to deal with the hard assimilation struggle of the Eastern European Jews. A remarkable document from Jessner's final years illustrates how the Jewish struggle for acknowledgement and civil equality in the Second German Empire marked his childhood and youth. In American exile in 1940 – more than half a century later, therefore – he reported concerning his childhood: 'I remember very vividly how I, the son of Lithuanian parents and raised as German-Jewish, was called "Litvak Yid" (Lithuanian Jew) by my German playmates and "Yackke" (Jacob)[1] by the Lithuanian ones. Eastern European Jews thought themselves superior to the Western European Jews, while the latter looked down superciliously on their Eastern brothers.'[2]

Such statements about his private life are extremely rare for Jessner, and they also vividly portray his divided native city. Jessner felt his social isolation and role as an outsider deeply and had not forgotten them even fifty years later. By contrast, his strict renunciation of public statements concerning his private life during the years of his great professional successes is striking. His Jewish identity played a central role in his life, and yet, with the exception of his later years in exile, he virtually never spoke of it. He was aware that the Prussian authorities' attitude towards the Jews was hostile. We should not forget that Jessner never received an appointment to a court or state theatre before the founding of the Weimar Republic, and yet – or precisely for this reason – he was a professing Jew in matters of faith as well.[3]

Youth in East Prussia

We do not know when Jessner's ancestors fled their Lithuanian homeland. Lithuania in the vicinity of Königsberg was not an autonomous state, but rather belonged to the Russian Empire, where anti-Jewish sentiment not infrequently erupted into pogroms. We only know that at the time of Jessner's birth there were something close to 4,000 Jews living among the approximately 200,000 inhabitants of Königsberg and that this minority was split into two very contrasting groups: German Jews, who were for the most part well assimilated and typically belonged to the middle class, and the Eastern Jews, who had fled Russian oppression and were trying gradually to become a normal part of the population.[4] Jessner's family initially belonged to the latter group, although fitting into German society was one of the young man's highest priorities. According to the oral testimony of Alfred Perry, a friend of his American exile, Jessner's cultivation of Jewish traditions and observance of religious rites were always a matter of course. In this Jessner formed a stark contrast to most stage artists, provided they did not have, as he had, an Eastern European Jewish background.[5]

Besides his Jewish roots, Jessner's embracing of Social Democracy played a great role in his adolescent years. While many Jews sympathized with liberal parties during the nineteenth century, shortly before the turn of the century they were increasingly joining the socialist movement. A small number of the Königsberg Jews had established themselves in the liberal professions as doctors, lawyers, merchants and bankers – access to the military, the civil service and the teaching professions remained almost completely closed to them until 1918 – but with Königsberg's industrial development, which brought strong population growth and new waves of immigrants from Russia, the majority of Jews now found work in the docks, the shipyards and the metal and timber industries.[6] These changes led to social tensions, the demise of the Liberals and the emergence of Social Democracy as Königsberg's strongest political party. This meant that the most unambiguously important political personage in the city of Königsberg was the charismatic Social Democrat Hugo Haase. From 1897 Haase worked as a directly elected representative in the German Reichstag. The son of a Jewish shoemaker, he had a meteoric career in Germany's Social

Democratic Party, which culminated in his sharing the party chairmanship in 1911 with August Bebel, its chairman of many years.

These historical circumstances are important for understanding the later theatrical personage, because the Königsberg experiences determined Jessner's later political engagement. The parallelism between his commitment to a humane socialism and his Jewish-messianic hope for equal justice and treatment of all human beings became the determining factor of his whole life and work. Jessner's lifelong determination to portray oppression and affront on the stage and to advance the influence of workers' unions was connected with his experience of the all but dehumanizing humiliations of his fellow Jews, who, like his parents, had come to Königsberg from the tsarist neighbourland, and the distressed social condition of the dock, shipyard and metal workers. He knew that the future of Germany lay only in the removal of the barriers imposed by class.[7]

Beginnings as an actor

Jessner's humane and idealistic socialism did not prompt him to a political career. As early as at the age of sixteen he decided to become an actor. Training according to today's standards did not yet exist, especially in the Reich's East Prussian border zone. Thus Jessner was forced to seek his earliest stage experiences in the provinces. He acted both in small theatres in Graudenz, West Prussia and Cottbus and as a member of travelling ensembles, until his breakthrough came in the form of a fateful encounter with the director Carl Heine in the threshold year of 1900. The meeting took place at the Deutsches Theater of Breslau where Jessner had been hired in 1899 and was first introduced to the novel form of popular theatre (*Volkstheater*).[8] Jessner was fascinated by the idea of using low admission prices to generate enthusiasm for literary works, shape aesthetic sensibility and even develop an appreciation for classical works among broad swathes of the population, including underprivileged classes and workers. In 1911, during his Hamburg years, he took up this idea again as the Director (*Leiter*) of the unionized Hamburger Volksschauspiele (Popular Plays).

Carl Heine, who engaged Jessner in 1900 for his Dr. Heine-Ensemble, became his decisive teacher. 'Through him I became acquainted with the concept of *direction* (*Regie*)', Jessner later claimed.[9] His time with the Dr. Heine-Ensemble was distinctly different from his experiences with the other travelling companies. Heine's troupe played every year in practically all the North and East German capitals and was also invited abroad, especially to Scandinavia and Russia. Heine's spectacular achievements included the promotion of young contemporary authors such as Wedekind and a completely new presentation of the plays of Henrik Ibsen, the greatest living dramatist of the period. Around the year 1900 almost all theatrical innovators were oriented towards the great Norwegian dramatist. Ibsen's works did not lend themselves to a clichéd style of dramatic presentation. His characters demanded individual treatment. To replace the histrionic speaking style and professionalized overacting of traditional theatre a new kind of actor appeared on the German stage, conspicuous for a subtly differentiated way of speaking and a sparing use of gesture, who could analytically develop individual characters with nuance and ambiguity. What Heine demanded as a director was the rejection of unsophisticated formality. Jessner later summarized the actor's responsibilities as follows: 'Instead of ungovernable superficiality, to give play to the understanding. To proceed first by dissecting. To analyse what is to be acted both psychologically and technically. To express the sense of the work, the sense of the character, the sense of each individual word.'[10]

The revolutionary aspect of Heine's and Jessner's demand for analytic penetration of a role was its unabashed rejection of Naturalism, the directorial style that still dominated the German stage at the end of the nineteenth century. Otto Brahm, the Director of the Deutsches Theater in Berlin, was likewise a great admirer of Henrik Ibsen, but staged his dramas as scrupulously faithful copies of life in the naturalistic manner. Jessner, on the other hand, regarded the closely realistic depiction of scenes from daily life as a fatal mistake – especially in the case of Ibsen's plays. Anyone who understands theatre as the precisely detailed reproduction of real events can only give a superficial picture of social behaviour and fails to recognize hidden ambiguities, symbolism and the idea lurking behind what is said. Instead of an art of everyday life and the most realistically faithful representation of events on the stage, Jessner and Heine advocated the connection of realistic activity with the psychological development of individual characters.[11]

Regietheater

The term *Regietheater* (director's theatre) is probably most justifiably first applied to the Ibsen productions at the Dr. Heine Theater. A freer treatment of plays that had in mind more than the mere reconstruction of a drama on stage was completely new territory at that time and points to the establishment of theatre as an autonomous art form. The idea that a play could be performed in various ways with the recognizable conceptual signature of a director meant that the interpretation of a classical or contemporary work did not depend on the individual style of an actor, but was rather subject to the creative refashioning of a stage director.

The director's role emerged from that of the earlier *Spielleiter* (play manager), who simply organized the course of rehearsals, managed and supervised the coordination of actors, scenery and technical aspects, and saw his artistic job exclusively in terms of copying a literary template or reconstructing a text on stage. With Carl Heine and the young Leopold Jessner a few years later, the director became the dominant power, who through his interpretation created an independent artwork by reconceiving what was to be represented upon the stage.[12]

The important collaboration with Carl Heine was of short duration, however. With international tours the ensemble had to be continually reconstituted, with the result that the Dr. Heine Theater broke up for organizational and financial reasons. Jessner joined a competing company run by Gustav Lindemann, later the Director of the Düsseldorfer Schauspielhaus. But even there he stayed only a year. His next engagements were with the Deutsches Theater of Hanover and the Residenztheater of Dresden. This instability during the early years of the twentieth century reflected Jessner's dissatisfaction. The young man in his mid-twenties wanted to establish himself as a director and theatrical innovator according to his own standards on a more than regional level. He wanted to put his own mark on a playhouse, which he succeeded in doing, starting in 1904, at the age of twenty-six, when he took over the position of head director (*Oberspielleiter*) at the Thalia Theater in Hamburg. There are no records to determine when Jessner finally completed the transition from actor to director. In Hanover and Dresden, in any case, he had already 'surprised with his unconventional stagings of the classics'.[13]

Thalia Theater of Hamburg – the first station

Theatrical cognoscenti were aware of the young but self-confident directorial innovator, with the result that Franz Bittong and Max Bachur, the Thalia's Directors, decided to bring him to Hamburg. He was to give an artistic-literary boost to an upscale entertainment theatre.[14] Before Jessner, the Thalia Theater was a tradition-rich, but down-at-heel comedy stage (*Lustspielbühne*). Once he began his work there, the house rose to prominence as the most important dramatic theatre in the city, alongside the Deutsches Schauspielhaus, because of its ambitious repertoire. The Thalia retains this ranking to the present day. More than a few people referred to the 'North German Burg', alluding to the most famous playhouse in the German-speaking world at that time, the Viennese Burgtheater.[15]

Jessner proceeded cautiously, but deliberately, with the reorganization. His directorial function at the Thalia Theater was supposed to last eleven years, an astonishing change after the mostly one- or two-year positions he had held previously. He knew that the most important element for a theatre's vitality was the cultivation of a contemporary and international repertoire. Besides, the circumstances at the theatre with its short rehearsal times made it difficult to stage the great classics. Jessner's public expected frequent premieres, if only because of subscriber demands, something hardly credible by today's standards. Approximately two weeks had to suffice for learning parts, even though Jessner reduced the quantity of the repertoire in favour of quality. Instead of witty French 'conversation plays' Jessner opted for English (Wilde, Shaw and so on) and, especially later, Russian authors (Gorky, Andreev, Tolstoy and Chekhov) in his step-by-step literarization of the repertoire. He was profoundly convinced that it was possible to shape and educate the audience's taste.[16]

In his second season in Hamburg Jessner gave a sign of where he was heading with *College Crampton*, a seldom-performed contemporary play by Gerhart Hauptmann. Here the reviews were already using terms like *Grundstimmung* (prevailing mood), which later characterized the directorial style of his great successes in Berlin. To create a prevailing mood – in the case of the title character, the social isolation of an embittered outcast – all stylistic means have to be subordinated to the desired effect. The set design consisted of a three-storey configuration. The space was not used for scenic purposes, but rather emphasized the confinement and encapsulation of the protagonist. Even the lighting reinforced the squalid, dark and depressive mood. Jessner's anti-naturalistic approach generated much attention and met with lasting success.[17] After two years of reorganization he was in a position to make calculated changes. Although classics occupied a surprisingly large place in the repertoire during his early years, he later gave up on them almost entirely. Big Schiller dramas, for example, were feasible on the Thalia's stage only with major concessions because of the shortness of rehearsal time and the relative lack of technical resources. The result was that Jessner renounced the focus on Schiller that would mark his later years in Hamburg. Instead, from 1907 on he devoted himself to another major objective: making Frank Wedekind a fixture at a repertoire and subscription theatre in a capital city.[18]

The director of Wedekind

Jessner had honoured Frank Wedekind more highly than his contemporary Gerhart Hauptmann by calling him 'the writer who really left his mark upon our age'.[19] Much later in an essay on Jessner, the German critic, journalist and author Günther Rühle even went so far in his exaggerated enthusiasm as to call him the 'writer who really left his mark on world literature'.[20] What drew Jessner to Wedekind was the same thing that made him the object of attacks: his pitiless analysis of the hypocritical state of morality and power in the Wilhelmine epoch, his provocative depiction of an age characterized by a petty bourgeois stink and the ostracism of prostitutes, performing artists, bohemians and other social outsiders. Such themes had earned Wedekind bitter animosity, threats, chicaneries from the censors and even personal persecution that included a prison sentence. Jessner showed solidarity with him and wanted to bring the artistic problems that Wedekind himself had suffered to the stage in an uncompromising form. We can assume that a great part of Jessner's fascination had to do with parallels he found between his own person and Wedekind's tragic figures. Jessner began his promotion of Wedekind in 1906 with *Erdgeist* (Earth Spirit), the first part of the *Lulu* tragedy. The Hamburg production was a huge success and went on tour for eleven performances. Wedekind himself appreciated Jessner's advocacy, especially since many other performances of the play were either banned by the censors or disrupted by continual riots.[21] Jessner's staging not only centred on the social taboo of sexuality, it also consciously thematized its connection with the brutality of power in a contemporary male-dominated society.

This was followed in 1907 by a new production of Wedekind's *Frühlings Erwachen* (Spring's Awakening) shortly after its premiere by Max Reinhardt in Berlin. The Reinhardt production was also brought to the Thalia Theater as a guest performance, so that both the audience and the press were deliberately invited to make comparisons. Jessner's fundamental idea was to highlight the play's subtitle *Kindertragödie* (Children's Tragedy), the downfall of adolescents who suffer from an upbringing that is as prudish as it is authoritarian. In order to circumvent the censors, Wedekind had written a stage version in which aspects of masochism, homosexuality and a masturbation scene were eliminated from the text. Jessner, however, succeeded in having the masturbation scene from the uncompromising book version represented on stage. Evidently, he found some way to placate the censors. Jessner's Hamburg production was practically the only public performance before 1918 in which this important scene was retained.[22]

The production of *Die Büchse der Pandora* (Pandora's Box) also occupied a special position. Wedekind's second part of the *Lulu* tragedy experienced an endless history of bans and confiscations. Because the focus here is on the homosexual connection between Lulu and the Countess Geschwitz, this second part was infinitely more provocative and scandalous than the first. Here, too, Jessner succeeded in presenting one of the few public performances of the play in pre-democratic Germany. In full accord with the author's intent, Jessner made Countess Geschwitz the central figure.[23] It is her self-sacrificial disposition and devotion to her lover rather than Lulu's fate that take centre stage. Wedekind's popularization – which made him one of the most performed authors after the lifting of censorship and his premature death in 1918 – was very much due to Jessner. Less successful was the 1913 five-act version of *Lulu* that played in a single evening: its excessive length and thematic overload met with a mostly cool response. Perhaps it was not by chance that Peter Zadek, one of the so-called 'Jessner grandchildren', chose Hamburg for a first staging, seventy years later, of the five-act version with resounding success.

Jessner's most influential Wedekind production for posterity was probably the *Marquis von Keith* of 1914. By Jessner's own statement it was an early anticipation of the 1920 Berlin production.[24] A radical stripping away of subject matter and a concentration on purely ideational aspects without a realistic nucleus were the goal; the time and place of the action were secondary. Jessner focused instead on the play's intellectual content, the stark contrast between the motivations of the main characters Keith and Scholz, the former a fraudulent striver after material pleasures, the latter an extreme case of an exaggerated and masochistic sense of duty. The whole action played out before a uniform scenic background without representational features, where the actors moved like silhouettes against a back wall. The idea was to suggest shadows in mutual pursuit. Barbed repartee without the least spatiotemporal concreteness and only symbolic colouration on a practically empty stage was revolutionary in 1914 and contradicted all previous experience.

The fundamental motif

Surprisingly, both the audience and the critics in Hamburg were mostly on Jessner's side. It was the same with his stagings of other dramatists, though Wedekind remained the heart and core of the Hamburger years. The 1908 production of Maeterlinck's *Pelléas and Mélisande* was also groundbreaking. It occasioned Jessner's first use of the term *Grundmotiv* (fundamental motif), a more precise description than the ambiguous *Grundstimmung* (prevailing mood).[25] In the case of *Pelléas* everything was subordinated to Goland's longing for love, in relation to which even the title characters were distinctly required to recede. Jessner understood fundamental motif as an exclusively core-oriented revision that entailed the elimination of entire scenes and a streamlined tautening aimed at a greater uniformity. Graphic scenery was almost entirely missing in these productions, replaced by changes of mood-creating lighting.

We see a similar procedure in the staging of Ibsen's *Peer Gynt* two years later. This 'Nordic Faust' made do without scenes of national orientation. The fundamental motif was Peer's life journey as symbol of humanity without a specific Nordic atmosphere.[26] The epic character of the play and the frequent changes of scene were indicated exclusively by changes of lighting and the first use of the vertical zoning of space which made it possible to present simultaneous scene shifts without loss of time. New productions of *Peer Gynt* accompanied Jessner everywhere he went (Hamburg, Königsberg and Berlin). Likewise, in 1910, just a few months after *Peer Gynt*, Jessner decided to take on Georg Büchner's *Dantons Tod* (Danton's Death), a drama that was regarded as unplayable at that time because of the multitude of its scenes and characters. Jessner was not interested in the specifics of the French Revolution, nor in the unbridled pathos of Robespierre's and St Just's speeches, but rather in revolution as a fundamental disposition with the people (*Volk*) as the fulcrum, partly in agitated tension during the convent and tribunal scenes, partly in crushing resignation in the prison. With *Danton's Death* political theatre became a reality on a former comic stage.[27]

With still greater logical consistency Jessner put on the same play in the summer of 1911 at the Volksschauspiele (People's Plays), set up by the Central Commission for Workers' Education. There the scenery consisted only of a red curtain.[28] The actors had to fill the space by themselves. It was not Paris in 1791 that was being played, but revolution itself and its failure. A passionate trade unionist, Jessner energetically supported the idea of people's theatre, for it offered the chance of financial compensation for actors who were without work and income during the summer. And in this way the common people could become familiar with world literature in contemporary *mises en scène* attuned to workers' interests. Despite limited resources, the performance of *Danton's Death* came off as a piece of world literature on the highest level, and the little money the actors earned from the low ticket prices would come in handy.

Intendant in his native city during the war

However, Jessner's final years in Hamburg were spent under the pall of impending departure. Rumours that he might leave Hamburg had been circulating for some time. Despite relative independence in artistic matters at the Thalia Theater, he was seeking a theatre directorship that would confer all responsibility on him. In 1913 he applied for the directorship of the Volksbühne (People's Stage) in Berlin. This was exactly the kind of position he had in mind, where pedagogical skills and social engagement were desired. Later the great theatre critic Herbert Ihering very much regretted that Jessner was passed over for the position at that time.[29] Jessner was piqued by his non-consideration, in which extra-artistic reasons may well have played a part, and almost defiantly had his candidate's speech published in the central organ of the Stageworkers' Association.[30] Also, his work was hardly made easier by the First World War. Aggressive militarism dictated what artistic work should be like; foreign authors, with the exception of the neutral Norwegian Ibsen, vanished from the stage.

Thus the appointment as *Intendant* (Director) in his native city of Königsberg in 1915 came to Jessner at a very opportune moment. War conditions complicated the task of directing a theatre here, too, of course. But Jessner's Neues Schauspielhaus (New Playhouse) was able to avoid being closed throughout the war, which was not the case with the rival Stadttheater (Municipal Theatre). The Neues Schauspielhaus was a new theatre building that had opened for operation just five years earlier, equipped with a modern lighting system and boasting a seating capacity of 660, which stood Jessner in good stead for staging the great classical dramas as well as a contemporary repertoire. But there was no question here of privileging the classics over contemporary drama. Jessner's tenure began with the staging of *Peer Gynt*, and Hauptmann's *Das Friedensfest*

(The Reconciliation) followed a mere month later. We should not forget that Jessner had to keep a repertoire going in a time of war. Besides the problem of limited financial resources, the politics of the time demanded the staging of heroic plays, but also divertingly cheerful comedies. Jessner remained unfazed, and put a considerable amount of effort into premieres.[31]

His productions of Shakespeare's *King Lear* and Schiller's *Don Carlos* during the first year gave a clear indication that Jessner was also moving in a classical direction rather than bending to national or heroic interests. Just the opposite: his *Don Carlos* was an almost blatant portrait of the human void at the heart of the Spanish court. It was not Schiller the historian whom Jessner admired, but Schiller the keen observer of human nature. In Jessner's comprehensive reworking of the play in the Königsberg version the treatment of the Carlos–Posa relationship took a back seat to the tragedy of Philip – not the tragedy of a king, but the tragedy of Philip as a human being. For this it was necessary to elaborate the conspiracy of Alba, Domingo and Eboli.[32] This *Don Carlos* was another milestone on Jessner's way to stage direction as an independent artistic achievement. He claimed ever more independence from the textual source. Traditionalists, who sensed a reinterpretation of literary monuments, were already seeing themselves challenged by Jessner's treatment. It was similar with *King Lear*. His abbreviated version of the scene with Lear, the Fool and Edgar on the heath met with incomprehension in the Königsberg reviews.

Nor was there to be any lack of Wedekind productions in Königsberg. The now almost forgotten *Karl Hetmann, der Zwergriese* (Karl Hetman, the Giant Dwarf) in 1916 was the first production, followed by *Earth Spirit* in January 1918 and finally, as one of Jessner's last works in Königsberg, *Pandora's Box*, the second part of the *Lulu* tragedy, in February 1919. Because of censorship the latter premiere was only possible after the proclamation of the Weimar Republic. But in contrast to the audiences in Hamburg and Berlin, the Königsbergers remained aloof in their response to Wedekind's subjects. The attitude to Jessner's art was split in his hometown. Most people respected the native Königsberger out of local patriotism and admired his ability to maintain the 'culture fortress of the East' during the war, but they regarded him with 'quite a bit of scepticism' in regard to his repertoire policy.[33]

For Jessner himself one high point of the Königsberg tenure was certainly his first production of *Wilhelm Tell* (William Tell) in November 1916. Jessner considered Schiller's *Tell* the '*opus ultimum*', and his engagement with it lasted his entire life. The portrait of the Swiss mountain world and the national character of its inhabitants were radically expunged in Jessner's version. In the First World War especially, the significance of *William Tell* lay in its example of liberation from despotic servitude and in the longing for human revolution leading to a sovereignty of the people. A declaration of faith in democracy as the *Kaiserreich* was receding was not only courageous, it contravened everything the audience was used to seeing on stage: expectations were for a folkloristic drama in an atmosphere coloured by regional patriotic leagues. Jessner's legendary start with *William Tell* in Berlin in many respects built on the Königsberg blueprint.[34]

The production of Jessner with the gravest consequences from the theatre-historical perspective was probably Friedrich Hebbel's *Judith*. Although the premiere in the autumn of 1917 occurred before the end of the war and the German Revolution, it anticipated the new period. Ludwig Marcuse, who met Jessner during this time and remained his friend until his death in exile, saw in it a call for democratic reforms and foreign-policy rapprochement after three years of war. Jessner gave Hebbel's Old Testament material an optimistic finale and 'had Hebbel's Judith fading into the Jewish Hanukkah song'.[35] The subject was not the individual act of a humiliated woman with which the biblical source and numerous Judith depictions in the history of art have made us familiar; it was rather that Judith's murder of Holofernes documented the prospect of retaliation for the sufferings of Jews all over the world. In the gruelling course of the war the old elites in the *Kaiserreich* had, in 1917, already begun marking down Jews. The so-called 'stab in the back myth' was prepared for at that time, according to which the imperial army would have remained undefeated in the field, but Jewish and socialist manipulators had subverted it through peace negotiations with the Entente powers and were thus to blame for the German defeat. Jessner was therefore an ideal bogeyman in a double sense. With his *Judith* interpretation Jessner prophetically anticipated that the war's end and the victory of the revolution would entail the integration of the Jewish minority. As a matter of course, he also saw this in terms of his own situation. In a democratic Germany without bans on Jews in government positions he would play a leading role in the life of the theatre.

Appointment as *Intendant* of the Staatstheater in Berlin

The revolutionary events a year later proved Jessner right. 'The ardent socialist and patriotic East Prussian was now quite certain that Germany was rescued.[36] Marcuse impressively describes how Jessner used the chaotic situation after the Kaiser's abdication to advance the restructuring of the German theatre. In an appeal in the *Berliner Tageblatt* he called for a close collaboration between the German Theatre Association (Deutscher Bühnenverein) and the workers' union, the placing of all former court theatres under state or municipal administration and the subordination of all private theatres to public supervision in material respects. He expected that these moves would lead to both a higher level of artistic quality and economic advantages for everyone connected with the theatre.[37]

But more than this it was a matter of a new direction in content. Conservative and monarchical forces seemed to be paralysed during the events of the autumn of 1918. In the transitional phase (1918–19) from the abdication of the Kaiser to the constitution of the Weimar Republic, prominent progressives, Social Democrats and Liberals in government and society succeeded in creating new theatrical conditions in Prussia by exploiting the state of shock that prevailed among the old elites consisting of industrialists, Junkers and the military. The well-known progressive theatre critic of the *Berliner Börsen-Courier* Herbert Ihering wrote of this time of disruption: 'It was a challenge and like a signal finally to put an end to this inconsequential theatre ... I knew at that point that a theatre of the times must arrive ... a theatre of fundamental engagement, of passionate affirmation of new contents.'[38]

The conditions at the Königliches Preussisches Hoftheater (Royal Prussian Court Theatre) at the Berlin Gendarmenmarkt were especially backward. The first stage in Germany to be turned directly into a state playhouse was sunk in irrelevancy because it had declared the taste of the court the official taste and concept of art. Other theatres, too, such as Max Reinhardt's Deutsches Theater in Berlin, had lost their connection to the time and the revolutionary present. They remained stuck in the world of lovely illusion and theatrical literarization. Therefore, the choice of Prussian Culture Minister Konrad Haenisch to fill the position of *Intendant* at the Staatstheater in the spring of 1919 fell on Leopold Jessner. His membership in the Social Democratic Party was certainly advantageous – Conservatives on one side and communists on the other continually made the charge that the appointment was made according to party affiliation[39] – but the fact that Jessner in Hamburg had been able to convert a light comic theatre into one of the most important theatres in Germany for contemporary drama and to keep the Königsberg theatre operating throughout the war was a decisive point in his favour. In the last analysis, the Culture Ministry saw no one as better suited for restoring the house both artistically and as a business to an exemplary and representative theatrical concern for all of Germany.

They were not wrong. Wolfgang Drews, a leading German theatre critic from the time of the Weimar Republic to the Federal Republic of Germany and an occasional deputy director of the Deutsches Theater under Heinz Hilpert, formulated Jessner's objectives, citing in the process Ferdinand Lassalle, the founder of the German Workers' Association (Allgemeiner Deutscher Arbeiterverein) of the nineteenth century, a forerunner of the Social Democratic Party:

> The tall, hulking man from East Prussia, who boldly professed his Jewishness and even more boldly his socialism, heeded Lassalle's demand that we 'Express what is.' He undertook to formulate the feel of the time; he formulated the theatre of the time. A formed theatre of external and internal tempo, of sober passion, of logical structure, of accent, of certainty.

Unmistakable his relationship with Meyerhold, Tairov, Vakhtangov, the Russian innovators who turned away from Stanislavski's realism.[40]

Drews places Jessner here in proximity to the socialist 'Theatre October', which formed after the establishment of the Soviet Union and demanded that theatre take part in agitation for a socialist society. The resolute democrat Jessner was not uninfluenced by the Russian reformers, but claimed a different path for himself, although many of Jessner's opponents put him in the camp of the agitators. Jessner rejected any commitment to a fixed political attitude:

> After the war and the revolution had set their seal on the time ... the theatre of enjoyment, the theatre of nothing but play, lost ground. The world of semblance was destroyed by the attacks of reality ... Gone is the idyllic time when it was still the sovereign site of magic, of uplift and diversion ... And a new concept has arisen: theatre politics. To be politically oriented means to have the face of the time. According to this world-view, the theatre is political and cannot escape the fact. But political theatre does not mean a party political theatre.[41]

Jessner's statements are in accord with the witness of many historians. The theatre was one of the areas in which the revolution of 1918 had left real and lasting traces, where people's sense of the time manifested itself upon the stage. Such political theatre, however, was clearly demarcated from propaganda for a party or a particular ideology. In the area of parliamentary politics the demarcation was much less consistent. Philipp Scheidemann's words on 'finished militarism' on the occasion of the declaration of the Republic were only valid for a few months. The vast modernization process in art and culture, in which Leopold Jessner rose to become a typical representative of this epoch, did not continue in the political realm. The old elites in officialdom and the military were only discredited for a short time. They were soon hard at work on the restoration of a nationalist climate from the pre-war era and doing battle with the Jewish spirit, which they made responsible for intellectuality and decadent big-city civilization. In this Jessner became their target par excellence.

A new chapter of theatre history

William Tell, his debut production, already showed Jessner's courageous aplomb and marked the launching of a new theatre-historical epoch. It was a signal that the mildewed, convention-bound state of the former court theatre had been swept clean. It also marked the final demise of naturalistic stagecraft and became the manifesto for a democratic theatre, a theatre that addressed itself to the time and to society and its current problems. Of course, it came to bitter conflicts at the very outset, and the premiere ended in a scandal. The young generation and the democratic press celebrated this Schiller interpretation because the theatre now served the interests of the present age and no longer exclusively those of poetry and this or that author. Jessner gave the new epoch of the Weimar Republic a democratic face, at least in the realm of theatre. For the same reasons, conservatives and regular patrons of the old house raged against the break with tradition. That Jessner of all people, a professed Jew and Social Democrat, had taken over the greatest playhouse of the Republic made him a more hated figure by nationalist adherents of the old order than many a statesman. Jessner's dramaturg Eckart von Naso remembers:

> The German Republic, hardly a year old, still suffered from the repercussions of its birth. The parties were in bitter conflict. Those on the right and in the middle drew their swords. Jessner was a Social Democrat and a Jew on top of it. As the first Jewish Director of a state theatre he remained a thorn in the eye of the right and middle-class parties until his fall.[42]

Jessner became the representative of the new epoch, and his work mirrors the deep polarization of the Weimar Republic. His fall eleven years later models the ostracism of Jews in the domain of German culture.

As we have already seen in Königsberg, he did not stage *William Tell* as a national drama with a patriotic, folkloric atmosphere. The rejection of local colour by Jessner's set designer and most important collaborator of the early Berlin years, Emil Pirchan, meant a frontal attack on the staging conventions of a century-old Schiller reception. The inauguration of Jessner's tenure with *William Tell* has become legendary and was vividly described by Fritz Kortner (1892–1970), the actor who played Gessler.[43] Gessler was Kortner's debut role at the Staatstheater. He was also Jessner's most important student, who later boasted many directorial ideas (*Regiegedanken*) of his own. He immediately became a star and the most important protagonist of the early years. The ensemble was very different from what Jessner had during the Hamburg and Königsberg years. The best German actors, who accepted the idea of *Regietheater* and stood for a natural, concise, concentrated, uncomplicated manner of speaking, came over from other large theatres to be part of the new beginning at the Staatstheater. Besides Fritz Kortner, Ernst Deutsch, Rudolf Forster, Lothar Müthel, Johanna Hofer and Elsa Wagner were among the most important actors of the early years. Later Helene Weigel, Gerda Müller, Alexander Granach, Veit Harlan, Walter Franck and Agnes Straub joined the group.

Jessner's structuring of space and objectively succinct directorial style were sometimes characterized as expressionistic, but this must emphatically be rejected. Jessner was too sober, of too tragic a disposition, to believe in the renewal of mankind or the world, a belief that authors such as Walter Hasenclever, Georg Kaiser, Reinhard Sorge, Oskar Kokoschka, Hanns Johst, Fritz von Unruh, Reinhard Goering, Paul Kornfeld and the young Ernst Toller sometimes expressed around the time of the First World War. Jessner never staged works by Hasenclever, Sorge, Kokoschka, Johst or Toller, and only took on Goering, von Unruh and Kornfeld at the end of the 1920s after the expressionist vogue had long since passed.[44] Georg Kaiser's *Gas* was the only play of the group that he staged in 1918 (Königsberg) and again in 1928 (Berlin). *Gas* appealed to him because of its fable of uncontrollable technological progress, but he gave the hit play of the day an against-the-grain treatment because he did not believe a man could be heroically transformed and had an instinctive mistrust of leader figures (*Führerfiguren*). Expressionism on the stage was not infrequently reproached for its histrionic mime and gesture and an exaggerated pathos in speech. Quite apart from the question of whether such tendencies ever really existed in the theatre or were stylistically influential (as distinct from expressionist drama which did indeed exist as a short-lived epoch between 1914 and 1924), Jessner worked hard to achieve an objective diction, a logically clear, taut language that was a basic component of his austere artistic model. This was the antithesis of an excessive pathos, and to this extent Jessner could be seen as a director of the New Objectivity movement rather than an Expressionist, insofar as we should use such terms (which have more justification in the history of art than in theatre) at all.

The sensational start continued. With *Marquis von Keith* Jessner quickly brought a Wedekind work into the Staatstheater repertoire. Here, too, the career of the huckster Keith fits the image of a time of upheaval. Fritz Kortner played the title role with the condescending tone of a war profiteer, a mythic figure for that era.[45]

Emil Pirchan's use of space was starkly separated into an upper and lower stage. Keith consorted only with his peers in a world of make-believe, while communicating with ordinary people, who never stepped onto the upper stage, in the form of condescending gestures. The revamped Wedekind *mise en scène* – which also emphasized the hectic busyness of the economic world with doors that seemed to spring open on their own and an almost caricaturistic black and white design – found numerous imitators. A veritable Wedekind vogue set in at the beginning of the 1920s. Unfortunately, early death prevented the author from experiencing it.

Jessner's first Berlin Shakespeare was not long in coming. With Fritz Kortner again in the lead, he staged *Richard III* as a cold ballad of intoxication with power.

With no relation to actual English history he had Pirchan construct a set of graded steps that took up almost the whole space. Richard became the universal symbol of rule by blood and terror. The delusion of reaching the top of the world through conquest, followed by precipitous downfall, played itself out on the different levels. At the conclusion Richard staggered

FIGURE 3.1 *Fritz Kortner as Richard III, 1920 (Schloss Wahn).*

down the red-lit stairs like a madman, to be stabbed to death by white-clad soldiers. Pirchan's famous stepped stage (*Stufenbühne*), occasionally satirized as a 'staircase' at the time, served the idea of the play as recognized by the direction (*Regie*) – or, better, the motif of the whole *mise en scène* – which in this case was the drive to wield power. Hugo Fetting explains its function in his afterword to Jessner's *Schriften*, a collection of numerous essays, lectures and public talks by Jessner:

> It was this desire for clear segmentation as the basic principle of the *mise-en-scène* that occasioned the 'invention' of the *Stufenbühne*, falsely termed a 'staircase' in theatre history, which was treated with sarcasm and hostility at the time, but is now universally accepted as a self-evident spatial and dramaturgical tool. It was no mere decoration, but rather served the particular scenic elucidation of the motif as applied in different variations.[46]

Jessner and Pirchan remained faithful to this space-organizing principle in later productions too. And in the early years the successes continued. With Ernst Barlach's *Die echten Sedemunds* (The Real Sedemunds) and Karl Zuckmayer's *Kreuzweg* (Stations of the Cross) Jessner promoted contemporary authors who were at that time unknown. Barlach's play he staged himself as a dark family history in which superstition and a

FIGURE 3.2 *Emil Pirchan's set design for* Richard III, 1920 *(Schloss Wahn).*

perfidious and mean-spirited communal life break through the façade of small-town cosiness.[47] Barlach remained controversial as a dramatist, as opposed to a sculptor, but Jessner's groundbreaking staging of *The Real Sedemunds* made him, for a short time in the 1920s, one of the most performed contemporary dramatists, although subsequently it was the director Jürgen Fehling who became the Barlach expert at the Berlin Staatstheater. Fehling was offered the appointment at Jessner's house in 1922 and stayed there for decades, into the Nazi period, as an influential director.

Jessner's second Schiller production, the youthful work *Die Verschwörung des Fiesco zu Genua* (Fiesco or the Conspiracy in Genoa) also had tremendous resonance. While Fritz Kortner played the intransigent republican Verrina, Ernst Deutsch portrayed the title character not as a charming and flirtatious ladies' man, but as an ambitious and self-assured striver. The exuberance that so infatuates women reveals itself as the disguise of a would-be despot.[48] Several months later another Shakespeare production was on the programme. In *Othello* the fundamental motif was the drama of loneliness. Fritz Kortner portrayed a for the most part gentle and profoundly melancholic general. Wild, chaotic outbreaks were rare. *Othello* was simultaneously a high point and a turning point.[49]

FIGURE 3.3 *Emil Pirchan's set design for* Othello, *1921 (Schloss Wahn).*

Kortner's temporary departure: A turning point

Jessner had uncontestably become Berlin's most important new impresario, and for twelve years after his debut success he had expanded his halo of artistic direction with Fritz Kortner as his lead actor and Emil Pirchan as his set designer. Now that Jessner had changed the theatrical face of the city, Max Reinhardt saw himself forced to retire from Berlin for a few years. Leaving the direction of his Berlin theatres to Felix Hollaender, he now worked predominantly in Vienna and Salzburg. Hollaender was never able to bridge the gap in Berlin. Along with Rudolf Bernauer and Carl Meinhardt, other directors of private theatres also gave up their positions.

Nevertheless, the 1922/3 season went ambivalently for Jessner. Kortner left the Staatstheater in the midst of the *Don Carlos* rehearsals where he was cast as Philip. The main reason was that he was lured away by rapidly growing film activity that left him no time for regular ensemble work at the theatre. He is recorded as having no fewer than eight film roles in 1922/3 alone.[50] This was a serious blow to Jessner, who did everything he could to retain him, although Kortner did return in 1926. Jessner's support in the progressive press disappeared, because the loss of his poster-child protagonist was blamed on him.[51]

In 1922 Jessner had success with a renaissance of the author Christian Dietrich Grabbe on the stage. The staging of *Napoleon* launched a regular Grabbe vogue in the aftermath. The bombastic historical drama, consisting of a scarcely intelligible welter of ideas, had previously been regarded as unplayable. Jessner cut untold characters, unimportant episodes and secondary plot threads, and concentrated the action on the character of Napoleon and his significance for the masses of the people. The fundamental motif was an anti-militaristic slant: the masses must bleed when a dictator falls. The apocalyptic slaughter at the end was held up to ridicule; the French army toppled into a deep ravine like tin soldiers, while above General Wellington cold-bloodedly surveyed the dying.[52] The set was designed this time by Cesar Klein, who from now on was frequently employed at the Staatstheater in Jessner's or Fehling's *mises en scène*. *Napoleon* makes clear that the vertical zoning of space was a product of Jessner's creativity and could be implemented by various set designers.

The classical productions during this period no longer received the sensational acclaim that greeted the early ones. The reactions to *Don Carlos* were coloured by the short-term departure of Kortner, although the shift of accent in the fundamental motif from the tragedy of Philip to the struggle for Posa's republic of free men is significant in comparison with the Königsberg production.[53] The *Macbeth* production, for its part, suffered from the not entirely felicitous choices of a set designer. And it was of no avail that Kortner returned for a few performances. Kortner also returned to the role of Gessler in the revival of the legendary *William Tell* production. Kortner accused Jessner of having removed the anti-nationalistic slant.[54] The claim is not quite credible. What we can verify is that the same set design was used. The *Tell* of 1923 departed so much from the 1919 premiere that part of the cast was no longer available, and the mood in the audience was fundamentally different. The revival took place at the time of the French troops' occupation of the Ruhr Valley. The top officials of state took part in the evening, which almost had the character of an act of state. Jessner did not change the fundamental motif: it was still the cry of the masses for freedom and the rebellion against oppressors. But the people's scorn was no longer directed at the 'tormentor of the peasants';[55] it was now directed at a foreign military power. As a Social Democrat Jessner unambiguously supported the government in its resistance to the occupation of the Ruhr. An interpolation to influence the audience regarding current political events was therefore completely intentional. Jessner consciously reacted to changed political circumstances, but in the case of *William Tell* this should not be confused with a fundamental shift of emphasis.

Jessner's 1923 production of *Faust* also met with divided opinion. All through his career he had less success with Goethe than with Schiller and Shakespeare. The national press could not get over its indignation that Gerda Müller did not play a blond Gretchen, but entered the stage with her own dark hair. Jessner had no interest in a conventional, angelic, typically German apparition as Gretchen, which was so violently attacked by the critics that the debate over the dark-haired, braidless Gretchen overshadowed the production's whole reception. Bertolt Brecht, who visited the *Faust* rehearsals as a young writer, wrote enthusiastically: 'Thus Goethe's *Faust* becomes Jessner's *Faust.*'[56] What the later theatre reformer Brecht meant as the highest praise was in the eyes of the opponents of *Regietheater* a monstrous violation of the greatest work of German literature.

Schillertheater as second playhouse and establishment of the theatre school

Jessner had to scale back his directorial involvement somewhat in view of these unpleasant events. In 1923 the once privately run Schillertheater in Charlottenburg was annexed to the Staatstheater as a second playhouse. Jessner greeted this merger as a matter of principle. He could present popular theatre there in the best sense of the term. The goal was to offer high-quality programming at a low price. To finance the operation leases, closed presentations for patron organizations were necessary; after all there were a thousand seats to fill at this 'small house'.

Jessner was likewise able to realize one of his life's dreams during this middle period of his directorship of the theatre. After a dogged struggle and much going back and forth, he had been able to convince the Ministry of Culture to set up a state theatre school.[57] Jessner was certain that the training of actors could only be meaningful if artistic aptitude was verified via a stringent acceptance process and subsequently schooled in a three-year curriculum, completely independent of the candidate's ability to pay. However, the amount of financing the Ministry could provide was limited, so that Jessner had to take over the direction of the school. The rest of the faculty was made up of ensemble members at the Staatstheater, which guaranteed a highly qualified teaching staff, but meant a strenuous double burden. Jessner's school produced people such as the director Hans Lietzau and actors Martin Held and Bernhard Minetti: all three of whom set the face of German theatre in the Federal Republic of Germany.

First protests in the Landtag (Parliament)

His new duties, especially the school directorship, drained Jessner's energies, though there was no drop in his activity as director. A premiere of a work by Hermann Essig with the title *Überteufel* (Superdevil) brought him widespread acknowledgement in the democratic press again. The addition of this play to the schedule, in which Agnes Straub played a femme fatale, caused an uproar. The parties of the right and middle class demanded its withdrawal for alleged perversities. 'The attacks against Piscator took place in the press, those against Jessner in the Landtag', as Ludwig Marcuse puts it in a nutshell.[58] Hostility in the arts sections could launch negative campaigns, but disapproval in Parliament had the character of a directive, calling Jessner's directorship of the theatre to account, and, in the worst case, threatening its existence. A state theatre was completely and utterly dependent on the Ministry of Culture's support, which in the case of *Superdevil* was still there. Nevertheless, a debate was launched on the so-called immorality of art. National parties openly voted for the reinstatement of censorship.[59]

Jessner was still able to survive unscathed this first open attempt by the opposition in the Landtag to discredit him. The middle years of his directorship in Berlin were marked by several triumphs. A fresh staging of Wedekind's *King Nicolo* met with a thoroughly positive, but almost matter-of-course reception, since thanks to Jessner the author's plays had already become established fare in all of Germany. The Schiller cycle was continued in 1924 with *Wallenstein*. Since Kortner was not available during these years, Jessner engaged Werner Krauss at the Staatstheater, the other great character actor of the 1920s. Krauss was less politically engaged than Kortner, but probably the ideal casting for Wallenstein. In this *mise en scène* he became an inward-directed implementer of a world mission who was trying to keep himself aloof from the atrocities of war. This almost pacifist interpretation of the Wallenstein figure became all the more evident when, at its beginning, the otherwise oft-neglected prologue *Wallensteins Lager* (Wallenstein's Camp) took up much of the space. Jessner presented the horror of war's barbarity with breath-taking force and repellent coldness. Anti-militarism remained a core theme of Jessner's political theatre.[60] In *Wallenstein* Jessner showed his gift for handling crowds of people on the stage. What was already apparent in *William Tell* appeared again in productions of Hauptmann's *Florian Geyer* and *Die Weber* (The Weavers), where the people played a chief role.

The cultivation of a contemporary repertoire

Besides the much discussed stagings of Schiller and Shakespeare, Jessner was continually working on the cultivation of a contemporary repertoire for the most important stage in the Republic. The critic Ihering gave him unqualified praise for this: 'Jessner has brought Brecht, Barlach, and Bronnen to the stage this year. He is the only one in Berlin who has directed a self-contained theatre, and he almost always makes a success of the play even if the *mise-en-scène* remains problematic.'[61] He let the premieres of Brecht's *Das Leben Eduards II von England* (The Life of Edward II of England) and Barlach's *Sündflut* (*The Deluge*) be directed by Jürgen Fehling, but staged Arnolt Bronnen's *Rheinische Rebellen* (Rhineland Rebels) himself. At this time it was Bronnen, not Brecht, who was the man of the day. The near-craziness of his fickle transformations has made Bronnen a forgotten figure today, although almost all critics of that time conceded his talent and temperament for dramatic intensification. The native Austrian with Jewish roots began as an expressionist author. The 1922 premiere of *Vatermord* (Parricide) in Frankfurt received a tremendous response; the venue was no happenstance, since the expressionist vogue had never really gained a footing in the capital. Bronnen wrote *Anarchie in Sillian* (Anarchy in Sillian) and *Katalaunische Schlacht* (Slaughter in Catalonia) under Brecht's influence. The two of them were close friends for a short time, although they agreed only in their fundamental opposition to capitalism and the total rejection of their expressionist beginnings.[62] After reading Ernst Jünger, Bronnen shifted to writing novels towards the end of the 1920s as well as becoming an early Nazi partisan, even though the nationalist press had decisively opposed his dramas. For career reasons Bronnen later categorically repudiated his Jewish ancestry, but his temporary acquiescence was of little use to him. He sank into obscurity and ended up a communist editor in the German Democratic Republic.[63]

Despite Bronnen's puzzling volatility, *Rhineland Rebels* (1925) struck the nerve of the time. At the time of Jessner's premiere people were celebrating the millennium of the Rhineland's belonging to Germany and simultaneously protesting against its ongoing occupation by French troops. At the conclusion of the play, the separatist leader succumbs to the female revolutionary leading the nationalist forces. There was heated discussion of the set design by Emil Pirchan, who placed a limply hanging black, white and green flag, the symbol of the Rhineland, at the rear of the stage. At the play's end it was replaced by the black, red and gold banner of the Republic, blowing proudly in the wind.

Before the founding of the Federal Republic of Germany in 1949, this banner, although it was the official flag of the Weimar Republic, was considered the symbol of the workers and Social Democracy.[64] The staging therefore clearly professed its support for the Weimar Republic. Jessner arranged the historical drama by making extensive textual cuts and employing a de-rhetoricized telegrammatic language. Like Erwin Piscator contemporaneously, Jessner and Pirchan introduced film media for the first time in the form of projections. *Rhineland Rebels* was a success because of its patriotic, republican sympathies and was re-enacted twenty times during these years. Five Bronnen plays, four of them premieres, came to the Berlin stage in the course of 1925/6.

Jessner himself took care of the next Bronnen premiere too, the monologue play *Ostpolzug* (Journey to the East Pole), a few months later in 1926. Kortner returned to the Staatstheater to do the solo piece. The title refers to the earth's highest elevation, Mount Everest, symbolizing the planet's third extremity. In terms of content, Bronnen connected the Asian campaign of the world conqueror of antiquity Alexander the Great with the British Himalayan expedition. The human will to conquer the world, to press forward into the unknown and unlimited was an immensely popular theme. As set designers Jessner engaged two film architects who worked with explanatory titles and projections, doing such things as making maps visible with lines of light. Jessner was attempting to master the epic structure of monodrama with the use of new technology.[65] Although the Bronnen premieres elicited much astonishment and even some enthusiasm, Jessner soon parted ways with Bronnen, who was distancing himself from his early work and whose transformation into a bitter foe of the Republic was becoming ever more evident.

The year 1926 was one of antitheses for Jessner. He silenced all his critics with a highly praised staging of Hebbel's *Herodes und Mariamne* (Herod and Mariamne) during the spring, which focused less on the Maccabee general than the millennia-long fragmented course of the Jewish diaspora. Kortner, who was now increasingly playing Jewish roles, had found the perfect role for him in this production's Herod.[66] But two directorial appointments gave Jessner trouble. With Erich Engel he brought a second director to the house on a lasting basis to complement Fehling. Engel was a Jessner pupil from the days of the Hamburg Volksschauspiele and unquestionably one of the greatest directorial talents of the younger generation. Trusting him with Wedekind's entire *Lulu* for his debut *mise en scène* was a gamble. The play with its unsparing depiction of female sexuality gave provocation even in democratic times.

Piscator at the Staatstheater and a new *Hamlet*

More serious was the engagement of Piscator as guest director for Schiller's *Die Räuber* (The Robbers) in the autumn of 1926. The production portrayed the revolutionary Karl Moor as having private motives – as a deviator and a lukewarm Menshevik – while the robber Spiegelberg, the revolutionary because of conviction, who entered the stage wearing a Trotsky mask, became the actual hero.[67] Yet it was not the *mise en scène* itself that became the dominant issue of the next few weeks – Piscator's style was not much different from his work at the Volksbühne (People's Stage) – but the fact that Jessner had called him to the Staatstheater at all. The German National People's Party in the Landtag enquired whether 'the subversive efforts of the communist agitator Piscator (were to be tolerated) on a state-run stage'.[68] The Minister (Becker) could not withstand the campaign, and his half-hearted defence was formally abandoned, so that Jessner could not repeat the experiment with Piscator. When towards the end of the same year Jessner directed his own staging of Shakespeare's *Hamlet* with Kortner playing the Danish prince as a victim of circumstances, it caused a tremendous uproar. The rottenness at the Danish court was the watchword of the production, and King Claudius fell down physically as the result of a psychological breakdown when his murder of Hamlet's father was made public. After the unmasking, the audience could see that the king had a crippled arm, for which the nationalists accused Jessner of a deliberate parody of Kaiser Wilhelm II's disability. All Jessner's attempts to explain that no foreign element had been added to the tragedy were of no avail.[69] The alleged mockery of the abdicated Kaiser unleashed a storm of indignation.

Jessner as the target of reactionary forces

In his following years as *Intendant* Jessner still celebrated many victories, but he was ever more aggressively vilified by the national parties and associations, for whom he was always the epitome of the 'system time' (as the Nazis called the Weimar period) and the 'jewified' Republic. Any means were valid for attacking Jessner's theatrical work. In 1927 the debate assumed grotesque proportions on the occasion of Jessner's broadly acclaimed restaging of Gerhart Hauptmann's *Florian Geyer*. The German Nationalists had nothing to say about Caspar Neher's grandiose stage design or the pressing poverty of the masses in the Peasants' War. Their only concern was whether a Jewish actor could by nature comprehend a German peasant leader. The fact that Walter Franck, who came from an old Bavarian officers' family, played the part of Florian Geyer had no effect on their far-fetched insinuations.[70]

The mobilization of all reactionary forces to bring Jessner down continued. The Jessner case was ultimately transferred to the political level. Jessner was the nearest target but the real objective was the Republic. To be sure, the director of the Staatstheater still celebrated occasional victories. Hauptmann's *The Weavers* of 1928 was one such. With an ingenious mass staging, Jessner portrayed the poverty of an entire distressed and bullied trade on the stage, first by using high stairs to separate off the world of the factory owner Dreissiger from that of the people, and secondly through a silent looting scene in the fourth act which provided a breath-taking demonstration of the browbeaten weavers' fear of revolutionary action.[71] About the time of this production, a group of his friends and comrades-in-arms celebrated his fiftieth birthday with Festschrifts and ceremonious occasions. In retrospect the great celebrations have the effect of obituaries, recollections of a once successful person. From the many contributions to the Festschrift we can single out Kortner's for the brave face it puts on Jessner's beleaguered situation:

> The Jessner crisis takes place annually during the ball season. Like the Press Ball, it is one the great social occasions of the year. One must have taken part in them … Just weeks ago it was necessary, from the Landtag to Schwannecke, to recall that Leopold Jessner had staged *Tell, Richard, Wallenstein, Hamlet*. Jessner was finished, and his future, his present, yes his very past were denied him. Today, after his *Weavers* production, he no longer needs encouragement. In his triumph, he can reciprocate his enemies' jubilation. My wish for Leopold Jessner, to whom I have very much to be grateful for, is that he remain controversial.[72]

A controversial personality as seal of excellence was not of much use to the *Intendant* of the Staatstheater. The resurgence of the *völkisch*-nationalist spirit spread to all areas in 1929. There were massive losses in revenue, even though what the theatre made in ticket sales amounted to something between 30 and 35 per cent of its total budget. Today that amount for state and municipal theatres is between 10 and 15 per cent. Discussions about firing staff and even closing venues were no longer a taboo even before 1929.

The fall of Jessner as *Intendant*

During this aggravated state of affairs, Jessner, together with Kortner, had success with an *Oedipus* production, which besides the premiere of Brecht's *Die Dreigroschenoper* (The Threepenny Opera) was the event of the season.[73] Following Brecht's pattern, Jessner strove for an epic-reportorial style. A matter-of-fact report concerning a sensational action was the basic thrust. With Shakespeare's *King John* this approach failed. Making it more difficult for Jessner was the fact that he was being attacked on two sides. Herbert Ihering, a supporter of Jessner in the early years and a leading voice of progressive theatre criticism, found fault with Jessner's supposed lack of courage in taking on new dramas.[74] It did not help much that the other great critic of the time, Alfred Kerr, took his side. Kerr made his famous remark about the 'Periclean age of the Republic'[75] that would be connected with Jessner's name. He later retracted this designation because of the looming Nazi catastrophe. Ludwig Marcuse defended Kerr: the designation made sense because after Pericles it went downhill for Hellas too.[76]

Jessner's demise was comparatively unspectacular. After an unsuccessful New Year's Eve premiere in 1929/30 his contract as *Intendant* of the theatre was changed, without loss of earnings, to a contract as director only. Officially there was even talk of a resignation. Bernhard Minetti, one of Jessner's earliest acting students, never tired of insisting that, even as resident director at the Staatstheater between 1930 and 1933, Jessner was at the height of his powers.[77] This is objectively true. Minetti, Alexander Granach, Walter Franck and Hans Otto (one of the first to be murdered by the Nazis) still celebrated many triumphs with Jessner. In Schiller's *The Robbers* with Minetti as Franz Moor, the reintroduced *Othello* with Heinrich George in the title role and Werner Krauss as Iago, and Hauptmann's *Gabriel Schillings Flucht* (The Flight *of* Gabriel Schilling) with Werner Krauss and Elisabeth Bergner, Jessner's energy had returned to the level of his early years in Berlin.[78] But this was another time, one in which National Socialism had already won influence in the area of culture. Jessner's forced resignation was an example of the ousting of Jews from the German cultural sphere and a first victory for emergent fascism.

Jessner's personal situation was also aggravated by the fact that the Ministry's financial promises were not kept. The deflation policy of Chancellor Heinrich Brüning demanded significant salary cuts for public officials. Jessner's definitive departure from Germany came immediately after a last staging of Richard Billinger's blood-and-soil piece *Rosse* (Horses). The Seizure of Power had already taken place by the time of its premiere at the beginning of April 1933. A few weeks later Jessner left Germany forever.

Jessner in exile

Jessner's years as an emigrant were one long odyssey. From the Netherlands, where he directed a touring ensemble, he arrived in London in 1934. He rigorously shielded his family circumstances from public view, but we know from a diary during Jessner's last stage of life in the United States that his wife Ellen and his stepdaughter Lotte had been living apart from him since the short intermezzo in London.[79] His loneliness was no secret to the actor Rudolf Forster:

> One had to love Jessner if only because of his enemies and his personal weaknesses. We were aware of his isolation, which he was unable to conceal ... Again with regard to his seclusion and loneliness. Compared with Reinhardt's charm, Jessner was awkward, withdrawn. He heaved along as if he had lead in his veins, as if he were constantly dragging a heavy load. The painter S. Sebba's portrait thoroughly expresses his whole divided state and essential awkwardness. He holds, as if forgotten, a cigarette in his hand, and a paper lies next to a chair in the background. The door is open and dissects his left shoulder. Politics. Compromises.[80]

The director Leopold Lindtberg has perhaps given the most impressive picture of Jessner. He connects Jessner's Jewish sagacity with his modesty and self-discipline, qualities that were transferred to his theatrical colleagues: 'He was a strange, guarded man, a sagacious Jew from Königsberg, tall, and really more like a Protestant pastor than a *Sturm-und-Dränger*. Jessner was the least vain man I ever met in the theatre. He could lead the new adventurous movement because he knew how to keep it within puritanically limited bounds.'[81] The mixture of Jewish sagacity and the Protestant work ethic is only an apparent contradiction. Here, too, is revealed the influence of his East Prussian and Eastern Jewish background, where nothing was more alien than a selfish craving for validation.

Jessner was twice invited to Tel Aviv in 1936, where he staged Shakespeare's *Merchant of Venice* and Schiller's *William Tell* at the Habima Theater, but this was only an engagement of a few months. On 26 October 1937 he arrived in the United States almost sixty years old. His last station was Hollywood, where he stayed until his death. He worked for the film company Metro-Goldwyn-Mayer as a reader. It was essential to prove one had means of livelihood in order to enter the United States. With Ernst Deutsch, Alexander Granach, William Dieterle and other emigrants, he put on another performance of *William Tell* in 1939. But this had nothing to do with the Berlin *Tell*. Performing a German play in English was bound to fail. 'Most of the actors, whose English was hardly sufficient, had to learn the script in a phonetic transcription.'[82] He tried to promote solidarity among the emigrants within the Jewish Club, of which he was the president and lively debates were conducted on Jewish identity. Jessner immersed himself in a deeply pious religiosity. Ludwig Marcuse remembers how strongly this attitude marked his life: 'I only remember one angry incident. Jessner as a pious Jew felt stung by some remark, and literally shouted out. Never before or afterward have I seen him so chafed – not after any review, not during any political conflict.'[83]

Politically Jessner was convinced that Hitler's fascism would be defeated. In 1945 the American occupation was thinking of bringing him back to rebuild the German theatre. Whether he was thinking along these lines himself is not known. He died in Hollywood a half-year after the liberation of Nazi Germany, on 13 December 1945, at the age of sixty-seven. In one of his numerous memoiristic essays Ludwig Marcuse, the companion of his life's journey until the end in California, describes the burial ceremony, at which no friend was to be present:

He lies according to his wish in Boyle Heights, the Jewish section of the broad city of Los Angeles. He arranged that only some Polish Jews, ten according to the rite, should lay him in his last resting place. They knew nothing about the great man of the theatre, the devout Socialist, the passionate Jew, and one of the talismans in the Germany of old.[84]

Jessner died as he lived, unspectacularly and without personal vanities. His obscure end – and Marcuse describes it accurately in the most forthright terms – stands in stark contrast to his former importance. In America only his friends and emigrant colleagues knew that his life's work represented a culmination point of the whole Weimar era. Two and a half years before Jessner's death, his sixty-fifth birthday was duly celebrated in Los Angeles by Lion Feuchtwanger, Ernst Deutsch, Fritz Kortner, Alexander Granach, Helene Weigel and Berthold Viertel. Viertel reminded them that California was the wrong place for this tribute and expressed the hope 'that a liberated Germany interested in finding its honourable precursors and early champions will thoroughly make up for its omission of this celebration. And soon!'[85] After all, he went on, it was Jessner who first showed the artistic face of the German people, before the Nazis with their murderous hatred drove him from the fatherland and nullified his art. Fate has decided otherwise, and yet the Nazis could not eradicate the spirit that Jessner played a great part in determining. Fritz Kortner got to the heart of the matter in an obituary:

> The progressive spirit of the Weimar constitution was not obliterated by the reaction that crossed over into barefaced murder under the Nazis. The same is true of that epoch's revolutionary art of theatre. Leopold Jessner is a symbol of that time with its seminal achievement, which has outlived its tragic errors. This will enter the history of German theatre under the name of Leopold Jessner and come to life again in a still to be liberated Germany. I only wish he could have experienced it.[86]

Jessner's legacy

After his return to the old homeland, Kortner saw what a difference Jessner's absence made in a weakened and uninspired theatre. He committed himself to the task of filling the gap and reviving German theatre from its sorry state in Jessner's spirit:

> Perhaps the image of Leopold Jessner, the *Intendant*, might become the paradigm by which the confusion and panicked aimlessness might regain its calm and orientation ... The *Intendant* crisis would be resolved if he were still with us. It is the difficult but exhilarating task of this old generation of authors and theatre people to help artistic Germany get past the tragic breakdown of a young [generation].[87]

Fritz Kortner returned to Germany from his American exile in 1949 and played only a few more roles. Instead he tried to revive Jessner's revolutionary art of the theatre as a director. In long, intense rehearsals Kortner focused on detailed truthfulness, setting up a counterpole to the classicism of Gustaf

Gründgens. In this way he became, at least indirectly, the model for the generation of Peter Zadek, Hans Neuenfels, Claus Peymann and Klaus Michael Grüber. Kortner's *Regietheater* was not crowned with a theatre Directorship before his death in 1970, but it relaid the groundwork for modern *Regietheater*, the influence of which is still felt today.

It remains to say that the 'birth of interpretation theatre',[88] as theatre historian Günther Rühle more than once insists, originated with Leopold Jessner. The hour of its birth was the *William Tell* production of 1919 that was repeatedly interrupted by the nationalists. It became a 'fundamental law in theatre work … After this event of 1919, there is no road back.'[89] In Berlin Jessner was able to establish his principle of *Regietheater* at the centre of events, on the state's own stage. As a director Jessner radically transformed the attitude towards drama that has been handed down from the past by resolutely questioning its topicality. He thereby not only contested the claim that literature has an immutable, enduring content, but also fundamentally shifted the directorial interest (*Regieinteresse*) from artistic value (*Kunstwert*) to temporal value (*Zeitwert*). When a play is viewed from the present, new questions and perspectives emerge from it. Jessner's claim – that 'each period takes from a writer's work what is appropriate to it. Any art which is not from the time lies rootless in an empty space'[90] – buttresses the importance of the director as an autonomous artist. Theatre thereby ultimately becomes the independent art of *mise en scène*, for which the director is responsible.

The idea that classical works are to be interpreted on the basis of the time released theatre from the illusion that it could achieve a universally valid rendition of drama on the stage. Jessner highlighted a play's characters from the present political perspective. This meant that if the present situation changed, a different emphasis would be given to the same drama. The filtering out of the central substance of a drama is distinctly different from all attempts to reproduce the work in its totality, and it completely redefined the concept of *Regietheater*. The shift in the idea of interpretation means that 'interpretation is now no longer understood as the accurate depiction – as the emphasizing, or sympathetic understanding, or elaboration – of what is found in the text, but as the extraction of what concerns us, the determination of an insight'.[91] The mediation of knowledge gives the play a political theme. To this extent, Jessner became directly involved in the daily struggle of the Republic before Piscator and Brecht. Piscator, Brecht and Jessner's student Kortner put their mark on the *Regietheater* of the post-war period and built the bridges to political directors of our own time.

4

Searching for Frictions in Time: Leopold Jessner as a Director of the Contemporary

Sascha Förster

On 12 December 1919 Friedrich Schiller's *Wilhelm Tell* (William Tell) opened at the newly founded State Theatre in Berlin. The production was directed by Leopold Jessner, who was also the theatre's Director, and it caused a massive uproar in the German-speaking theatre landscape. To some reviewers this production entered 'new territory and answered to a long-cherished yearning',[1] yet others criticized the minimal scenography for being a 'dangerous distraction'[2] and a 'failure'.[3] Not only did critics and audience members discuss heatedly about the aesthetic means of this *Tell*, they were also left baffled by a scandal that took place on the night of its opening. Some spectators responded to Albert Bassermann as Tell delivering the famous line 'He [Gessler] needs must pass along this hollow way' (4.3)[4] with boos and laughter. The play's set consisted of different levelled steps, but of no hollow way. Throughout the performance, audience members in the upper circle had shown their disapproval of the production by hissing, chatting and laughing. At this moment, however, they could not suppress their criticism any more and deliberately disturbed the performance. Bassermann asked for the curtain to be closed, went in front of the curtain and addressed the audience asking for this 'paid mob' to be thrown out. The remaining audience cheered, the performance continued.[5]

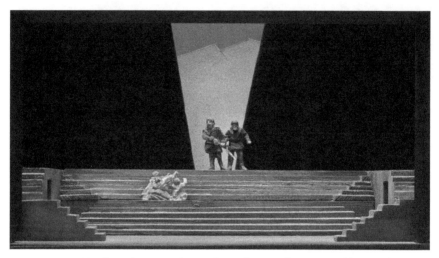

FIGURE 4.1 *Emil Pirchan's set design for* William Tell, *1919 (Schloss Wahn).*

In his study *Directing Scenes and Senses*, theatre scholar Peter M. Boenisch grants the production a seminal status for theatre history:

> *Regie* [directing] is often associated with the staging of an interpretive, even idiosyncratic 'directorial vision,' which is frequently perceived as ignoring the playwright's intentions and overwriting the instructions scripted in the playtext. The moment this new language of a *Regietheater* that reaches beyond the 'silent speech' of realist and naturalist *mise en scène* was born can be exactly dated: 12 December 1919.[6]

In this chapter, I will take a closer look at this milestone production by deciphering the aesthetic reasons that led to the scandal and presenting the innovations of the staging. I will follow up on the development of Jessner's approach to staging the dramatic classics by investigating his production of Shakespeare's *Hamlet* in 1926. As a first step, however, I will consider his essays, presentations and lectures – which were edited and published by Hugo Fetting – as early attempts at a theory of directing. Weimar Germany, especially its theatre will provide the backdrop for my investigation. Here, I am neither interested in too singular a focus on Jessner nor am I interested on any idea of rivalry with Max Reinhardt. I will rather regard Jessner as part of a broader network of theatrical innovators in directing, set design and dramaturgy. Theatre histories tend to focus on Berlin as the capital of the new German Republic, yet many innovations also took place in the theatre in Darmstadt, Wiesbaden, Frankfurt, Dresden and Düsseldorf, to name a few. These theatres appropriated innovations from the Berlin stages, but then presented new approaches to staging themselves which in turn inspired Berlin theatre-makers.

Equally influential were the experiments in stage performance and scenography the Bauhaus movement was interested in. Before the First World War, Heinrich Tessenow designed a unique performance building for the Festspielhaus Hellerau in Dresden. Such experiments continued to exert an influence in Weimar Germany. Any 'new' form of directing in Weimar Germany has its roots in the diverse theatrical languages that were discovered earlier and that were often as controversial as Jessner's *Tell*. Theatre-makers in Weimar Germany extended their explorations to include stylistic innovations and new aesthetic languages of the stage. Yet not every 'new' necessarily means a clear break with theatre history; the 'new' still negotiates with the past and therefore has connections with it. The great directors, set designers, playwrights and dramaturgs of the theatre in Weimar Germany are part of genealogies that are inherent to the history of German-speaking theatre. From Felix Ziege's point of view, Jessner continues an important path: 'Leopold Jessner is the theatre of the time [*Zeit-Theater*]. Leopold Jessner is making theatre of the time just as the Duke Georg von Meiningen, Otto Brahm and Max Reinhardt did.'[7] However, as the Director of the publicly subsidized State Theatre and owing to his personal backgrounds as a Social Democrat and Jew, Jessner had a singular position in this network of genealogies and within his contemporaries. For theatre historian and theatre critic Günther Rühle it is also the city of Berlin that enabled Jessner to become the director he is now known as: 'Berlin did not create Jessner. It let him emerge.'[8]

Towards a theory of directing

In 1979 East German theatre scholar Hugo Fetting, who also edited books on Max Reinhardt, August Wilhelm Iffland and Otto Brahm, published a collection of numerous essays, lectures and public talks by Leopold Jessner. Although Jessner himself never planned a cohesive publication of his texts, they nevertheless show essential foundations for a theory of directing. To Jessner, those contributions were merely a form of outreach in his role as Director of the State Theatre and as Chair of the Vereinigung künstlerischer Bühnenvorstände (German Association of Artistic Directors). That is why the texts were published in a variety of media as were the talks held at a variety of events. Yet read against and through each other, these texts provide crucial insights into his thinking about theatre and directing and their fundamental links with culture and society. The relevance of a culturally engaged theatre stems from Jessner's fascination with Schiller's lecture *Die Schaubühne als moralische Anstalt betrachtet* (The Theatre Considered as a Moral Institution, 1784). In this lecture, Schiller describes the lasting effect of the performing arts because they can offer their audiences guidance through a good life. Theatre, then, is an institution that can educate people in various aspects, even in those aspects that religion and the law ignore.

This lecture has been fundamental to the German idea of theatre as a site to reflect culture critically and one's own participation in social life. Schiller's piece affected Jessner greatly and offered him directions that he followed with his productions. Matthias Heilmann even describes the *Schaubühne* speech as Jessner's 'magna carta'.[9]

The idea of the contemporary stands at the core of Jessner's engagement with the art of directing. His interest echoes a general obsession of Weimar culture with everything 'new', contemporary or 'timely'; the German word for time, 'Zeit', was added to dramas, operas and the theatre generally as was the German 'neu' for innovations linked to acting styles, fashions or literature. Theatre scholar David Román conceptualizes the contemporary as 'a critical temporality that engages the past without being held captive to it and that instantiates the present without defining a future'.[10] Even though Román analyses performances in the United States in a much later time frame, his theory of the contemporary proves productive to understand fully Jessner's interest in the notion of the contemporary. The contemporary is more than the mere present; moreover, it is not just new. Through the contemporary present moments are tied to moments of the past that are being renegotiated through performance. At the same time, through the lens of the contemporary we are looking forward to the future while acknowledging that the moment for working towards the future is the here and now. Therefore, a contemporary aesthetics is not rooted in the 'infertile, slack soil of fashion'.[11] It is rather constituted by 'the people of its time'[12] with their stories and their 'hope for a renewal of society'.[13] Jessner characterizes the theatrical labour that must go into such an aesthetics as a work-in-progress as 'Es wird'.[14] This short sentence means both 'It is becoming' and 'It will be'. The notion of labour is as important to Jessner as is the notion of the contemporary. In his inaugural address as Director of the State Theatre, he calls on his staff as 'workshop comrades'.[15] By using the term 'comrade' he echoes a heritage of the political left. He also democratizes the staff at the State Theatre when addressing them all as craftsmen and -women while at the same highlighting the non-stop work that is a theatre of its time.

Jessner identifies a type of director who is able to capture the contemporary moment. This type he labels the 'dramaturgical director'.[16] Whereas a director like Max Reinhardt relied on his team of dramaturgs, Jessner combines the director and the dramaturg in one person. The State Theatre's dramaturgy department was responsible for reading new texts, putting together the programme and the like, but it did not play a relevant role within respective productions. A dramaturgical director will explore a play, especially a so-called classic, from a contemporary point of view and will look for a clear vision of what the text has to tell us in the time of the staging. This vision then becomes the aesthetic starting point for the production. A play is not merely put on stage realizing the playwright's stage directions; the director rather interprets and questions the play as a relevant piece of dramatic literature for today's culture. Lothar Müthel, who started his acting career under Jessner and later worked as director at the State Theatre under the leadership of Gustaf Gründgens in the 1930s, describes Jessner's approach to the play: 'Jessner's intuition is forced through the piece, shines a light on it and then re-creates the piece, not through psychologizing, but through disrupting it.'[17] Thus, the task of the director combines intuition and trust in a play while being able to step away from it and disrupting it, only to create a joint piece of art with the playwright.

The interpretation of the drama will affect cuts and edits. For every production Jessner therefore revised the drama according to his vision of the production. This process of revising dramaturgically allowed for a 'work of literature' to be transformed 'into a work of theatre'.[18] For instance, he staged *Tell* multiple times throughout his career. Since every time the contemporary world around the respective production was different, Jessner's vision of *Tell* changed and so did the revision. Like many directors nowadays, Jessner was confronted with criticism for not respecting a play. Yet he called himself the 'servant'[19] of the drama because it is the text that is the most important material of a production. However, even this important material must be updated to meet the needs of its time.

In an essay simply called 'Regie' Jessner describes the director as someone who is not so much a sculptor 'as a listener, as a generator, who, with sure instinct, tries to model his material, the actor, as he tries to harmonize each actor's individualities and their performing expression with the overall image'.[20] Working with actors is not so much cutting away material until the directors find what they are looking for. It is rather respecting the actors and their craft and creating a role collaboratively. Therefore the director needs to acknowledge the actor as an individual human being with specific features and specific ways to act and express him- or herself. The individual features can even become part of a production, but will need to fit with the aesthetic of the directorial vision. According to Jessner, even when working on the 'Regiebuch' – a form of prompt book compiled by the director before and throughout rehearsals – directors must have their actors in mind because it is they who will constitute 'the tone which determines the colours of the decoration'.[21] The *Regiebuch* should suggest scenic realizations while leaving enough freedom for the actors to make their own individual contributions under the director's vision. Jessner argues that every theatre production needs to deal with the core of human existence at the concrete point in time. It can be only through the actors that audiences can actually come closer to the meaning of the human condition as negotiated in a performance.

As Director of the State Theatre one of Jessner's responsibilities lay with the company of actors. He found it essential to think about the ensemble as a company consisting of individuals who, together, formed a bigger picture. That is why Felix Ziege compares the company to a 'mosaic'.[22] Jessner objects to the past practice of a company being assembled by different types, such as the young hero, the romantic female lead or the mother figure.[23] With his ensemble, Jessner was looking for strong individual human beings who reflected the diversity of the new German Republic and its equally diverse society. Furthermore, Jessner points out the importance of a production's ensemble as a major concern for the director because 'the casting very often decides the fate of the work ... even before the first rehearsal begins'.[24] Jessner even continues to emphasize the importance of the casting by calling it a 'sacred right'[25] of the director.

Jessner continues his debate of historic practices by accentuating the set designer as a 'set architect' in contrast to a 'painter of decorations'.[26] In the nineteenth century sets were mostly painted on two-dimensional pieces of scenery which were then combined with scenic props. Moreover, commercial studios sold finished sets to theatres which added those sets to their storage. Set designs were assembled from the different pieces in this storage but were not specifically designed for a production. In Germany, the Duke of Meiningen introduced the practice of designing a specific set for a specific production without reusing any other sets. At the beginning of the twentieth century, especially because of Max Reinhardt and his designers, sets were finally built as three-dimensional objects rather than painted on flat backdrops. Eventually, theatre-makers in the Weimar Republic were looking for new approaches to a three-dimensional set design. They aimed at getting away from realistic depictions of scenes towards designs that were artistic expressions in and for themselves. In Jessner's theatre the set designer became the 'master builder of a more or less space- and timeless scene'.[27] The First World War had changed the way audiences perceived reality on stage. Owing to the horrors of the battlefield they were not willing to believe any form of, says Jessner, 'bespangling illusion'[28] any more. In that day and age, audiences came to the theatre to be confronted with an idea and a vision instead of any kind of magic that could only conceal the harsh challenges of reality.

With his *Tell* Jessner introduced a radically new approach to set design which consisted of differently levelled and assembled steps. This scene was designed by the artist Emil Pirchan. Critics and audience members who disliked the new design labelled these steps '*Jessner-Treppe*', Jessner stairs. The director, however, called this scenic approach '*Stufenbühne*', stage of steps, and makes a strong claim for the steps not being reduced to a realistic image of stairs. The steps allowed for dynamic ways to structure stage action. They also offered new ways to unfold a play's nature which, argues Jessner, had been hidden by Realism.[29] Jessner regarded scenography as the main artistic component of his directing – scenography understood as the interplay of scenery, costume, movement of actors, light and props. Each production's scenography originated from the dramaturgical vision which translated it into radical images. Jessner worked with only a few designers who were then able to facilitate his visions through innovative scenic ideas.

In the early Berlin years Emil Pirchan, who also worked as a painter and illustrator, was Jessner's main collaborator and was responsible for multiple variations of the *Stufenbühne*. As theatre was changing as were the times, Jessner did not regard the *Stufenbühne* an everlasting solution. Yet, at this point in time, this scenographic approach was essential in radically reducing the scenery of the State Theatre to implode the traditions haunting this theatre. Such a reduction alone made it possible for theatre-makers and audiences alike to work on a new republican theatre – as soon as they were able to imagine this republican theatre the designs would shift to greater realism as we shall see with the more realistic designs of Jessner's 1926 production of *Hamlet*. In 1919 and the following years, the stages of his productions were left spare and empty refusing any realistic scenery, thereby challenging the audience's imagination and their 'spiritual economy'[30] while challenging theatre history and traditional images at the same time. Even props were rarely used in Jessner's performances as he wanted to focus the play of the actors on the texts they spoke without any unnecessarily diverting props. He identifies the kinship of his scenographic approach to the architectural and artistic movement of New Objectivity which also gave attention to the core of an artistic idea free of any unnecessary romantic decoration.

Jessner described the *Stufenbühne* as an 'abstract scene of mythic events'.[31] It is the director's vision that detects the timeless myths within a drama and makes their emblematic 'events' speak to the contemporary audience. Realistic sets only limit the interpretation of a drama to a specific temporal frame, thereby limiting the dramaturgical potential to the mere problems of the fictional characters on stage. Jessner, however, sees the stage as a site to reflect broader cultural and social conditions. The stage, then, will work like a mirror in which the audiences may find themselves reflected. Here lies the political potential of Jessner's theatre. The political theatre in Weimar Germany is heavily associated with the director Erwin Piscator who wrote a book of the same name. Piscator's political theatre was a leftist project used to enlighten audiences from a socialist standpoint. Although Jessner was a member of the Social Democratic Party, he spoke against such politically biased appropriations of theatre: 'Over and over I will say: the theatre, as it is approached by today's government, does not, shall not be operated as one party's policy.'[32] Theatre is political when negotiating the state of the contemporary society by offering new viewpoints on the classic plays or by championing young playwrights and their '*Zeitstücke*', plays that evolved around acute social issues. Jessner wanted the theatre to serve as a character witness of its time – a witness that reflects its contemporary environments critically and engages with the people living in it. The theatre, then, will also witness 'changes of time'.[33] A politically engaged theatre will also acknowledge the plurality of its audience members and their diverse political views. In the eyes of right-wing politicians, however, Jessner misused the State Theatre as a platform to advertise Social Democratic beliefs. The theatre in Germany, with the State Theatre at the forefront, became a site not only to fight over new theatre aesthetics, but to fight over the possible futures of this 'new' country.

In a text dedicated to the memory of Friedrich Ebert, president of Germany from 1919 to 1925 and head of the Social Democrats from 1913 to 1925, Jessner sums up Ebert's idea of the theatre in the new Republic: 'That the theatre might once again become a sociological event, that it might neither exist as a site of amusement nor as *l'art pour l'art*, but as an important member of our cultural community – that was his wish.'[34] The term 'sociological' might seem a bit odd at first glance, but reveals a bold approach behind this vision of republican performing arts. Germany was one of the main nations for sociological research. Especially at the beginning of the Weimar Republic, sociology was a massively productive field in German academia.[35] Jessner's and Ebert's use of the adjective 'sociological' instead of 'social' is intriguing. It elucidates how the theatre must not merely acknowledge the plurality of society, but engage with it and understand its particularities. Shedding a light on its contemporary society in all its forms is what makes the theatre political and can bring about change.

Not only did Jessner contemplate the aesthetics of his directing, he even thought about processes of production. For instance, he reflects on the short periods of rehearsals because these force directors to be punctual and precise in the ways they plan and structure rehearsals. A period of 'eight or more weeks' is a 'luxury',[36] a luxury that is productive and inspiring, as it will allow for improvisation and a more collective and collaborative exploration of a play. At the State Theatre, however, the general schedule did not allow for such extensive rehearsal periods. The necessary preparation would include weeks in which directors read and reread the play really to understand the literal quality of it and its contemporary meaning, the latter evolving into the vision for the production. This vision would be the outcome of directors being generally well read and having trained themselves as precise observers of their culture and society. As a next step, a director would work on the production's *Regiebuch* in which he noted ideas for spatial compositions and about the characters. At the first rehearsal a director would share her or his vision with the company. Despite the need for preparation, directors would need to schedule enough flexibility to invite the actors to offer individual contributions to the characters they would be performing.

While reflecting on production processes, Jessner discussed superstitions. In German theatre, the opening night of a production bears great meaning, thereby causing an enormous stress level for the company. In general, there are no previews of a production; the first time the actors face an audience is on the opening night which is also always press night. Even though the dress rehearsal takes place the night before the show opens and under the same conditions as every performance, there is no audience except for the theatre's staff. It is the dress rehearsal that is tied to superstition; it is said that a bad dress rehearsal will cause a great and successful opening night and vice versa. Most of the time, rehearsals take place in a quiet and safe environment and then, quite abruptly, the company must face the high-pressure situation of a 'fateful' dress rehearsal. Thus Jessner decided to split the dress rehearsal for his productions into two to three parts over the course of a few days, thereby ultimately abandoning the dress rehearsal. That way he took care of his actors navigating the emotional stress of the final rehearsals. However, Jessner warns that such decisions must be made individually and should never be turned into a general principle.[37]

Jessner's essays and talks contributed sustainably to the professionalization of the director. Hence, he advocated an understanding of directing as a craft in its own right, a craft that is rather creative than merely reproductive. In his writings, he constantly characterizes the specifics of directing with its own rights, values and challenges – like casting or the interpretation of the play, developing a scenographic idea or finding the contemporary vision. He regarded the journal *Die Scene*, edited by the German Association of Artistic Directors, as the central medium for the exchange of views about directing as a profession. Here, not only Jessner but other directors as well found a platform for their discussions about the role and meaning of the director. In 1924 the Association held a Directing Congress where it intensified the discussions. Throughout his career, Jessner even promoted a study programme to train emerging directors. Around 1910 he managed to lead a class in directing at a privately funded conservatoire in Hamburg. One of his students was Erich Engel who later worked as a director at the Deutsches Theater, the Theater am Schiffbauerdamm and directed movies too.[38]

As Jessner reflected on his position as director he also reflected on his position as Director of the State Theatre. In this position he addressed both the crucial role of the repertoire and the essential meaning of all staff. To him the theatre is not only based on actors, playwrights and directors. Technicians and workshops, dramaturgs and designers, dressmakers and ushers play an equally essential role in shaping the identity of a theatre. The Director is only a '*primus inter pares*', the first among equal and fellow theatre-makers.[39] Regarding the repertoire, Jessner looked for diversity which consisted of (1) classical plays, (2) contemporary plays that have become part of the canon, (3) experiments by young playwrights and (4) entertaining and popular plays.[40] All plays were shown and repeated as repertory productions. Jessner emphasized the importance of planning a repertoire sustainably and with patience to create effects that might only show in the long run. Leading a theatre subsidized by the state was for him both an opportunity and a duty. On the one hand, it meant that a repertoire had to appeal to the diversity of the city's audiences, on the other hand it had also to challenge them. A good Director had to be brave enough to follow his plans even in the case of setbacks. Jessner also had to decide who would direct which play. While Jessner mostly took on the task of staging the classics, he gave plays by emerging playwrights, whose place in the repertoire he championed, to other directors. As both Director and director, Jessner had to be constantly 'searching for something, looking after something, seeking something'.[41] Peter Boenisch characterizes Jessner's influence on the institution of the publicly funded German theatre as follows: 'Jessner became instrumental in shaping the system of subsidized public theatre in Germany, which has been much envied ever since.'[42]

William Tell (Berlin, 1919)

When the 1919/20 season of the State Theatre opened, it did not do so with a production by the new Director. Only the third production of the season was directed by him – Friedrich Schiller's great freedom play *William Tell*. The production's set designer Emil Pirchan, however, had already introduced himself to Berlin audiences when designing for a production of Schiller's *Maria Stuart*. Although audiences had a vague idea of Pirchan's aesthetic approach, they did not imagine such a reduced and minimalist stage that they were confronted with on the night of 12 December 1919. Throughout every scene the stage looked the same, stagehands did not change any scenery, only a few pieces were moved here and there. Most audience members were shocked about such a reduction occurring in a production of a play that had been so closely associated with spectacular scenic delights: painted backdrops of monumental Alpine mountains with icy tips or of the deep blue Lake Lucerne with the green meadows of the Rütli at its shore. A relatively fixed set of traditional images had been tied to any production of *Tell*. Therefore, Jessner's production, with its distinct break with German theatre history, came as a huge provocation. Yet Felix Ziege illustrates the meaning of this production for German history when he writes about the date of its opening night in the same context as he writes about 9 November 1918, the date of the birth of Weimar Germany, and when he metaphorically calls the production the 'cultural visiting card' of the new era.[43]

Schiller finished *Tell* in 1804 after studying encyclopaedias and travelogues about Switzerland. It is one of those everlasting anecdotes of theatre history that Schiller described the Swiss landscapes beautifully and with detail in the stage directions despite never having been to the country. It was also the last full drama Schiller would ever write. In *William Tell* the playwright shows Swiss people struggling with the rule of the Habsburg monarchy. Those people who are from different cantons set out to resist their oppressors.

On the Rütli meadow they swear the legendary oath which Schiller imagined like this:

A folk of banded brothers we will be,
Never in need or peril more to part.
(All repeat the words, with three uplifted fingers.)
We will be free as were our isles of yore,
And liefer die than live in slavery.
(All repeat the words as before.)
We'll place our faith and trust in God most High,
And never quail before the might of man!
(All repeat the words, and embrace each other) (2.2)

FIGURE 4.2 *The oath sworn on the Rütli meadow in* William Tell, *1919 (Schloss Wahn).*

William Tell, however, is not a part of this brotherhood; he accidentally becomes part of the movement when he does not bow in front of a cap that serves as a stand-in for the monarch. That is why Gessler, governor of the cantons by command of the monarch, orders Tell to take a test. If Tell manages to shoot an arrow through an apple, placed on the head of his son, he will be free of all charges. Although Tell manages to meet the target, Gessler orders his imprisonment because Tell professes that he would have killed Gessler if anything happened to his son. After managing to flee, Tell waits for Gessler at a forest pass and speaks one of the play's most iconic lines: 'He [Gessler] needs must pass along this hollow way' (4.3). He then shoots Gessler which causes the cantons' peasants to begin their successful revolt against their occupiers.

The play premiered in 1804 in a production directed by Johann Wolfgang von Goethe at the Weimar Court Theatre. However, August Wilhelm Iffland's production at the Berlin Royal National Theatre – the precursor institution to the State Theatre – was the more culturally influential staging. It was this production that introduced audiences to overwhelming naturalistic scenic images that tried to do justice to Schiller's descriptively rich stage directions. Like productions of Wagner operas that were directed by the composer himself, Iffland's *Tell* became a benchmark production for every performance thereafter. Schiller's drama gained a special place in German culture, not only owing to its topic, but also because many lines of the drama found their way into everyday culture as popular idioms. In November 1918 Friedrich Kayssler opened a production of *William Tell* at the Volksbühne Berlin in which Ewald Dülberg – who was to shock audiences and critics alike with challenging sets for *The Flying Dutchman* at the Berlin Kroll Opera in 1929 – introduced a more abstract scenographic approach to the play. The different sites of the scenes were still existent, but were transformed into geometric forms which a critic called 'a historical-cubistic muddle'.[44] Some reviews of Jessner's *Tell* mention this production from the year before, especially its sets, to criticize both productions' scenographic ideas. Despite the Volksbühne production, it was the production at the State Theatre in 1919 that caused a major scandal.

The example of Kayssler's production proves that it was not only the unfamiliar aesthetic approach which caused the uproar. It was also the biography of Jessner, a professed Jew and Social Democrat, who brought this aesthetic to this theatre at this specific point in time. To the opponents of the performance, such an aesthetic was the republican takeover of the glorious past of the former Royal Theatre. Hereby, references to the Royal Theatre and more generally to the past illustrate the dislike of the new German Republic which was regarded by conservative groups with hatred and distrust. Jessner's *Tell* made a strong statement about the contemporary world of this Germany while breaking with traditions known from Wilhelmine Germany. Not only did Jessner refuse scenographic displays of Naturalism and Alpine panoramas, but his interpretation also omitted many of the well-known idioms. He refused any familiarity with past performances of the play. For many young Germans over the centuries, visiting a performance of *Tell* was their first theatrical experience. Schiller's play was an important part of people's lives – they knew what to expect of it and a visit of any performance felt safe. It was this cultural safety Jessner withheld from audiences by breaking with tradition. Exploring the play for the contemporary society, however, allowed for new insights into the drama and its poetic quality. Owing to its production history the actual drama was hidden below layers of tradition and spectacular sceneries.

An English-speaking critic described Pirchan's set design:

> The background or underground of these settings – if one might use the term – consisted of a broad flight of green, moss-covered steps, with short flights of side steps, arches, ramparts and the like. This permanent feature of the stage-setting was constantly varied by the introduction of some essential or symbolic feature of the different scenes, a stone-wall, the slopes of mountains, a tree with a bench, Gessler's hat upon the pole in the market-place, the wall of an ancestral hall with windows, etc.[45]

Whereas there is no proof the steps were actually covered in moss – a scenographic sensuality that is more reminiscent of Max Reinhardt – many critics write about the strong impression the green steps had on them. In this design, the Rütli meadow with its intense green grass formed the foundation for the stage action. A closer look at a photograph of the performance shows that the steps were covered with a textured fabric. Unfortunately, no archival document of the production shows the green colour of the steps. In Pirchan's design sketches, the steps look mostly grey, in a model of the stage they are a bright wooden brown. This set of steps remained throughout the performance, scenic changes were marked only by specific pieces of scenery, such as the above-mentioned pole, a tree and so on. The set's backdrop consisted of flexible walls which could be arranged differently to mark specific sites. For example, in the stage model two black walls leave a V-shaped split in the middle through which a beige spiky form in front of a bright blue background can be seen. This simple image represents the mountains which the split aims attention at. Pirchan and Jessner do not reject images of the dramatic locations; they only reduce the traditional rich images to forms and shapes. They also did not illustrate a concrete time period; they rather turned the stage into a timeless space. So, instead of refusal of the past, the scenography of *Tell* can be understood in terms of imagination: the reduced images trigger traditional as well as individual images of *Tell*. The stage does not force everyone to see the same images; it rather enables a multitude of images. One critic phrases the same conclusion, yet negatively: 'The spectator had to have a lot of good will to imagine the green of the Rütli meadow, the canyons near Küssnacht, William Tell's farmstead, Attinghausen's hall and so on among these images.'[46] Jessner invited the audience to play a more active role as spectators – an invitation that challenged some to make rude comments and disturb the opening night performance.

Light played an important role in the scenography for *Tell*. The sketches, held by the Vienna Theatre Museum, show how Pirchan imagined density and contrasts of material, which each react to light in individual ways, through hatching and cross-hatching. In some more elaborate sketches Pirchan planned on using light to emphasize contrasts and focal points. Not only did the steps have a strong colour, but the production also used coloured light for atmosphere and symbolization. The strong blue of the backdrop in the model was lit in ways that gave the surface its deep colour. In the sketches, Pirchan draws entire areas in monochrome colours which translate concrete situations into flat images: yellow for dawn, blue for the sky, green for the meadow. A critic notes: 'the main aid for the scenic impacts were the diverse lighting effects'.[47] Another remarked how the 'warm sun' shed its light over Tell's home.[48] Theatre scholar Scott Palmer remarks: 'how light makes us "feel" is an integral aspect of how it makes meaning'.[49] Pirchan used coloured lights to evoke feelings – 'warm sun' – which played an important role within the production's dramaturgy. As another example, the actor of Tell, Albert Bassermann, wore an all-white costume which reflected bright light intensely. Thereby, the character of Tell was highlighted among the ensemble by giving him an otherworld-like appearance. The white of his costume must also be read as a symbol for his innocence in contrast to Gessler, played by Fritz Kortner, who performed in a dark costume.

The costumes harmonized with the lighting scheme, stylistically; however, they contrasted with the reduced and more functional set. On the one hand, costumes were reminiscent of peasants and knights; on the other hand, Pirchan managed to add a quality to the different pieces which made them look non-naturalistic while making them work as concrete signs for the respective role. The cuts of the different costume pieces, the hair styling, the caps and so on resembled contemporary fashion pieces without actually being fashion pieces. While the set design worked as a precisely stated break with tradition, the costumes felt more muted in their overall effect and helped linking past and present more delicately. Hence, some reviews criticized the design of the costumes feeling disconnected from the set. Pirchan equipped the main roles with singular, yet symbolizing props: Tell wore his crossbow and Gessler carried a horsewhip wherever he went. Generally, however, Jessner and Pirchan did without props.

Even though the critics judged the scenography differently, they agreed on labelling it as 'Stil', style. It was this 'stylistic' approach that broke with traditions of Naturalism and Realism in favour of a modern aesthetic vision by the director and his designer. Style then indicates that the design follows a theatrical will of its own and is not a mere illustration of the playwright's stage directions. On the one hand, the term recalls the Dutch De Stijl movement which was seminal for a new Western European conception of arts, architecture and applied arts. De Stijl artists favoured colourful shapes and forms whose use they, just like Jessner, justified by the changed times. The label of 'Stil', on the other hand, highlights the innovations behind Jessner's scenographic approach which ultimately comprises the play of the actors, the design and the relation of acting and design as a new way to explore a text without illustrating it. 'Stil' then serves as a means to label a specific aesthetic approach by a director as happened earlier in Berlin when referring to Otto Brahm's production style as 'Brahm-Stil'. Jessner elevated the intermediality of theatre – which Richard Wagner had introduced to German theatre with his concept of the *Gesamtkunstwerk* and which had been turned into new multisensual experiences on Reinhardt's stages – by acknowledging the diverse media and arts that constitute theatre. Unlike Wagner and Reinhardt, however, the play too was turned into a material which was both taken seriously and regarded as only one part of many that resulted in a stage production. These different parts were made into a coherent whole by the director's vision.

As Carl Theodor Bluth points out, this scenographic approach also affected the ways Jessner arranged the actors on stage.[50] Refusing the actors any unnecessary prop resulted in accentuating their bodily presence. Jessner also reduced the play of the actors to conscious and precise movements. Repeatedly the ensemble remained in static positions and was arranged in spatial images. A photograph of the Rütli oath illustrates the quality of Jessner's scenographic arrangements. In front of a pillar with a cross on top stands Leopold von Ledebur as Rösselmann leading the oath with his clenched hand raised high. He looks straight ahead into the distance while the men around him look directly at him. Rösselmann is positioned on the highest level of the steps while Theodor Becker as Melchthal and Eduard von Winterstein as Stauffacher are positioned on lower levels, both clenching their hands but holding them at their sides. The other actors are grouped in a half circle around Rösselmann, thereby highlighting him. Yet Melchthal and Stauffacher stand in a blank space, therefore being highlighted as well. They look neither to Rösselmann nor to each other; both look into a respective distance. The different viewing directions can be read as the different cantons the characters are identifying themselves with. Therefore, the lack of an exclusive viewing direction refers to the unity of distinct areas succeeding from the oath. As the bigger group of actors look up to Rösselmann, the neighbouring cantons of Melchthal and Stauffacher are redirected towards him as the leading speaker of the foundational oath. The apparent lack of unity resists a romantic reading of this essential scene in support of a complex exploration of symbolism through an innovative spatial arrangement. The dynamics of the scene do not originate from movements, but from positions, looks and precise gestures.

Even critics who disapproved of the production praised Jessner for his composition of crowd scenes which they found effective, harmonious and electric. They also applauded him for bringing leading actors and extras together to form a whole. Jessner even managed to balance the different acting traditions the company represented because some had been trained in the conservative style of the former Royal Theatre; others represented a new approach to acting that stemmed from Reinhardt. All of them fitted well within Jessner's aesthetic, even if a few exceptions might have challenged the rule. One critic presumed from this performance that even a bad production will be 'ennobled' by such an ensemble.[51] The director's innovative explorations of Schiller's drama extended to the interpretation of specific parts. In this regard the most prominent example is Albert Bassermann as Tell whose performance received mixed reviews. Bassermann was one of the great German actors who, for example, received the famous Iffland Ring, which was given to him by Friedrich Hasse. Yet it was this great German actor who stripped the heroic potential from that great Germanic hero William Tell. His performance was described by some as a fairy tale character, a fool or simply as too complicated. To those critics Bassermann lacked the archaic quality that was inherent in the role. His acting was also viewed as too naturalistic and thereby seemed out of place on the stylized stage. Others, however, praised the performance for being more humane and ordinary than any Tell before. Unlike Bassermann, Fritz Kortner was quite unknown at the time, but with this performance he was working towards his breakthrough. Josef Bondy portrays his Gessler: 'With satanic bleat, he [Kortner] savours every whipping word, he rattles the words like the horsewhip that is dominating their dancing beat with authoritative passion.'[52] This Gessler was a sadistic antagonist whose sleek modern performance was positioned against the more rural and naturalistic performance of Tell.

With this production, Jessner set out to explore *Tell* for a new generation and for a new time. He was fascinated by this play which he staged six times in his career, including an altered Berlin production in 1923. The drama fascinated him as a theatrical text with possible intentions he explored again and again every time finding new meaning. Heilmann states: 'Jessner regarded staging Schiller's plays, first and foremost *William Tell*, a lifelong task.'[53] In 1919 Jessner found an opera-like quality within the play which became particularly apparent in the beginning of the first scene which he turned into a prologue. In this scene, peasants describe the lake and the surrounding mountains. The director stages these descriptions as a poem to emphasize the poetic quality not only of the scene but of Schiller's play generally. The actors were not enacting the text, rather they were performing its words and its rhythm. With this prologue Jessner sought an absolute reduction of theatrical play: there was neither interaction between characters nor movement on stage; this tableau served as a static image out of which the lines of the prologue were spoken. *Tell* here was not only a well-told story, Jessner saw it as a strong piece of dramatic literature. The production emphasized both the latter and the story. By omitting lines which had become common sayings, Jessner directed the audience's attention to the remaining text of the drama, not only to lines which had become commonplace. The ensemble spoke the text quite quickly – a mode of speaking which had been called 'Jessner speed' – to further highlight the poetic quality of the text. The strangeness of the quickly spoken delivery invited audience members to hear the text anew. Boenisch concludes that Jessner 'invited his performers to exploit paralinguistic means, pushing for a genuinely theatral [*sic*] delivery of the text'.[54]

Many of Jessner's strategies had been heard of before, but here he was combining them while staging such a traditional drama. The reviewers refer to aesthetic predecessors and traditions. The costume of Tell reminded critics of the Swiss painter Ferdinand Hodler who had painted a *Tell* image in 1897, but also of the Austrian painter Albin Egger-Lienz and the German painter Max Klinger. All three artists were influenced by the impact of modern art, such as Expressionism, yet they were not fully committed to the artistic ideas of the coming century. Thus the three artists build bridges between the diverse aesthetic approaches at the *fin de siècle*. The critics' references acknowledge that Pirchan picks up on aesthetic approaches which had been established before the First World War. Theatrical references are also mentioned: in 1913 naturalist playwright Gerhart Hauptmann directed a production of *Tell* at the Deutsches Künstlertheater in Berlin which already brushed off some of the play's stage traditions. The steps reminded some critics of the Grosses Schauspielhaus, the former Zirkus Schumann, in which Reinhardt staged his spectacular productions of *König Ödipus* (Oedipus Rex) (1910) and *Orestie* (1911). Here, too, spatial dynamics played an important role, although in these productions actors were performing in the auditorium whereas *Tell* was staged on a proscenium arch stage. Another reference is made to the Tribüne, a small Berlin theatre well known for its expressionist stage experiments. The theatre was founded only four months before the opening night of Jessner's production. With these references, reviews manage to illustrate how Jessner did not invent from scratch. Jessner rather resumed aesthetic achievements made by modern artists and theatre-makers before the war.

At Iffland's National Theatre and its successor institution, the Royal Theatre, which was built at the same site but as a new building designed by Karl Friedrich Schinkel, performances of Schiller's *Tell* were 'hours of consecration'.[55] Jessner's new *Tell* was a 'revolution drama'[56] that glorified the revolution of 1918 which eventually turned Germany into a republic and made it possible for the state to take over the theatre and turn it into the State Theatre with Jessner as Director. The range of criticism in the reviews is also a sign of the range of political positions for and against this new state. At the Gendarmenmarkt, the location of the State Theatre, the Republic with its politics and cultural spirit took over the leading theatre of Prussian royalty. It was at this site that Jessner broke with tradition for the sake of innovation. We may not know if the audience members who disturbed the opening night performance were paid to do so or if they came to cause a scandal. But we do know that those audience members had to face losing what was familiar to them and that they had to find orientation in this new country. It is in such moments that theatre becomes a place to negotiate politics.

Hamlet (Berlin, 1926)

In his memoir, the State Theatre's dramaturg Eckart von Naso remembers the negotiation of theatre and politics: 'Lipmann [Heinz Lipmann, the State Theatre's second dramaturg] and I, too, had to suffer. Because every inquiry at the Landtag consumed batches of paper. For every parliamentary party, we composed apologies.'[57] Owing to the theatre's political engagement, the dramaturgy department became responsible for public relations and had to defend the productions intellectually, not only Jessner's, but also productions of new plays such as Hermann Essig's *Überteufel* (*Superdevil*). Furthermore, Jessner himself was involved in politics, for example serving as an expert in a lawsuit against the homosexual journal *Die Freundschaft* (Friendship) in 1921. *Freundschaft* was charged for its literary supplement and the advertisements which were considered obscene. Consequently, the journal condemned the lawsuit as a general campaign against homosexuality. Jessner was asked to speak about the literary quality of the journal and denied any criticism of obscenity. He certainly did not shy away from political involvement while challenging the old order. On 3 December 1926 Jessner caused yet another scandal, this time with his production of William Shakespeare's *Hamlet*. In this staging, Jessner parodied monarchic structures, thereby taking a strong – for some far too strong – republican stance.

Between 1919 and 1926 Weimar Germany faced enormous inflation which the government eventually managed by introducing a new currency, the *Rentenmark*. In the following years, the country experienced social stability and new prosperity, but was still under constant attack by conservatives and nationalists. It was in this period that Jessner introduced German society to his new reading of *Hamlet*. Like *Tell*, *Hamlet* was regarded an essential piece of the German repertoire.[58] The contemplative hero, who faces tyranny, and revolts against his uncle to defend the legacy of his father, attracted German audiences over the centuries leading to Ferdinand Freiligrath stating: 'Deutschland ist Hamlet' (Germany is Hamlet). Not only has *Hamlet* been appropriated as German, this drama, too, has been played in specific traditions with which Jessner's production broke. However, Jessner was not the first director to attempt an innovative staging of the drama; many more had tried to explore the drama for their respective new times. Rühle states: 'The stage innovations in this century [the twentieth century] were closely tied to Shakespeare.'[59] Jessner, however, was the first to combine his reading of the drama with anti-monarchist views at a theatre that inherited the Prussian monarchy's legacy. Some critics and audience members even perceived the crippled arm of King Claudius, played by Aribert Wäscher, as a reflection of the paralysed arm of former Prussian king and German Kaiser Wilhelm II who was forced to abdicate in 1918. The mere potential of such a reading in this theatre could not avoid offending conservative Germans. This time, however, Jessner addressed the criticism publicly. In the *Vossische Zeitung*, Jessner published the short piece 'Hamlet der Republikaner' (Hamlet the republican). He rejects any criticism claiming similarities between the disabled Claudius and the former Kaiser as being offensive. His counterargument is the production's dramaturgy: Claudius' disability was not shown from the beginning, it was an illustration of the king's 'bodily decay as a consequence of the spiritual decay' following the 'mousetrap' scene.[60]

Jessner's staging of *Hamlet*, for which he chose August Wilhelm Schlegel's Romantic translation, was more complex and aesthetically less reduced than *Tell*. Still, Jessner chose a distinct dramaturgical approach: the decay of Claudius follows an interpretation of *Hamlet* that highlights the narrative frame of Fortinbras and thereby the political storyline of the drama. Jessner established a scenic frame for Act 1, Scene 2, especially its opening monologue. Here, Claudius mourns the dead king and mocks the young Norwegian prince Fortinbras. Jessner repeated the scenic frame in the end of Act 5, Scene 2 which he detached from the main part of 5.2. Horatio gives a brief account of the reasons that led to the many deaths while Fortinbras accepts his fate as monarch of Denmark. The scenic approach to both scenes was set up as a council of the Danish king, Claudius's monologue was handed to him as a speech by, in the eyes of critic Julius Bab, his prime minister. Wäscher did not deliver the speech in a tragic tone, but rather monotonously and unaffected while turning every line about Fortinbras into a joke about the Norwegian prince. Jessner placed this scene at the beginning of the performance followed by Act 1, Scene 1. The end of the performance saw the same council, this time with Fortinbras in the position of the Danish king. To Jessner, however, Fortinbras does not represent a new beginning; rather, he represents history repeating itself in the worst way possible. The German Republic the audience and the theatre-makers live in is quietly presented as the only way out of this vicious cycle of a rotten state.

The example illustrates the director's approach to Shakespeare's drama and to his revisions according to his dramaturgical reading and directorial vision. Elsinore was parodied as a court where everyone is serving the king by, among other behaviour, constantly bowing before the king and when 'The king's royal household stands in soldierly organized groups'.[61] Jessner's emphasis of the political mechanism led to a reduced emphasis on the personal tragedy of Hamlet, which had been the cornerstone of actor's careers. Star actors such as Josef Kainz, Alexander Moissi and Adele Sandrock toured Germany with their renditions of Hamlet and manifested an approach to the play that focused in the main on his personal tragedy. Jessner, however, was interested in the entire drama, which offers more narratives than the title character's storyline. Jessner also balanced the tragic tone by highlighting the comic scenes or by staging scenes as comic that had been interpreted tragically before. Jessner challenged his audience to rethink their interpretation of *Hamlet* and encouraged them to explore the drama through new eyes.

Caspar Neher, who was to become one of Bertolt Brecht's main collaborators, designed the sets and costumes. In contrast to Pirchan's design for *Tell*, the design for *Hamlet* was less reduced, there were no steps and there was different scenery for individual scenes. The highlight of Neher's design was a court theatre in the mousetrap scene. When the curtain opened to reveal that court theatre, the view was spectacular. The spectators were bedazzled by looking at an auditorium with boxes, including a royal box, and a large group of audience members sitting in front of a stage equipped with footlights.

The statues and ornaments of the auditorium were painted in broad brushstrokes, thereby always presenting an aestheticized idea of a Baroque theatre instead of a perfect representation. The fictional stage was set at the location of the real State Theatre's curtain, turning the proscenium arch into a form of mirror that reflected the actual auditorium. Especially the royal box reminded audience members of the significant royal box in the theatre they were sitting in; in 1913, 'The Court Theatre became the "Kaiser's Theatre," the Kaiser's box was the second, yes, the actual stage'.[62] In his analysis of the production, theatre scholar Peter W. Marx concludes: 'It is obvious that the set mirrors the interior space of the State Theatre itself.'[63] Instead of 'mirroring', I argue that the set created a double of the auditorium of the State Theatre. Theatre scholar Alice Rayner conceptualizes the double: 'The double is not simply a copy that stands in relationship of otherness to the true, nor can it be stated in positive terms. It is between the lines, in the syntax and performativity of a text, of an act, of a work.'[64] Thus the double is not exactly like something else; rather it seems like it and makes the consequential gaps and uncertainties of similarities which help spectators to resist losing themselves in a fictional world. Because of the rough brushstrokes of paint and the two-dimensional elements, Neher's theatre imitates but does not copy Schinkel's auditorium. By this means the set challenges the audience to look on their surroundings with fresh eyes. If audience members saw the State Theatre with its legacy reflected in the design, it was owing to their active interpretation.

FIGURE 4.3 *Caspar Neher's set for the 'mousetrap' scene, Hamlet, 1926 (Schloss Wahn).*

The interior of Elsinore consisted of slanted walls and multiple doors. The latter allowed for a quick rhythm of entrances and exits more reminiscent of comedy. Emil Faktor sees a shift from a linear storytelling to a mode of intertwining storytelling that was achieved through these doors.[65] Together with Neher, Jessner sped up scenes that traditionally consumed most of a performance's time while he slowed down other scenes that got cut or were played without any emphasis in previous productions. For example, Neher built a fully equipped sailing boat for the scene in which Hamlet is sent to England and Jessner expanded the scene to stage this specific moment of a ship setting sail. Thus, not only did his version cut scenes while keeping others, but it also highlighted the scenes in different ways by exploring new and different speeds to play the drama. Ernst Heilborn explains: 'Lending the speed of our time to the action was something Leopold Jessner insisted on.'[66] Varying the performance's speed even included a scene change at the end of the performance only to stage the last bits of the final scene like the beginning of the performance. As Jessner balanced tragic with comic scenes, Neher balanced simpler sets (the castle walls) with more elaborate and spectacular scenery (the theatre, the boat).

The costumes were as diverse as the sets. Critics saw references to different years from the early nineteenth century to the present – one even suspected the production team just used the theatre's costume store resulting in indecisively looking ideas.[67] The costumes certainly referenced a Germany pre-1918, a Germany under royal command. That is why the male actors wore richly decorated uniforms which showed they belonged to the royal household of Denmark. Yet Neher added alienating pieces here and there. In the photograph of Claudius, Polonius, Gertrude and Hamlet in the mousetrap scene, Claudius is wearing a metallic piece around his neck which is more reminiscent of a medieval suit of armour than of the modern-looking uniform he is wearing.

In the same photograph, Hamlet, who was played by the Gessler actor Fritz Kortner, is wearing an all-black outfit that seems rather curious because of its monotonous and simple look that does not offer any associations. In the gravedigger scene, Kortner was wearing a shiny black coat that looked like a modern raincoat. All of Hamlet's costumes were intentionally ill-fitting to reinforce the image of an anti-Romantic Hamlet. Jessner and Kortner proposed a new Hamlet, one that was not nervous like his famous predecessor Kainz. Kortner's Hamlet was an intellectual who acted rationally and clearly planned his actions. He suffers from the corruption that happens within the royal household and not from a psychological disposition. Bluth characterizes this Hamlet 'as a fighter who is smart and well alert, not contemplating or just seeming to be contemplating, knowing immediately ... what his enemies are after, that is worming and wresting a secret out of him'.[68] Kortner performed Hamlet with a blond wig which Peter W. Marx reads as a strategy to hide Kortner's Jewishness while playing this 'German' hero Hamlet.[69] In his review, Felix Hollaender described traces of the 'bonhomie of the wise Jew, who manages the art of dialectics' as well as of the 'villainous face of Richard III'.[70] Hollaender brings together the biography of Kortner with this other major Shakespeare role he played at the State Theatre in 1920. Kortner's Hamlet was an ambivalent character who could be perceived as manifold as the costumes.

Jessner worked with the entire company on rethinking the roles of which many had been overshadowed by traditions of production and interpretation.

Especially, Blandine Ebinger introduced new aspects to Ophelia. She spoke in a Berlin dialect which inspired the critic Curt Hotzel to call her 'Ophelia from Wedding'.[71] Wedding is a borough of Berlin that was known as a working-class district. Thus Jessner turned Ophelia into the girl from the lower classes who is astonished by the interest the Danish prince shows in her and who is easily misused as a tool to go against Hamlet by Polonius. Jessner reads Hamlet and Ophelia's relationship in a sexual way which led to a quite scandalous moment in the mousetrap scene. When Hamlet asks Ophelia 'Lady, shall I lie in your lap? … I mean, my head upon your lap?' (3.2), Kortner laid his head between Ebinger's thighs, indicating a passionate sexual longing. Moreover, Hollaender mentions Hamlet laying his head in the lap of his mother when both die in the end, thereby echoing the moment with Ophelia and anticipating Laurence Olivier's Freud-inspired reading of *Hamlet*. Albert Florath who played the clown in the gravedigger scene also spoke in dialect, thereby adding another comic dimension to the role. He spoke in Low German, a form of German spoken mostly in Northern Germany and parts of the Netherlands.

Jessner even introduced a new way of staging the ghost of Hamlet's father. Before, it was common to show the ghost as a spiritual and eerie being. Fritz Volk's ghost, however, was quite concrete and rather real. He played the ghost in a uniform, tying him to the royal household and illustrating a royal lineage that is absent in Hamlet's costume, while walking downstage close to the audience and displaying his corporeality. Volk played the ghost trance-like, thereby presenting the part as an undead creature who haunts this rotten state of Denmark.

Whereas Jessner's production of *Tell* was timeless and explored the poetic quality of its dramatic text, *Hamlet* convinced as a bricolage of temporal references and exploration of forgotten aspects of Shakespeare's popular drama. *Hamlet* did not break with its traditions, but rather addressed and transformed them. The programme presents an extract from Johann Wolfgang von Goethe's *Wilhelm Meister*, in which Wilhelm Meister acts in a *Hamlet* performance, together with images of David Garrick and Johann Franz Hieronymus Brockmann as Hamlet. It therefore ties the State Theatre production with past productions and makes the genealogies clear. Jessner now addressed the various ghosts that haunt the drama while updating the play, which was historically appropriated as a German drama, to speak to the year 1926. In *Hamlet* Shakespeare describes a society that experiences two changes in government. However, Shakespeare seems more optimistic, looking forward to the second change, than Jessner who is not able to spot any good argument for another government led by a monarch.

Conclusion

At the beginning of the new German Republic, channelling the mostly progressive spirit of 1919, Jessner confronted his audience with *Tell* and staged human beings who fought against a ruler ultimately to be able to govern themselves. Seven years later, Jessner presented his audience with a vicious cycle of monarchist rule where nothing changes for the better no matter who is king. Eventually, the escape out of this cycle lies in the republican state the audience lived in. Not only did Jessner adapt and adopt his aesthetic approach over time, but he also adapted his views on culture and society again and again to be a true contemporary. For Jessner, plays were a means to challenge one's perception of the world. With his challenging productions, he encouraged spectators to be open to look at their world anew, to be open to different futures and leaving the past behind. The State Theatre was a site of exchange, of challenge and of openness. With such a programme, Jessner led the theatre in stark contrast to the former Royal Theatre. Before November 1918 the Director of the Theatre was appointed by the Kaiser himself, mostly because of loyalty and allegiance rather than artistic talents. While some great actors could be counted among the company, the production styles were conservative and classic, naturalistic plays were ignored and so were the stage innovations that took place at the Deutsches Theater. The last Director of the Royal Theatre was Georg Graf Hülsen-Haesler who had to hand over the theatre to Leopold Jessner.

Jessner now was willing not only to challenge others, but to challenge himself as well. His *Tell* worked as a ground zero to establish a new aesthetics for a new theatre. From then on, the director developed his directing style further. The experiment of 1919 was only intended to open a more diverse approach to the craft and art of directing. At the end of the 1920s, influenced by Erwin Piscator, Jessner was to work on a 'reporting' kind of directing,[72] which Brecht would develop further into his Epic Theatre. The set designs became more realistic again because the reduced stage was not necessary any more. For example, in 1929, he staged an entire boxing ring for a production of Ferdinand Reyher's *Harte Bandagen* (Boxer). Constantly challenging himself artistically, Jessner's productions might have looked different, yet they were tied to each other through this feeling of activation: being an active spectator, being an active observer of one's own culture and being an actively engaged citizen of this new republic.

At the beginning of Felix Ziege's short book on Jessner is a cartoon by Marga Santelmann.[73] The image, which stylistically looks like a silhouette, shows a tall man standing on a small tower, holding his glasses in his left hand. Around the small tower, birds are flying through the air and a boat sails on the stormy sea. In the black of the water it reads 'Der Leuchtturm', the lighthouse. The man on the tower is Leopold Jessner whose relaxed pose is contrasted with the turbulent atmosphere of the water. Just like a lighthouse, Jessner will stand quietly no matter how disquieted the environment around him becomes. His focused glance will both observe what is going on out there and offer orientation in stormy times.

FIGURE 4.4 *Marga Santelmann's cartoon of Leopold Jessner, 1928 (Schloss Wahn).*

Harley Granville Barker

5

Harley Granville Barker: Director Extraordinary

Colin Chambers

'Art is not mere entertainment, although it can be most entertaining', wrote Harley Granville Barker in 1945, a year before his death. 'It is a moral exercise, although it need never be depressingly solemn. It should leaven the daily life of a community. It frees men's [*sic*] imagination, and controls it.'[1] Barker, who is credited with if not inventing the role of director in the English-speaking theatre then of establishing it as an indispensable feature of the modern landscape, was an emancipated slave of art himself, and his chief and enduring passion within that bondage was theatre. Born in London in 1877 he was immersed in theatre at an early age and spent the rest of his lifetime in ethical and utopian pursuit of its truths, a pursuit rooted in and shaped by extraordinary and highly intense practice as actor, manager, and writer (of plays and commentaries) as well as director.[2]

With little formal education but driven by a restless, endless curiosity, Barker excelled in each of these disciplines, and what he learned in one nourished his work in the others, guided by implacable and often high-minded seriousness in his commitment to what he called 'aesthetic honesty', to him an extension of moral honesty.[3] 'The teacher must have his doctrine pat,' he asserted,

> but the artist sets out to discover truth itself with each new book or play or picture he begins. In a single devotion to that search lies art's integrity;

let him respect this, and though the result may make the simplest show, some flush of a deeper truth may be manifest through it. The search is never-ending, and the search itself is the thing.[4]

An inveterate reviser of his own work, Barker was animated by the thrill of the ceaseless search, and this trait can be seen in the catholic choice of plays he directed. They number around eighty and belong to different cultures, dramatic conventions and times, from Euripides and Shakespeare to Ibsen, Maeterlinck, Hauptmann, the Quintero Brothers, Schnitzler, Sierra and Shaw; many of Barker's productions were premieres, including of his own plays, and the range of styles required – whether Realism, Expressionism, Symbolism, or Farce – showed he was responsive to the needs of each and did not reduce a production to his own, preconceived view. At first, Barker often replicated the prevailing actor-manager role, appearing in productions he directed, but he soon discovered that the demands of the two roles meant it was not possible to continue combining them, particularly as he was also writing, if he wished to achieve the results he was seeking; he gave up acting and subsequently regular directing as well.

The work that created his directorial legacy was largely concentrated into the first fifteen years of the twentieth century, although he did direct occasionally after that and advised on productions until a few years before his death. He was only twenty-six with a handful of short-run productions to his name when what became seen as the legendary seasons he ran with J.E. Vedrenne and which made his name as a director opened in 1904 at the Court in London. His promethean and groundbreaking activity there over three years involved choosing and casting the plays, directing them all except those by Shaw (with whom, however, he collaborated as co-director) and playing eleven different roles, six of which were leading Shavian parts, and of those he created three.

Barker's Court offered an unprecedented repertoire in range and content, mixing old and new: eleven plays by Shaw, establishing him as a leading international playwright; three by Euripides in new translations by Gilbert Murray; two by Ibsen; first plays by John Galsworthy and John Masefield; and new plays by among others St. John Hankin, Elizabeth Robins and himself.

Although these seasons were not run as true repertory as Barker wished, he nevertheless produced remarkable – and for Britain, exceptional – ensemble acting dedicated to the needs of each play. Further directorial work, primarily at the Savoy Theatre, where his revolutionary Shakespeare productions took place, the Duke of York's, Little, Kingsway, and St James's theatres in London, and both indoor and outdoor venues on a visit he made to the United States in 1915, cemented his towering reputation. This was later enhanced by the wide impact he made through the work of his disciples and other followers, and through his extensive writing about theatre, which is characterized by continual reference to practice. Indeed, of his most influential writing, his *Prefaces to Shakespeare*, Barker said, 'it is intended to present the plays from the point of view of their performance upon the stage,' and he continued that they 'may best be thought of as the sort of address a director might make to a company upon their first meeting to study the play'.[5]

FIGURE 5.1 *Barker (left) as Adolphus Cusins in Shaw's* Major Barbara, Court Theatre, *1905 (Getty Images).*

Guiding principles

Barker's ideas on theatre and directing, as well as coming from reading, observation and reflection, derive, above all, from practice. This perhaps made him wary of programmatic systems – 'of all the arts, drama can live least in the light of theory' – while remaining firm in his beliefs about the role of theatre, ways of organizing it and methods to create it, all of which, for him, were guided by underlying principles.[6] These principles, which animated and provide context for his directing, evolved for Barker in much the same way as he believed they did in Shakespeare's work; Shakespeare's plays, he wrote, show 'such principles as the growth of a tree shows. It is not haphazard merely because it is not formal; it is shaped by inner strength.'[7] Yet Barker knew the limitations of principles in the theatre: 'We may sense what is wrong, yet wisely be chary of dogmatising upon its putting right' because the process of putting a play on stage was to him 'a very incalculable thing. And incalculable it must to some extent remain if its chief aim is to be the endowing of the play with anything we are to call life; for the term will escape aesthetic definition.'[8]

This 'endowing a play with anything we are to call life' lay at the heart of Barker's directing and was rooted in his belief in theatre not only as a human medium – 'what more wonderful instrument has man to play upon than is this living self?' – but also as a social endeavour.[9] 'Dramatic art ... is the working out ... not of the self-realisation of the individual, but of society itself', he wrote.[10] A play is 'a microcosm of society' and the laws of a play's being are 'moral laws, the guiding one that only in the fullest expression of each individual will the whole be expressed and only by mutual thinking in terms of the whole will each one of us find his place and fulfil it'.[11]

Barker's crucial emphasis on 'the whole' links his theatrical and social aspirations. As far as theatre was concerned, Barker believed with other reformers that the anarchy of the star-based, commercial system, while it might occasionally produce outstanding shows ('lucky chances by which play and company fit together'), was not able to provide the conditions necessary for the theatre they envisaged and were working towards.[12] 'What we want, then, it seems,' he wrote, 'are plays that will compel the actor's interest in something besides that mental looking-glass he carries about with him; directors who will think more of the spirit than the letter of a performance, and a system which will encourage us in these virtues, not compel us towards the opposite vices.'[13]

He joined with and came to the forefront of the movement to organize the theatre and replace the old order, which he knew well from his time as an actor, with a new one, and in the process he found the need for theatrical reform both influenced and was influenced by the need for social reform. He was active in the ethical socialist movement, was a trade unionist and suffrage supporter, and found his theatre companies enlivened by political debates that were often reflected in the plays he chose for them to perform.

A common theme of the early plays he directed and of the plays he wrote himself, for example, was the position of women, and his production of John Galsworthy's *Justice* in 1910, seen by the then Home Secretary Winston Churchill four times, led to important prison reform. His productions in the United States during the First World War of two Trojan War plays by Euripides, which expose the terrible cost of war, were deliberate contributions to an international self-examination triggered by the carnage in Europe.

Barker's belief in building a new society had its parallels in building a new theatre and in the forms that organizing the new theatre would take, namely an ensemble-based repertory system. Running through this interdependent social and aesthetic ideal was the notion of partnership. He insisted drama was 'above all an art of collaboration', and often wrote of its benefits.[14] 'What greater capacity for an orchestration of humanity, with all its thoughts and passions, will [man] find than lies in a company of men and women highly attuned, performing a play?'[15] Within the larger cooperative whole, the director's role was as go-between, the glue connecting the various collaborators, from playwright to actors and, eventually, audience. 'An audience there must be', wrote Barker. 'Not the finest playing of the best play in the world can fully exist without it. Its presence is the logical extension of the co-operation between actors and playwright, and between the actors themselves, upon which the whole art rests.'[16]

He held this conclusion despite a history of disappointment with audiences. In his attempt to escape coterie drama and build a new audience through his repertoire at the Court, he moved the company to the larger Savoy Theatre, only to be met by boos from those who saw his arrival in the West End as a betrayal of the reformists' ideals. Unsurprisingly, he confessed a preference for addressing minorities, because 'one can make them hear better'.[17] In 1918 he even wrote: 'I do believe my present loathing for the theatre is loathing for the audience. I have never loved them.'[18] He lived at a time when his idea of making an audience sit through a play without an interval was seen as outlandish, yet his ambition was always to expand theatre's horizons, and he always acknowledged the audience as an essential collaborator in the theatrical process, however complicated its relationship to that process might be.

Barker was adamant that this process – a theatrical compact between playwright, actor and audience – was based on performance, an emphasis which, odd as it might seem now that the idea of theatre as performance has become commonplace, was then unusual. 'What livelier microcosm of human society ... can there be,' he asked, 'than an acted play?'[19] A play, he asserted, was 'material for acting. It may be far more, but it must be that to begin with.'[20] It must not be 'judged by the printed page – where it lies inanimate, incomplete.'[21] In bringing a play to life, Barker also understood, again before it became routine, that performance produced meaning. 'In the collective consciousness so formed by playwrights, actors, and audience we can gain from the acted drama an understanding of human relationships deeper and subtler than words and their reasoning can give.'[22] If a play's performance were 'a mere intelligent repetition of the author's words accompanied by the necessary action, its object merely to let the audience *understand* what was going forward, no more,' it would be 'a very lifeless business'.[23] But, he asked by way of contrast, 'what do we find in the theatre at its liveliest?'

> We find actors and audience in a concord which certainly no mere verbal, no mere intellectual give and take of the author's meaning will set up. The play is being interpreted, and its meaning enriched in a dozen other ways. There is the emotional value in the very sound of words, the allusive value of familiar phrases, there is a whole vocabulary of demeanour and gesture.[24]

For Barker, the value of the director, a role in its infancy, was to be found in this enriching of a play's meaning in 'a dozen other ways' than merely through understanding the playwright's words. Conventional practice also brought enrichment but not necessarily in bringing a play fully to life. It was common for productions to follow a preset pattern. Actors would arrive with their costumes and moves, requiring little rehearsal, and actor-managers would arrange the actors on stage, or it might be the dramatist if it were a new play. The result of whatever enrichment occurred was usually deadly. 'There is hardly a theatre in the world,' wrote Barker, 'where masterpiece and trumpery alike are not rushed through rehearsals to an arbitrarily effective performance, little more learned of them than the words, gaps in the understanding of them filled up with "business" – effect without cause, the demand for this being the curse of theatre as of other arts, as of other things than art.'[25] If a director did not search for the cause and then the appropriate effect, the new role would not represent an improvement on conventional practice.

The role of director had been evolved for several reasons, Barker wrote, but mostly 'by the growing complexity of the processes, mechanical and other, in the theatre itself'.[26] Yet he observed that the

> work of the modern theatre … is done, as a whole, upon the basis of a compromise by which the author provides essentials and the actor incidentals to taste. That modern invention, the director, is the honest broker brought in to effect it. It answers, doubtless; and the bulk of the work done under it may be pleasing enough. But is there no more to be said? For there is no future in a compromise.[27]

In order to transcend such compromise, Barker proposed proper collaboration in the search for and service of the play's cause or overall purpose and its subsequent realization on stage.

In keeping with modernist thinking, Barker believed that such successful collaboration relied on surrender to the demands of the art. 'The best play director,' he wrote, 'is he who ostensibly does least, not most.'[28] In the collaborative and imprecise art form of theatre that was Barker's domain, this subjugation was a complex and continuous undertaking that channelled personality in the service of the higher purpose:

> What is great drama but the repetition of words and the movements of men and women for an hour or two upon a lit and painted stage? And yet, by furthering with their best thoughts the thoughts of the poet, and more, far more, by yielding themselves utterly, body and spirit, as instruments to the harmony of the play's purpose, a company of actors does bring to birth a thing of powerful beauty that was not in the play before, that is not in themselves, but has now some of the absolute virtue of fine music, some of the quality that can make small things great. There is honour in this art.[29]

Appropriately, in writing about a director searching for the 'harmony of the play's purpose', Barker often turned to musical analogy. (When preparing a production, it was said he played for hours his pianola, a wedding present from the Shaws.) 'There are purists who deny [the director's] right to existence, but some co-ordination is needed, and he is probably less to be dispensed with than is the conductor of an orchestra.'[30] But he offered a clear warning:

> It is tempting to compare conductor and director, but one must do so mainly to remark that their powers, if not their functions, are very different. To wield a baton at rehearsals only, and even then to have neither terms nor instruments of precision for explanation or response – the limitation is severe. It is better to remember that compared to music – and to a far greater degree in comparison with painting, sculpture, and poetry – acting is hardly capable of verbal definition. For by admitting the weakness, by abjuring fixation and finality, one can the better profit by the compensating strength, the ever fresh vitality of the purely human medium; and so the art will gain, not lose. Some fixity, however, there must be, for the practical reason, if for no other, that co-operation would be impossible without it. But there is the aesthetic reason too, and the theatre's problem is concisely this: how to attain enough definition of form and unity of intent for the staged play to rank as a homogeneous work of art and yet preserve that freedom of action which the virtue of the human medium demands.[31]

In this summary of the theatre's problem – fixity against flexibility – Barker encapsulated the challenge for the director. He rejected an excluding and prescriptive approach that might have made life easier, although circumstance, such as shortage of rehearsal time and resistance from actors, did lead him to compromise and take shortcuts in order to achieve his vision.

His aim, nevertheless, was to bring together all the collaborators within his overall vision. Barker believed it had been 'proved beyond doubt that the "team work" of a well-practised company serves this cause better than the most brilliant temperamental despotism,' and concluded: 'A director may direct the preparation, certainly. But if he only knows how to give orders, he has mistaken his vocation; he had better be a drill-sergeant.'[32]

Holding firm, the director must realize the singular vision step by step, through the combined and concerted work of the varied contributors. All the functions of the director's role, such as scholar, playwright's interpreter and champion, encourager of actors, and critical audience, come into play during the process, which begins for Barker with a text, then casting and choice of other collaborators – in design, music, movement – followed by rehearsal in preparation for performance in front of an audience. Along with Barker's ability to work with actors, this insistence on delivering a unified vision serving the play rather than its stars is his chief contribution to directorial practice.

Unified vision

The starting point for Barker is what he called finding the 'plan of thought' of the play. In 'nearly all plays (except, of course, those of pure mime) the physical action is extraordinarily unimportant'; crucial was 'the mental and the emotional action'.[33] As a playwright himself, and major activist in a movement for a new theatre that was being created and led by writers, with Ibsen at their head, it is understandable that this 'plan of thought' would be discovered in, and through close study of, the text. Actors commented on Barker's arriving at rehearsals thoroughly imbued with the text and with all its details at his fingertips, a trait evident also in the many *Prefaces* he wrote to Shakespeare's plays.[34]

Barker believed the writer's intentions were discoverable in the text, which offered guidance as to how the play should be understood and therefore staged. Purpose was bound up with effect: 'Gain Shakespeare's effects by Shakespeare's means when you can', he wrote, and he brought the same approach to all dramatists.[35] Barker became associated with fidelity to the text, through both his championing of new plays and playing Shakespeare in full versions. Following the example of director William Poel, with whom Barker worked as an actor, he restored the most complete versions of Shakespeare's plays seen since the first performances.[36] But Barker was not mechanically supine in relation to text, which he saw as the embodiment of a living organism and notation for its realization in performance. He would often revise his own plays after directing them and would challenge on textual matters the living playwrights whose work he directed. He even said that he would have argued with Shakespeare, whom he treated as a living writer, 'if I could have got at him'.[37]

A text for Barker was only the beginning. It had to be read dramaturgically, not literally or a-historically, if it were to come alive from the printed page. 'Reading a play,' he wrote, 'is comparable to reading the score of a symphony and asks as much skill.'[38] In his reading, he researched the conventions and buildings of the theatre for which a play was written, and sought to understand both why and how the playwright chose to tell a particular story in a particular way and to identify the dramatic means chosen to do this (for example, the formal structure of a play, scene and character selection, and what a character says and does not say and to whom). 'How much of the total effect of a play will be explicit in its literary record will partly depend upon the sort of theatre for which it is meant,' wrote Barker, but 'whatever the theatre, the less there is likely to be on the plain surface of the record of a play of any quality and the more underneath. It will be like the iceberg, floating one-ninth above water and eight-ninths submerged.'[39]

To express 'the total effect of a play' in performance, or – to borrow from Brecht – to express a play's overall *Gestus*, the director has to find a theatrical syntax that on stage articulates a whole understanding and realization of that text. This *Gestus* must transcend any literal meaning of space, word, gesture, costume, scenic design and sound, and embrace the metaphoric richness of the complete *mise en scène*, or what Barker elsewhere called the 'commonwealth of effect'.[40] By way of example, Barker wrote: 'the attention of an audience can be focused upon the smallest details without either words or action being used to mark them, light, darkness, and silence can be made eloquent in themselves, a whole gamut of effectiveness has been added. It has brought new obligations – of accuracy, of sincerity, of verisimilitude in general.'[41]

He applied this approach to plays regardless of their time and place of origin because he believed the aim of drama, which he considered was to create an emotional intimacy between actors and audience, had not changed throughout history. He did see, however, a great divide in method and, therefore, in manner of representation between the presentational theatre of the ancient Greeks and Elizabethans and the then dominant pictorialist or, as he called it, illusionary theatre of the proscenium arch and footlights. The old method brought the stage and the actor into the midst of the audience, whereas in the new, the audience is lured in its imagination on to the stage; 'if it can be hypnotised, even, into forgetting that such a thing as a stage exists,' he wrote by way of explanation, 'so much the better'.[42]

Plays written for the latter, new method – the majority of which, including his own plays, are set in a recognizable and familiar social milieu – might look as if they required a naturalistic setting, but Barker was not interested in the failed literalness of paint and canvas but rather in a different kind of expressive verisimilitude or imaginative authenticity. This was to be achieved through the poetic and minimal use of real objects that carried a metaphoric weight within a particular stage arrangement. Barker placed great importance, for instance, on the choice and use of furniture, which had to be real in order to convey symbolic meaning. In his own play, *The Voysey Inheritance*, for instance, much of the action unfolds in a domestic dining room dominated by a huge dining table, the hub of family interactions, and in his play *Waste*, he places a pair of settees back to back to act as a barrier between two political factions who have to fight across it. Furniture was also arranged to force actors to negotiate their way round it as they would in life, and consciously placed to prevent actors from smoothly sweeping across the stage in pre-planned perfection or from making a grand theatrical exit. Barker cited examples from Ibsen, the writer who for him initiated the reform crusade: Hedda Gabler's surroundings – 'she herself such a contrast to them' – are very much a part of the play, he wrote, as is the gallery in *John Gabriel Borkman*; as for 'the studio and that queer garret in *The Wild Duck*, there is as much dramatic life in it, one could protest, as in any character in the play.'[43] It is interesting to remember, he noted, that the 'end of *The* [sic] *Doll's House* – of the play which began this movement – was the banging of a door'.[44]

Studying the contrast between theatre from different periods stimulated Barker's major breakthroughs in staging and his understanding of how to make the theatre responsively modern. His desire to capture a past spirit led him to the recognition of the importance of the ideas that animated the use of theatre space in the cultures and times of the creation of a particular text and which might be inscribed in that particular text.

His search to find spatial and visual correlatives for a play's poetic vision, however, was not slavish interest in architecture (he rejected the idea of replication) but part of the learning process in which he hoped to discover the *Gestus* of the play. 'We can play the *Agamemnon* in the very theatre for which Aeschylus wrote it, but it cannot mean to us what it meant to his audience. We can rebuild Shakespeare's Globe, but can we come to accepting its conventions as spontaneously as the Elizabethans accepted them?', he asked.[45] Although he wanted to capture again the spirit of past intimacy without returning to the past, he was equally uninterested in false modernity ('Nor does it take modern costume to make the politics of Coriolanus modern enough').[46]

The problems posed by staging classical Athenian drama, a practice then confined to the universities and schools, were crucial in the development of Barker the director, and fed into his innovative directorial work on other playwrights, especially Shakespeare. Barker's productions of five Euripides plays, the first in British professional theatre, presented the ancient texts translated afresh by Gilbert Murray as new plays, and, also in keeping with his approach to Shakespeare, they were not attempts at archaeology. It was with Euripides that Barker opened the celebrated Court seasons, and he added another when the company moved to the Savoy Theatre in 1907.

The arc of Barker's directing was taking him away from the picture frame towards the more overtly presentational style of the pre-illusionary theatre. During his 1910 season at the Duke of York's Theatre, while he was not able to stage Euripides as he had hoped, he deepened his exploration of poetic symbolism in apparently naturalistic drama, particularly in his own play *The Madras House*. The following year, he took over the Little Theatre with his then wife, the actor Lillah McCarthy, and inaugurated their season with Schnitzler's *Anatol* (Barker played Anatol) and Ibsen's *The Master Builder*, two experimental productions designed by Norman Wilkinson. In the age of the grand proscenium theatres, the Little was like a studio space found in the latter part of the twentieth century, with a 250-seat auditorium laid out on one level without an orchestra pit. Barker did not use scene cloths, and, in the manner of Reinhardt, whose work Barker had seen in Germany the year before, lighting was central and overhead, and, in the absence of traditional backdrops, beams were cast in blocks to help create the environment in which the action took place. Wilkinson was to be Barker's chief scenographer for the radical Savoy Shakespeare productions as well as designer for him of the epic production of Thomas Hardy's *The Dynasts* at the Kingsway Theatre in 1914.

The clearest break in Barker's attitude to staging came when he was able to return to Euripides in March 1912 and he directed *Iphigenia in Tauris* at the Kingsway Theatre, which was under McCarthy-Barker management; design was by Wilkinson, and McCarthy played Iphigenia. The forestage covered the orchestra pit and the first rows of the stalls, there were two enormous doors in the centre, and the raised upstage temple was reached by five steps; some entrances and exits were made from the auditorium on a sloping gangway, and there were no curtains.[47] Wilkinson, evoking blood, used red as the dominant colour, with contrasting huge gilt doors patterned in black and white, and the eleven-strong female chorus clothed in brown hoods and bluish-purple robes. Stationary, muted red lighting came from above, fixed in the temple roof (hidden), on the side columns and on top of the proscenium. The chorus, choreographed by Margaret Morris, moved in simple patterns often far downstage, and they faded when in the shadows because of their dark costumes, thus allowing Barker to bring them in and out of focus as he required and to overcome the problem of what to do with a block of actors when not directly involved in the action.

Several critics saw this production as being influenced by Reinhardt, who within the previous few months had directed three revelatory productions in London which challenged prevailing staging conventions. Barker had attended rehearsals for the latest of these, *Oedipus Rex*, which featured McCarthy, whom Barker coached in the role of Jocasta. He tested *Iphigenia in Tauris* at His Majesty's Theatre, a larger auditorium than the Kingsway though still proscenium in design, and, more significantly, at Bradfield College's open-air Greek theatre, built in a redundant chalk pit. The exhilaration and freedom of these latter performances convinced him Greek plays had to be staged as originally in the open air, something he achieved when he mounted *Iphigenia in Tauris* and *The Trojan Women* in the United States in 1915 'on a scale even Reinhardt and Meyerhold would not match'.[48]

FIGURE 5.2 Iphigenia in Tauris *at the Yale University Bowl, 1915*
(Yale University).

The Savoy

That American tour marked the end point of Barker's continuous directing. He did not direct another production for five years, and after that only sporadically while he concentrated on his writing. He had gone to and returned from the United States at the height of his fame, featuring in New York before the Euripides tour his productions of *Androcles and the Lion, The Doctor's Dilemma* (both Shaw) and the last of his stunning Savoy Shakespeares, *A Midsummer Night's Dream.*[49] With *The Winter's Tale* and *Twelfth Night*, both staged in 1912, this 1914 production had formed the modernist trilogy of Barker productions at the Savoy that shook audiences and critics and changed the way British theatre stages Shakespeare.

Euripides did not come with the cultural baggage that Shakespeare did, hence Barker's innovations with Shakespeare, being central to the English repertoire and the nation's cultural sense of self, were more influential and profound. His only previous production of Shakespeare, an intelligent account of *Two Gentlemen of Verona* at the Court, had represented a bargaining chip in his bid to mount a season at that theatre, and though not lavish, maintained habitual practice of text cutting and altering scenes to accommodate set changes. Barker was not ready or able to tackle the enormous challenge of Shakespeare until he returned to the Savoy.

The Savoy was a conventional, end-on theatre, designed for comic operetta, and Barker changed its configuration for all three productions to allow fluid staging and to emulate the basic spatial relationships of an Elizabethan stage, including bringing the action to the audience. Developing

FIGURE 5.3 Twelfth Night *at the Savoy Theatre, 1912*
(ArenaPAL/University of Bristol).

his Kingsway layout for *Iphigenia in Tauris*, Barker removed the footlights and built a curved apron over the orchestra pit and into the stalls, wider than the theatre's proscenium. Entrances and exits were through boxes left and right. Two steps up from the permanent proscenium was a large central acting area, and four steps up from that, inside a bespoke proscenium, was another acting area, similar to the Elizabethan inner stage.

Norman Wilkinson, the scenographer for all three productions and costume designer for the latter two, provided a generally white floor and surround, and used this background to highlight the colour of the costumes: Oberon in magnificent gold, for example; Puck in brilliant red; Leontes in deep, vivid blue and silver. Props were minimal and chosen for impact; in *The Winter's Tale*, for instance, critics were struck by Hermione's enormous regal umbrella. Aside from a few (non-realistic) settings, such as Leontes' palace or Olivia's garden, scenes were played in front of light and patterned drapes, which were used to vary the depth of the revealed acting area and allowed for uninterrupted playing. The speed and sound of the drapes became a notable aspect of the productions, which were controlled, as at the Little and Kingsway, by the lighting. Barker lit from the front with a set of high-wattage lamps suspended in full view from a rail on the dress circle. Fellow director William Bridges-Adams described the effect as 'a hygienic light, the sort a surgeon likes to have at an operating table' and 'a strictly democratic light, falling equally on principals and supers'.[50]

This anti-illusionistic scenographic display, boasting clarity of line and architectural, geometric design, emphasized the importance and reality of the stage world in which the plays took place in order to focus on and free the plays themselves. Albert Rothenstein, costume designer of *The Winter's Tale* and art editor of *The Players' Shakespeare* for which Barker wrote the *Prefaces*, commenting on the drapes, said they 'were meant to be suggestive only of the time, place, and mood of the action ... There was no attempt at scenic illusion, only such colour and form being employed as were sufficient and appropriate both to the material being used, and the suggestion which had to be implied.'[51]

Norman Wilkinson corroborated this approach. He had 'attempted to give the design and plan that was necessary for the action of the play,' he wrote, 'and the charm of light and line and colour that might result from that and that alone'.[52] He also confirmed that the choreographed composition of the abstract stage pictures was informed by and designed for a particular type of audience engagement. As Barker was to write: 'If [Elizabethan playgoers] stopped to ask themselves where such and such a character ... was supposed to be, "On the stage" might well have served for an immediate answer.'[53] To underpin this presentational, playful element, Barker had Puck act like a stage manager, bidding gilded fairies to open curtains and lights to be lowered.

In responding to the shock that greeted the productions, Barker acknowledged his debt to Gordon Craig, for destroying any illusions Barker had held about the need for representational stage scenery. The challenge, said Barker, was to 'invent a new hieroglyphic language of scenery,' explaining that as 'a new formula, a new convention, has to be found, the audience must learn to see, even as we learn to work in it'.[54] When he took *A Midsummer Night's Dream* to the United States, he elaborated on this in an interview, and gave the journalist a quotation that turned out to be prophetic: what theatre needed, Barker said, was 'a great white box. That's what our theatre really is.'[55] Barker's embrace of a liberating minimalism predated the use of just such a stage in the post-Second World War years, notably at the Royal Shakespeare Company, most famously in Peter Brook's 1970 production of the same play designed by Sally Jacobs, and the widespread use of simple but versatile box studio theatres. Barker's advocacy was in line with the revolutionary, actor-centred experiments of Swiss designer Adolphe Appia, whose use of light to create a stripped-down, dynamic performance space Barker had admired in Germany in 1913. In terms of impact on the future, it is also worth noting that on Barker's American visit, he gave Robert Edmond Jones his first professional job, as designer of Anatole France's *The Man Who Married a Dumb Wife*, a production that introduced radical scenography to the United States and became a milestone in American theatre history.

After objections to the decor, the commonest complaints about Barker's Savoy Shakespeares concerned the speaking. Barker's break with the usual slow, extended delivery through a rapid, energized clarity seemed scandalous to many. Again, he was ready to acknowledge debts; although departing from

William Poel's antiquarian approach, Barker thanked Poel for teaching him 'how swift and passionate a thing, how beautiful in its variety, Elizabethan blank verse might be when tongues were trained to speak and ears acute to hear it'.[56] Barker rehearsed his casts long and hard, often until the early hours of the morning, to achieve the pace and emotional rather than purely intellectual meaning he was looking for, both of which were essential to the vitality of the performance. A note he left Cathleen Nesbitt (Perdita) before opening night read: 'Be swift, be swift, be not poetical.'[57] He left similar notes for other actors, and maintained this approach when advising or commenting on productions by other directors, typically urging actors not 'to be so damned explanatory'.[58]

It was all of a piece with his countering conventional interpretation, not for its own sake, but for the sake of what he believed to be the meaning of the play; in A Midsummer Night's Dream, for example, he dropped the almost obligatory Mendelssohn score for folk music arranged by Cecil Sharp, the leader of the folk song revival, made Puck a descendant of English hobgoblins (reputedly the first time a grown man had played the role in Britain), found individual personalities in the lovers, removed the other-worldly fairies from fey Victoriana, and returned Oberon to his now familiar central role. As had been the case with the Court seasons, Barker was lauded for his attention to detail, especially in the care he took with small parts, and for his ability to manoeuvre and enliven blocks of actors. The fairies, for example, instantly established as non-mortals by their startling golden appearance, moved in often synchronized and abstract configurations, displaying the formalized verve of Asian drama. They showed that Barker's reputation for energizing crowds, gained particularly from the Trafalgar Square scene at the heart of Votes for Women! (1907) and the choreography of the strikers in Strife (1909), was justly warranted.

As with the Court productions, too, major praise was afforded the quality of performance Barker stimulated in his casts, both individually and as a whole, in particular their naturalness, a persuasive and authentic verisimilitude consonant with his overall vision. The quiet inner strength Barker sought in his actors, a feature Shaw was known to find frustrating in both Barker the actor and Barker the director, sometimes led critics to complain of poor audibility, but, as with other facets of his productions, calm intensity was designed to engage the audience in the meaning of the play and ask them to, if not demand they, listen rather than have them assailed by waves of barnstorming noise.

Centrality of the actor

If Barker's espousal of a unified aesthetic vision has been identified as his distinctive directorial contribution, then the core of his achieving it in performance must enjoy equal standing, and that is his belief in the centrality of the actor. Regardless of period, pre- or post-footlights, the key for Barker was the transformative power of acting. 'The written text is not a play's final and complete manifestation', he wrote. 'This it will owe to its actors and their interpreting.'[59] A director, he believed, must 'see, no doubt, that the scenery is of the right shape and colour, the furniture placed usefully, costumes as they should be; but this is simple enough and comparatively unimportant. The acting is what matters.'[60]

The director's 'first care', said Barker, should be the 'constant credibility of the actor', and to achieve this he sought in his casts his own qualities as an actor: speed, lightness, intelligence, understatement, subtlety, and, overall, a vital naturalness in speech, gesture and movement.[61] He asked more of his actors than usual in exploration of their character on and off stage and in discipline; he encouraged spontaneity and hated the conventional, and loathed fixing a production before it was ready or seeing a production becoming too fixed. It is 'the letter that killeth,' says Barker, 'and only the spirit that giveth life'.[62]

Yet to achieve Barker's chief aim of vitality, the actor needs both freedom (the spirit) and boundaries (the letter). 'A book must be finished with, or a picture, but the moment an actor ceases to vary his part he should stop playing it; he *has*, in fact, stopped playing it; repetition is not acting. The director's problem then is how to shape the play stably but not statically, to give it what will be a living form.'[63] To do this a director 'has to struggle constantly against one temptation: to get everything, at any cost, just so. With a long run in prospect, the certainty that after production the actor will gradually become mechanical, and with ample time before production to see that at least the mechanism is perfect, the temptation is overwhelming.'[64]

A highly successful and creative performer himself, Barker took a clear view in the contemporary debate that divided the profession; actors were not mechanical puppets simply doing someone else's artistic bidding; they were interpretive artists themselves embodying the 'living form':

> To my taste, if acting cannot seem spontaneous, it is nothing. It can only seem so by the actor coming fresh to his work, his whole personality like a sensitive plate, which he exposes untouched to the light of his conception of the part. The image produced, valuable according to the rightness of the conception, will vary from time to time according to the condition of the plate, but each time it must be a fresh image. A director's business is to help an actor in the study of his part, especially to help him find the relation of his part to the whole play; at later rehearsals to constitute himself as far as possible an ideal audience, registering each effect or each failure, and a critic analysing the causes. Let the director, in fact, do all he can before-hand in grouping this sun-picture, the performance of a play; but let him not touch the plates, not anticipate the final process.[65]

Barker applied the same principle to actors as he did to all collaborators in the production process; they had to supress their individual personality in the collective personality of the whole endeavour, to allow the variety of each individual contribution to be enhanced through this mutual sacrifice. 'An actor must realise the part in his own person,' according to Barker, and to do this 'he must surrender himself to it, even as the dramatist surrenders it to him.'[66] In writing about this complex process, which, for Barker, was critical, he distinguished between the conscious and subconscious action of a play. The former category (conscious action) provides relatively straightforward challenges, while, for the latter:

> we are to bring everything in the play's acting – movement, expression, emotion, thought – which may, without disturbance of the production's structure or to the distraction of fellow actors, be carried forward in any one of fifty different ways. We say fifty, as we might say a dozen or a hundred, simply for comparison with the single way of the first category.[67]

He went on to argue that 'the sub-conscious self has still to be regulated. But practically what we are after is a consciousness of complete freedom.' He was, however, aware of the problem this raises:

> And though the freedom can never be quite complete, neither can any action in the first category be made perfectly accurate, for in each case the work is done in the incalculable human medium which defies (and perhaps despises) exactitude. We aim, then, through this freedom at an appearance of spontaneity. This may seem to some people a very little thing; if it does they have not a very discriminating taste for acting.[68]

For Barker, the overriding need was to help an actor find a cohering, stimulating, inner conviction:

> If the actor anchors himself to this bit of business, to that intonation, even to a particular trick of thought or emotion which he finds he can command, his performance will become in time a mosaic of excellent fragments: disturb one, a dozen others are loosened, and then, with the oncoming of fatigue, the whole may begin to break up, for there is no vital principle to unite them.[69]

He summed up what he had been describing as a double process: 'first the mental search and the provocative argument into and around the character and the play ...; then the sensitizing of the actor's receptive faculties, mental and emotional, too. It should be a concurrent process'.[70]

Rehearsals

This 'concurrent process' takes place in rehearsals, where the director has to create the conditions in which actors explore together and make themselves the instruments by which the play can become itself. Barker wrote in detail about this preparation, the conduct of rehearsals, and the journey to performance on the stage, always with the concerns of the actor in the forefront. Rehearsals, for Barker, were informed by 'the community of interest implicit in all acting'.[71] Their main object was to enable 'an actor to forget both himself and them [i.e. the rehearsals] in the performance'.[72]

The discovery implicit in the process was built into Barker's scheme. In line with his thoughts on finding the 'plan of thought', he began with study of the play and put that before the acting. 'Far from encouraging a company to act, a director will need, as a rule, to prevent them trying to, before they know what the play and the parts are about. Beware of the actor who comes to a first rehearsal word perfect, his mind made up about every detail of his part.'[73] He even proposed the 'cast should be formed into a committee upon the play, sitting to discuss it with the director as chairman,' and added,

> just as seventeenth-century music teachers used to lock up the instrument on their departure, and carry off the key, so should the actors leave their parts on the committee table and cease to worry about them till they all meet again. The task of the committee should be to arrive at a common understanding and a unity of intention about the play.[74]

Barker's view of the nature of acting informed his ideas for shaping and managing rehearsals to the needs of the play and not to a dogmatic plan: 'No play should move in an efficient straight line between first rehearsal and performance. This time of survey and discovery is the time, too, when the first tendons are being formed which will come to unite the actor's personality with the crescent figure of the character itself.'[75] He warned that 'the physical action of the play must not be defined while the thought and feeling that should prompt it are still unsure ... Quite literally the company should be allowed to feel their feet in the play, to stamp up and down and restore the circulation which too much talk may have slackened.'[76]

Not all plays require lengthy discussion but once the 'plan of thought' has been found, said Barker, the 'plan of action' will at the right moment develop itself with 'surprising ease', and it is the responsibility of the director to select that moment.[77] Having 'decided upon the barest skeleton of action', the director's role changes:

> To suggest, to criticize, to co-ordinate – that should be the limit of his function. Even plays that seem to need the exactitude of orchestration must still, as far as possible, grow healthily and naturally into being. We must never forget that to put a play into action on the stage is to pour it into its mould; once there it tends very quickly to set. If the performance of such plays as these is not to become mere repetition of ritual they must be kept fluid and experimental in their preparation till appearance and purpose both, fineness and sincerity united, can be relied upon for the tempering.[78]

Acting as the 'ideal audience', the director works patiently, by elimination: '"No, that does not quite express it. Try again." His simple rule at this stage will be that though in the last instance he may veto, say definitely what is not to be done, he may never dictate what is to be.'[79] How long this process should take Barker found impossible to say. He was particularly frustrated by the restrictions of the commercial system and looked to the repertory theatre as an answer. He was fond of quoting a conversation he had with Konstantin Stanislavski when he visited Moscow in 1914 and asked him how long he liked to rehearse a play. 'Till it is ready' was the reply, which Barker took to be conclusive.[80] He also quoted the Russian director on the critical issue of how to maintain freshness:

We are indebted, again to Stanislavski, for a rule of thumb solution. Establish, he says, a certain number of fixed points, rendezvous for the players, physical or mental, where they may be sure of meeting. Let there be enough of these to ensure that the action never drifts awry. You will need more in scenes of crisis and quick movement than in those of exposition and discussion, but always keep them as few as you can, for they tend to multiply unawares. Between these points actors must encourage themselves to wander, they must resist habit.[81]

Barker had been working along similar lines to Stanislavski without being aware of his work, and had discussed rehearsal methods with both him and Reinhardt when he wrote the above (1919) at a point in his life when, apart from a few instances, he had left directing behind and had devoted himself to writing. With Stanislavski, he found common ground in the primacy of the text, the indispensable need for repertory and ensemble acting (and the consequent abolition of stage 'business' and the distinction between large and small parts), and an insatiable interest in finding the subjective character of a role. This search for an interior life in a part, another facet that aligned Barker's work with Modernism, can be seen not only in his productions but also in the detail with which he writes about character in the *Prefaces* and elsewhere, in the subtle and complex exploration of character in his own plays, and in his correspondence with actors and directors regarding roles and their casting, all of which show constant tension between an ideal view and the theatrical reality of the day.

In the shadow of the devastation of the First World War, Barker was all too aware of the theatre's shortcomings, and this often brought him low, but he continued to hope and plan. He remained firm in his commitment to a new kind of theatre and also continued to advocate proper training for actors as integral to its creation. He told William Archer in 1923 that there was no English company that could act his latest play, *The Secret Life*; yet the following year he relaunched a campaign to establish a National Theatre. Ten years on, after co-directing a revival of *The Voysey Inheritance*,

Barker judged the theatre had not changed in forty years, but believed that was why '*real* repertory and a permanent company are the only solution'.[82]

Reputation

The notion that when Barker stopped regular directing during the First World War in order to concentrate on writing he in fact abandoned the theatre, and in particular the cause of reform with which his name had become synonymous, has undermined his reputation. The first biography, published almost ten years after his death in 1955, aroused little curiosity and sanctified the legend of the lost leader who had deserted his post. He remained known as a director from a bygone age and as the author of the *Prefaces*. His standing as a playwright, high before the First World War but diminished afterwards, began to be repaired in the 1970s, and three plays, *The Voysey Inheritance, The Madras House* and *Waste*, have since come to be regarded as classics of the Edwardian theatre. Academic interest has also increased; yet the fracture in his life between writing and directing, despite some rebalancing of the account, has left him a respected name but not a known one. His curiously elusive status, in accord with the private man he was, is out of kilter with the enormous and unquantifiable influence his work exerted and continues to exert on English-speaking theatre.

As a director during the birth of modern theatre, much of his legacy has become so commonplace that the nature of his contribution has been forgotten. In trying to uncover that legacy, commentators have traced many influences on his directing, from those he acknowledged, such as William Poel and Gordon Craig, to the many theatre reformers with whom he worked in the early part of his life, such as (to list a few) Max Behrend, J.T. Grein, William Archer, Charles Charrington, Janet Achurch, Gilbert Murray and Bernard Shaw, as well as those whose work he saw and admired, such as Max Reinhardt, Adolphe Appia and Konstantin Stanislavski. It is impossible, however, to identify direct influences clearly, and Barker was an assiduous magpie, who was always looking for whatever might prove useful. The related notions of director and ensemble came from mainland Europe, and, at a time when ideas about change in the theatre were circulating rapidly and enthusiastically across borders and cultures, Barker absorbed ideas on theatre and art from wherever he could find them – William Morris, John Ruskin, George Moore, George Meredith, Henrik Ibsen, W.B. Yeats and Maurice Maeterlinck could be added to the mix, for instance, along with many others. It should be remembered, nevertheless, that Barker was very much his own man, even at the outset of his directing.

Elisabeth Fagan, writing when Barker had become the most famous director in Britain, offers a cameo portrait of him two decades earlier directing *The Weather Hen* in 1899. The play was written by Barker and an actor friend of his, Berte Thomas, and the production was probably Barker's first in the professional theatre, albeit uncredited. He was twenty-one. Even then, she wrote, Barker 'was a splendid director'. He had

> the peculiar director's talent ... of making his company *see* what the part means – such a different thing to showing them 'how to do it'. I used to say he could make a cat act. (He certainly made me.) But young as he was, he was very strict at rehearsals. From the stall would come his quiet voice, just as one felt one was really beginning to get a grip on the scene.
> 'One moment, please. What was your last line, Miss – ?'
> 'No, thank you,' you would read from your part, wonderingly.
> 'Ah, I thought so. You said, "*Oh*, no, thank you." Would you mind keeping exactly to what I've written? So sorry to interrupt you. Go on, please.'
> And you went on, somewhat crushed – but not nastily so, the reprimand had been said too kindly for that, and he was quite right.[83]

Unlike Poel, Craig and other directors who helped establish the modern art of directing, Barker placed the actor at the heart of the production and performance process, and was good at communicating with actors. As Lewis Casson recalled, he gave actors the confidence to use 'their own imaginative ideas'.[84] Harcourt Williams, another actor-director who was a Barker disciple like Casson, offered this summary of Barker's directorial style:

> Roughly one may say that Barker worked from the inside to the outside. He had an exceptional interest in what was theatrically effective, but never got it by theatrical means. It had to be won by mental clarity and emotional truth – in fact, the very opposite to the methods of most directors. Besides his intellectual attainments he had gone through the rough and tumble of an actor's training and knew to a hairsbreadth what an actor could put up with and how he could best be handled. I have known him change readings without explaining why he did it, on purpose to break down the inhibitions of some actor, and at last, out of the subconscious if you will, would emerge the right way of doing it.[85]

The relatively new role of director was not universally accepted, and many actors, steeped in the old conventions, resisted new ways of looking at theatre and new ways of working. Casson noted: '[Barker] always assumed that everyone was as keen as he on research into and expression of the author's meaning, and the motives, thoughts and emotions of his characters, evoking the actor's enthusiasm and making everyone contribute his utmost.'[86] Faced with actors who were not as keen, the response of Barker the perfectionist unsurprisingly sometimes combined the two extremes of the role: the enabler and the despot.

While there are a few dissenting voices, Barker, generally, has been praised by actors with whom he worked. Sybil Thorndike, who appeared in small parts in Barker's Duke of York's company, said he was one of the biggest influences in her life. She recalled with amazement 'one of his gestures ... that no one but God would have thought of – and things he does with his voice when he's showing people what he wants'.[87] John Gielgud, who played Lear in the 1940 Lewis Casson production on which Barker advised, was 'so impressed' with the few hours he spent with him on stage: 'He seemed to know exactly what he wanted and how much to give and how much not to give.'[88] A critic, writing in 1912 during Barker's pomp as a director, saw in his vision 'the birth of the art of the theatre'.[89] Indeed, there is a consensus among those contemporary with Barker, both actors and critics, that he was the best director of his day. A 1913 description of Barker the playwright as 'the first experimentalist in the modern English theatre' could also, it seems, be justifiably applied to Barker the director.[90] The critic Kenneth Tynan, writing after Barker's death, even believed that, aside from Tyrone Guthrie 'intermittently', Barker was the only director who had exerted 'much perceptible influence on English acting'.[91] For Richard Eyre, National Theatre Artistic Director from 1988–97, Barker stands 'not only as the first modern English director but as the most influential'.[92]

Barker passed on his reflections on directing in his extensive writing on theatre, much of which, apart from the *Prefaces*, is not as well known as it deserves to be; the *Prefaces*, however, have secured their central place in the history of Shakespeare production in the English-speaking theatre. More directly, Barker passed on his methods to his actors and to important directors, such as Lewis Casson, Harcourt Williams, Ben Iden Payne, William Bridges-Adams, Barry Jackson, Robert Atkins, Basil Dean and Norman Marshall. They were prominent in the years before the Second World War in the production of Shakespeare and the classics and of new plays, particularly in the repertory movement, which also featured many plays Barker had championed. The repertory idea, of which Barker was the chief proponent, extended beyond the Second World War in many manifestations, and in one form or another became the bedrock of the majority of publicly funded post-war British theatre. It gave rise to the widespread phenomenon of the university-educated director and artistic director (a role Barker pioneered and wrote about in relation to the National Theatre), combining the qualities of theatre practitioner and scholar found in the (non-university-educated) 'man of theatre' Barker, who, with little formal education, had taken to the stage as a youth.

However difficult it is to identify influence, Barker's imprint can surely be found in theatres such as the Royal Court after 1956, the Royal Shakespeare Company and the National Theatre, as well as in the few repertory theatres outside London that remain. Barker advocated a collective production process rather than the atomized practice of the nineteenth century, and championed theatre performed by amateurs as well as theatre beyond the capital in his concern with new forms of organization that would take the new theatre he was trying to create away from its coterie status. In a more general sense, his legacy can be seen in any group that champions new writing, produces fluid, full-text Shakespeare, and interprets classic texts as if new, or one that espouses his directorial principles based on the primacy of performance: research into and fidelity to text, discoveries to be made together in rehearsal (from round-table discussion to interpretation of a role and actors' finding a backstory for their characters in order to understand them better), ensemble playing and the need to find an integrated production style (rhythm, pace, gesture, sound and look) in the service of the play's overall purpose.

Although many of the innovations associated with Barker, whether the approach to directing outlined above, for example, or particulars, such as overhead and frontal lighting, and projecting the forestage, were not exclusive to him or introduced by him, Barker gave them prominence and impact through the outstanding quality of the work he achieved. His belief that 'spontaneous enjoyment is the life of the theatre' meant that his extra-textual readings embraced theatricality (unlike some modernizers) but with purpose derived from his view of the play's meaning and not as stage 'business' to win admiration.[93] His approach led to directness and simplicity, if not austerity, compared to late Victorian/Edwardian excess, an expressive minimalism and restrained intensity that celebrated playfulness derived from integrity to the perceived needs and intentions of the text. Later commentators have successfully challenged this 'intentional fallacy', which allows fidelity to the text to be claimed by a wide and disparate collection of interpreters, often with contradictory readings though seemingly equal authority; yet, in the context of Barker's time, given the random and often idiosyncratic way text was treated then, his insistence on the overriding weight of the text proved vital to the rejuvenation of theatre.[94]

Barker, especially in the Savoy Shakespeares, has often been bracketed with Modernism because he ran against the grain and because of the look of his productions, with their use of architectural shapes, evidence of abstraction, clarity of line, simplicity of impact and imaginative, anti-pictorial presentation. This visual connection, founded on the work of the artists with whom he collaborated, from Norman Wilkinson and Albert Rothenstein through to the illustrators of the *Prefaces*, such as Paul Nash, was reinforced by his sometimes stylized choreography of actors. But Barker was no Craig, and his eclecticism, though controlled by a unifying vision, was ultimately pragmatic. He did not sacrifice actors to directorial dogma or scenic elements, which remained a background against, in and on which actors performed. Barker was also conservative in his belief in a canon and in its hierarchy, with Shakespeare's place impregnable at the summit (and with a decided ladder of merit within Shakespeare's plays). His use of the past to illuminate the present was shared by modernists, and in particular his fascination with Greek drama is echoed in Yeats and Eliot. Barker also shared the modernist drive for change, but it was change predicated not on the privilege of wealth and class but on taste, on ethics, judgement and quality, a cornerstone of the liberal democracy he defended in the face of rising totalitarian systems and the spread of mass culture.

As a director, he was not part of a modernist avant-garde, though he grappled with form in his productions both of seemingly naturalistic and of presentational plays, looking for an authentic poetic verisimilitude to express their vision. As a director, he also echoed many of the modernist interests he had as a writer in countering conventional representation of the relationships between human beings and exploring the interior world of a subject within this social nexus. Prefiguring the stage world of Beckett and even of the later notion of post-dramatic theatre, Barker summed up his theatrical direction of travel in an essay he wrote in 1922:

> One is tempted to imagine a play – to be written in desperate defiance of Aristotle – from which doing would be eliminated altogether, in which nothing but being would be left. The task set the actors of it would be to interest their audience in what the characters *were*, quite apart from anything they might *do*; to set up, that is to say, the relation by which all important human intimacies exist. If the art of the theatre could achieve this it would stand alone in a great achievement.[95]

In all his writing about the director, he never saw the role as one of authority in the way that it has subsequently become. For Barker, the twin poles of imaginative might were the dramatist and the actor, and in his 1930 book on the National Theatre it is still not the director who occupies the key role but, again, the actor. Barker repeats his constant view:

> acting is not an individual art. It attains full development only in the complete accord of a whole company of actors. Nor can this accord be reached by the sudden throwing together for three weeks' rehearsal of even the most brilliant and generous individual talents. It comes with time and patience, variety of expression, and the cultivation of a mutual sympathy which will be instinctive, not calculated.[96]

Barker may have abandoned directing but he never abandoned the theatre or his search in art for what he considered the truth, a search that underpinned his directing as much as his acting and writing, and which can stand as a summation of his legacy:

> To say that one strives for perfection in art and wishes never to attain it is no paradox, it is only to assert the intimate relation of art to life. To sit while the action of a play grows, goes its own way, not insisting on this or that – for in art as in life how many good roads to a given point there are – caring only that the roads are good, testing sympathetically step by step that the way *is* its own.[97]

6

'The Mind Goes Back to the Golden Fairies …': Harley Granville Barker's Choral Work

Philippa Burt

Amid the mixed and, at times, violent reaction to Harley Granville Barker's production of *A Midsummer Night's Dream* at the Savoy Theatre in February 1914, the woodland fairy scenes quickly emerged as the focal point of critical discourse.[1] Barker's and designer Norman Wilkinson's decision to dress Oberon, Titania and the fairies from head to toe in gold, complete with gilt faces and hands, astounded the critics. While some praised these 'elegant creatures … tall and graceful, clad in the soft metallic shimmer of their web of gold over gold armour',[2] others denounced them as 'grotesque figures'.[3] However, although critical opinion was divided with regards to the appearance of the fairies, there was almost unanimous praise of their performances and positioning on the stage, particularly for their arrival at the beginning of Act 2, Scene 1. *The Athenaeum* declared that this 'first scene in which the fairy nation appears is a triumphantly beautiful spectacle'[4] and J.T. Grein described the scene, and the production as a whole, as 'a beautiful dream … a gallery of statuesque groups … a vision of something eerie, remote, supernatural'.[5] For A.B. Walkley, whose titular quotation has become almost synonymous with the production, the impression of the group gathered together in gold was 'wonderfully beautiful'.[6]

While the fairy chorus was singled out for particular acclaim, it was, in reality, one in a long line of similar experiments conducted by Barker that foregrounded the notion of the unified group, beginning with his legendary

FIGURE 6.1 *The fairies surround the sleeping Titania,* A Midsummer Night's Dream, *1914 (ArenaPAL/University of Bristol).*

seasons at the Court Theatre between 1904 and 1907. These experiments manifested themselves, on the one hand, in a new approach to rehearsals that centred on collaborative study to establish a shared understanding of the play in question and thus a sense of ensemble among the actors.[7] Barker argued that 'co-operation was the first and last law of the theatre', and that it was impossible for an actor to know and understand her or his part without also knowing and understanding the play as a whole, which could only be achieved with corporate study.[8] To achieve this, he sent company members complete copies of the script, as opposed to the conventional cue scripts, so all could get a sense of the totality of the play and how each character fitted into its structure. Likewise, he dedicated time and attention in the rehearsals to every actor regardless of the size of her or his role. The result was even and balanced productions, where 'the unity of tone, the subordination of the individual, the genuine striving for totality of effect ... the abolition of the "star" system – all were noteworthy features of these productions'.[9]

On the other hand, and most pertinent to this chapter, Barker's interest in the ensemble saw him develop new ways of presenting groups on the stage in order to create a cohesive unity that was centred on visual and aural harmony. In this, as with his work in rehearsals, Barker's innovations went hand in glove with the introduction of the role of director, which, as Colin Chambers has already argued, was a role Barker pioneered in Britain at the time. An illustrative example is his production of Elizabeth Robins' *Votes for Women!,* which opened at the Court on 9 April 1907. For Act

2's famous suffragette rally in Trafalgar Square – the centre point of the play and its dramatic crescendo – Barker countered the conventions of the time and the tendency to hire in walk-on supernumeraries to simply fill the space and create an appropriate stage picture. Instead, he worked hard with experienced actors, including regular Court players, to create a crowd that comprised lifelike, recognizable and realistic individuals that spanned the spectrum of Edwardian society.

This crowd responded to and interrupted the platform speakers, speaking alternately as a unified group and as a cacophony of individual voices. Thus:

Old Newsvendor   It's true, wot she says! – every word.

Working Woman   You say we women 'ave got no business servin' on boards and thinkin' about politics. Wot's *politics*?

(*A decisive roar.*)

It's just 'ousekeepin' on a big scale. 'Oo among you workin' men 'as the most comfortable 'omes? Those of you that gives yer wives yer wages.

(*Loud laughter and jeers.*)

Voices   That's it!
          Wantin' our money.
          Lord 'Igh 'Ousekeeper of England.[10]

FIGURE 6.2 *The suffragette rally in* Votes for Women! *Court Theatre, 1907 (British Library).*

The critics responded enthusiastically. 'I have never seen so good a stage crowd', remarked the *London Daily News*. 'Its humblest members had character, from a costermonger with his flashes of crude wit to an elderly gentleman fresh from his lunch at the club and full of pompous platitudes.'[11] *The Times* similarly praised Barker for his 'admirably managed "living picture" with as realistic a crowd as we have ever seen manoeuvred on the stage'.[12]

The positioning of the crowd was also significant. Barker set the scene around the base of Nelson's Column, where the speakers, including Edith Wynne Matthison as the outspoken suffragette Vida Levering and Edmund Gwenn as Labour leader Mr Walker, delivered their orations from a small platform that faced the audience. In the small space between the speakers and the auditorium was a crowd of more than forty actors, the majority of whom had their backs to the audience. The speakers therefore addressed the audience directly, giving the scene a 'sense of reality' and encouraging the latter group to listen carefully to the messages from the stage.[13] As Dennis Kennedy rightly observes, this placement of the crowd in the liminal space between stage and auditorium meant that it adopted a role akin to that of the Greek chorus, commenting on the dramatic action and representing the audience on the stage.[14] Barker's close orchestration of the crowd was thus not solely for aesthetic reasons; it also served to foreground the political debate at the heart of the play and promote female suffrage at a time when campaigning was becoming increasingly visible and violent.

Although brief, these introductory observations highlight the need to re-evaluate Barker's work with groups on the stage and to consider it as an integral part of his ongoing assault on the individualistic and naturalistic theatre of his time, with its emphasis on illusion, spectacle, declamation and theatrical effect. Nowhere was this penchant for illusion and spectacle more apparent than in the Shakespeare productions of the period. The common practice was to present the plays as 'star' vehicles, which often entailed rewriting the text to create a central lead character.[15] The staging similarly foregrounded the individual 'star' actor, while the heavily decorative sets and slavish reproduction of minute everyday detail – as epitomized by the live rabbits seen hopping around the stage for Herbert Beerbohm Tree's 1911 *A Midsummer Night's Dream* – created productions that were overly elaborate, slow and drawn out.

By way of a response, Barker staged a series of three Shakespeare productions at the Savoy Theatre, which is the primary focus of this chapter. The tendency is to focus on the iconoclastic design of these productions, where the stripped-back minimalist sets, the use of drop curtains and the Leon Bakst-inspired costumes provided a startling antidote to the conventional emphasis on naturalistic illusion. However, the productions also introduced an entirely new way of performing Shakespeare that centred on lightness and a swift tempo, where Barker again placed precedence on the unified group working together in harmony over any single 'star' actor. In this, Barker sought to bring the plays back to life, encouraging the actors to listen to Shakespeare's text and work in collaboration with him in order to communicate the plays' meanings and make clear their relevance to a British public on the brink of war. The emphasis was on making the plays 'true' or 'real', even if not realistic in the conventional sense of the word.

This same goal of resuscitation underpinned Barker's work on Greek tragedy, which is a secondary concern of this chapter. Gilbert Murray's recent translations of Euripides' tragedies demonstrated to Barker the timeliness of the plays, and he saw their potential as a means of identifying and examining the problems that beset Edwardian society. The plays quickly became a trope of his work as a director and featured in the repertoire of each of his ventures into theatre management, where they sat alongside such leading proponents of the New Drama as Robins, George Bernard Shaw, John Galsworthy and St. John Hankin.[16] His production of *Hippolytus* inaugurated the Court Theatre seasons in October 1904 – a production that was first staged for William Archer and Elizabeth Robins' New Century Theatre five months earlier – while his 1915 *Iphigenia in Tauris* and *The Trojan Women*, staged at various university stadia on the east coast of the United States, were among his last practical work on the stage. The Euripidean productions also marked one of Barker's significant contributions to the field of theatre: the 1904 *Hippolytus* was the first professional staging of a Greek play in Britain and brought a new interest in the work, thus laying the groundwork for William Poel's production of *The Bacchae* and Max Reinhardt's 1912 *Oedipus Rex* at Covent Garden. Yet, despite the clear significance that these plays had for Barker, little scholarly attention has been placed on this aspect of his oeuvre. Noel Thomas noted in 1955 the overwhelming tendency to remember Barker as a director of Shakespeare and Shaw at the expense of Euripides, and it is a tendency that is still adhered to today.[17]

The aim, as Barker explained in 1932, was not to present Euripides' plays as antiquarian artefacts, but rather 'to take a play which was a living thing two thousand years ago and provide for its interpreting as a living thing to an audience of to-day'.[18] In order to avoid any accusation of museum theatre, there needed to be an emotional connection established between the audience and the performers, and Barker acknowledged the integral role played by the chorus in securing this connection. Its speech, song and movement provided the necessary counterpoint to the action of the protagonists, becoming, in Euripides' plays, 'an instrument with which to weave music of the most subtle and exquisite rhythm'.[19] The chorus correspondingly became the central concern of Barker's productions, where the challenge of creating a unified ensemble on the stage without reducing the individual actors into a homogenized mass was emblematic of his whole quest for – and struggle with – the notion of ensemble theatre.

Barker in context

In order to understand fully Barker's innovations in group work on the stage and the development of what I term his choric aesthetic, it is necessary to consider it in the context of his wider ideas on the theatre and, in particular, the deep-rooted conventions that he was challenging. Barker's arrival on the British theatre scene at the turn of the twentieth century came at a time when the long-standing domination of the actor-managers was being threatened. Such managers as Henry Irving, Herbert Beerbohm Tree and Charles Wyndham continued to occupy positions at the pinnacle of the British theatre hierarchy, which they had won by staging sentimental melodramas that appealed to large crowds and by avoiding work that was experimental or commercially risky. However, the Independent or Free Theatre Movement that was spreading across continental Europe saw the emergence in Britain of new theatre groups and societies to challenge these positions. These included J.T. Grein's Independent Theatre Society (founded in 1891), the New Century Theatre (1897), the Stage Society (1899) and, slightly later, the Actresses' Franchise League (1908) and the Pioneer Players (1911).

The overriding aim was to provide an alternative to the commercial, 'assembly-line' and 'star'-oriented productions that 'treated plays as commodities and audiences as consumers of products'.[20] These groups sought to use the theatre to expose the problems facing British society by providing a platform for new experimental drama that would simultaneously bring the British theatre into touch with developments happening across the Continent. Thus, Archer and Robins founded their New Century Theatre with the aim to stage plays 'of intrinsic interest which find no place on the stage', while the Franchise League and Edith Craig's Pioneer Players produced plays that foregrounded women's suffrage.[21] It is not within the remit of this chapter to detail the activities of each group, but it is illuminating to note the atmosphere of change and progress that surrounded Barker and into which he was immersed. He was himself a member of the Stage Society, directed plays for the New Century Theatre, as noted above, and his first wife Lillah McCarthy was a member of the Franchise League. It is also worth noting, as I have done elsewhere, Barker's political position as a member of the Fabian Society, which placed him at the centre of the growing socialist concern in Britain.[22]

Among the many criticisms levelled against the actor-managers, Barker was most vocal in his critique of their unwavering adherence to the two central components of the Victorian theatre: the long run and, in particular, the 'star' system. The latter was integral to a theatre establishment that, much like the commercial theatre in Britain today, worshipped 'star' names and famous faces. This system created a hierarchy among actors and foregrounded the 'star' personality in a production at the expense of the other elements. Managers such as Irving and Tree embodied this system and organized their companies with a substantial level of self-promotion, placing their own interests ahead of the rest of the company. Edwardian author Leonard Merrick, writing under the pseudonym Stanley Jones, criticized such actor-managers, who did not 'allow the members of his company to increase their experience, to improve their reputation, to become his own possible rivals'. The first concern of the actor-manager, by contrast, was to 'find a play in which he shall have a good part, and the second to look to it that nobody else shall have so good a part as himself'.[23] With the emphasis placed on the 'star' actor, there was little more for the supporting actors to do than fit around him. These actors became mere 'props or '"sticks"', whose ignorance and stupidity serve to bring the star into prominence'.[24]

The tendency to perceive the other actors as mere wallpaper to act against influenced how they were treated in rehearsals, where they were either overlooked entirely, save for some more general comments on blocking, or closely drilled in set movements, with little consideration for character development or interpretation.[25] Irving was a prominent proponent of the latter approach, and would coach his actors to fulfil his vision for the play in question. He dedicated the first rehearsal to reading the play aloud to the assembled company, playing each role and setting the template of what he wanted the actors to reproduce: 'He acted every part in the piece he read, and in his mind the tones of his actors' voices, the moves of the characters, the processions, and the order of the crowd scenes was already set. All the actors had to do was to come up to the expectations which lay in his mind.'[26] Irving's aim was to create a pictorial ensemble, where the various visual elements worked in harmony with each other: 'It is important that an actor should learn that he is a figure in a stage picture, and that the least exaggeration destroys the harmony of a composition.'[27] In this sense he transcended the practices of his time and was, at least, attempting to create cohesion on the stage. However, the purpose of this ensemble was to provide an appropriate background that would accentuate more keenly his 'star' role. Indeed, he developed his own performance in isolation, which meant that there was no room for dialogue between the 'star' character and the supporting parts. The focus was, again, on the individual and so was far from the ensemble that Barker sought.

The prioritization of individual actors engendered by the 'star' system was a necessary consequence of the economic state of the British theatre. Without the security of a permanent, subsidized company or a regular income, actors were subject to the pressures of the free market and the principles of *laissez-faire* capitalism, and so their futures were determined by public taste and their ability to meet its demands. Michael Baker explains: 'Alone among artists, the actor was now obliged to present his work to a mass audience, which paid for his services directly and in cash; his livelihood and his success or failure became dependent upon the immediate reactions of this audience.'[28]

This dependence on the reactions of the audience encouraged a strong sense of competition between actors, who developed distinctive personalities and promoted their own celebrity in order to make themselves recognizable and memorable. Hence the 'star' system, where those at the apex were actors who successfully individualized themselves and became synonymous with, and indispensable to, the British theatre and its audience and so were able to reap the economic rewards.

Barker condemned the 'dog-eat-dog' attitude of survival that this system cultivated, where actors were encouraged to perform 'star' turns regardless of the demands of the play. This attitude, along with the practice of limiting rehearsal periods as much as possible to reduce overheads – a practice that remains all too common in the British theatre today – made actors untrusting and violently protective of any previously acquired symbolic power. He warned: 'To surrender this personal power to whatever unity of effect can be gained in three weeks' work or so among a strange company might be to lose it all together, and to get nothing in exchange – so thinks the theatre-wise actor.' The actor worked separately and developed her or his own performance that demonstrated this power or 'personal charm', 'exercising it, though, as often as not directly upon the audience rather than primarily on the play'.[29]

The 'star' system on the stage

The emphasis on the individual during rehearsals manifested itself on the stage in a number of related ways. The need to maintain a carefully cultivated personality, for example, determined how an actor interpreted a particular role, regardless of the playwright's intentions. Max Beerbohm observed to readers of *The Saturday Review* in 1901 that a great actor made little attempt to become a new, unrecognizable character, but, rather, tried 'merely to absorb the part into himself – to reveal himself through it ... [A great actress] may play tragedy one night, and comedy the next, and be equally fine in both; but in both she will be frankly the same woman, seen from different angles of herself.'[30] As usual, Shaw did not pull any punches in his critique of such practices, especially when it came to Irving. 'A prodigious deal of nonsense has been written about Sir Henry Irving's conception of this, that, and the other Shakespearean character', he told readers of *The Saturday Review* in 1896. 'The truth is that he has never in his life conceived or interpreted the characters of any author except himself ... There was no question of a bad Shylock or a good Shylock: he was simply not Shylock at all.'[31]

The stage design was, again, oriented around the individual 'star' actor, where the lighting, costume and positioning of the other actors on the stage all served the purpose of focusing the audience's attention on this 'star'. Christopher Innes recounts Irving's decision to dress himself in flaming scarlet for his 1886 production of *Faust* to ensure that he stood out from the rest of the actors and the other design elements, which were all in a grey-green colour. Likewise, when rehearsing a duel scene for *The Corsican Brothers*, his sparring partner stopped to ask whether he would share part of his limelight: 'Don't you think, Guv'nor, a few rays of moon might fall on me – it shines equally on the just and the unjust.'[32]

Other actor-managers insisted on maintaining a certain amount of stage space between themselves and the supporting actors as a way of enforcing their authority and asserting their status and distinction from the crowd. In such companies 'the magic circle around the star was not to be violated with impunity by a lesser actor'.[33] Again, the lot of the supporting actor was simply to provide a backdrop and avoid becoming too obtrusive. Cathleen Nesbitt, Perdita in Barker's 1912 production of *The Winter's Tale*, recalled the common experience of working under an actor-manager: 'One never "marked" anything, we just kept out of each other's way. If there wasn't an empty space you sat on the nearest chair.'[34] It was such practices and the perception of supporting actors as inferior that saw crowds on the stage being presented as homogeneous masses whose function was to fill the space, as epitomized by Tree's *Henry VIII* in 1910, where cardboard cutouts were used for many of the extras.

The effect of all of the above was inconsistent and dissonant productions. George Moore complained that the unevenness in the acting and incongruity of the production elements engendered by this approach succeeded only in distorting the meaning of the play, leaving it 'mutilated and disfigured *as a musical work would be if the musicians did not play in tune*'.[35] The surprised tone with which critics greeted the ensemble playing of Barker's actors at the Court indicates the extent to which they had become used to the usual fare of top-heavy 'star' productions. Max Beerbohm, again, noted that 'acting at the Court seems so infinitely better than in so many other theatres where the same mimes are to be seen', explaining that this was due to Barker's insistence that his actors play as an ensemble and follow closely the intentions of the playwright: '[The] mimes at the Court are very carefully stage-managed, every one of them being kept in such relation to his fellows as is demanded by the relation in which the various parts stand to one another – no one mime getting more, or less, of a chance than the playwright has intended him to have.'[36]

Desmond MacCarthy similarly argued that the success of Barker's ensemble highlighted the flaws of the 'star' system and showed the London theatre-going public that an alternative was possible:

> When will other London managers learn that the dramatist who is worth his salt needs the co-operation of every part, however small, in order to drive his meaning home; that we want to see plays, not to have our attention riveted perpetually on the same personality for three hours at a stretch?[37]

As these observations suggest, Barker positioned his productions and his whole approach to theatre-making in direct opposition to the 'star' system and its associated conventions and practices. The *New York Times* summarized this position accurately in 1915:

> He is against the star system. He is against the 'long run' system. He is against what he calls the 'rampant individualism' of the ordinary commercial system of play producing ... the theatre, to Granville Barker, is perhaps the most important of all possible agencies as a social expression and a social instrument.[38]

Warning of the potentially destructive force of a dominant individual – 'Much could be learned, no doubt from seeing a theatre glorified and destroyed by an individual genius' – Barker argued that it was only by acting as an ensemble that the actors could remain true to the intentions of the playwright.[39] This suspicion of the 'individual genius' extended to the director. Barker was adamant that the role of the director was not to command or dictate, but to work with his actors as a committee to achieve the unity of effect to which all plays strove. By giving the actors the space to develop their own performances in relation to each other, as opposed to competing with each other or merely following the orders of an overbearing director, the resulting performance would be organic and would help to keep the production 'a healthy living body'.[40] It was for this reason that he sought a cooperative approach to rehearsals, as alluded to briefly at the beginning of this chapter.

The security offered by a long-standing ensemble company would similarly facilitate a sense of trust among actors, elevating them from the demoralizing position of casual labourer and the need to compete on the free market of the commercial theatre. At the same time, it provided an alternative to the long run, where the need to perform the same role repeatedly for months on end could easily turn an actor into an automaton, stripping away any sense of truth or spontaneity from the performance. Despite not being able to establish such a long-standing company, Barker created this sense of trust and communality among the nucleus of actors with whom he worked regularly at the Court Theatre. Speaking in 1907, Matthison observed that 'there have been no rancours, no jealousies, no groans of the ill-paid and sweated in our midst'. There was instead 'a very real and a very precious sense of human brotherhood and sympathy, firmly based on economic equity and artistic opportunity'.[41]

Lillah McCarthy gave a similar account two decades later, explaining how the absence of the hierarchy that prioritized the 'star' role made the Court one of the only theatres in London where actors were willing to perform in smaller roles:

> Any of us would cheerfully take a small role, for we knew that even so we would not have to be subservient, negative or obsequious to the stars – for, as I have said, there were no stars. We were members of a theatrical House of Lords: all equal and all Lords.[42]

Barker's method of treating the entire company as part of a composite whole limited the competitive tension between actors who felt the need to vie for the director's attention, and so encouraged actors to work together and to serve the play as opposed to any individual. Not only did this mean that actors were willing to perform in smaller roles, but it also encouraged them to work as a group on the stage, as will become clear in the discussion of his Shakespeare and Euripides productions below.

Barker was, of course, far from alone in Europe in his quest for unified productions performed by an ensemble of actors. The influence of the Meiningen Ensemble was felt across the Continent during the 1880s and 1890s, where its unity of expression, its close attention to historical accuracy and its meticulously organized large-scale crowd scenes inspired a range of actors and directors, including Irving, Otto Brahm, André Antoine and Konstantin Stanislavski. The last's influence on Barker was more direct, although the pair only met towards the end of Barker's directorial career, when he travelled to the Moscow Art Theatre in 1914. Barker spent a week in Moscow, where he attended performances of *The Cherry Orchard*, *Three Sisters* and *The Blue Bird*, among others, and discussed rehearsal techniques and actor training with Stanislavski. The experience was revelatory for the British director, and the company became a major point of reference in his subsequent writings on the theatre and a model to be followed.[43]

What impressed Barker most was the sense of synthesis and spontaneity with which the ensemble performed, where productions that had been in the repertoire for a number of years still had the feeling of being fresh and alive. He described the acting as 'operatic' in the sense that 'it was harmonized as fine music is into a unity of effect by which the themes and players are given not less value but more and more meaning, not less, as parts of an ordered whole'.[44] Stanislavski was able to achieve this owing to the familiarity and shared understanding that came from working with a permanent group of actors and his insistence on allowing each production to develop organically through extensive rehearsal periods: 'It is because plays are produced there when they are ready – are born, not aborted as Stanislawsky [*sic*] says – that they are living things, that their power over the audiences (such audiences sitting to such fare) is the amazing power of interpreted life.'[45] Barker argued that it was this insistence on theatre as the expression or interpretation of life, and not, therefore, separate from it, that distinguished Stanislavski from directors like Reinhardt.

Barker stopped in Berlin on his way to Moscow to see Reinhardt and his Deutsches Theater. While his experience of the Art Theatre had made all other companies pale in comparison – 'Moscow is nearer to me now than Berlin will ever be' – the German director had been a presence in his life for a number of years.[46] Barker travelled to Berlin in 1906 and again in 1910 to see Reinhardt's work, attending rehearsals during the latter visit. He was also among the audience of Reinhardt's productions in London, and, in the case of *Oedipus Rex*, attended rehearsals in order to provide McCarthy with copious detailed notes for her performance in the role of Jocasta. The extent to which Reinhardt influenced Barker and his choreography of group scenes is shown more closely below, as is the undeniable influence of a figure who was pioneering the role of the director in Britain at the same time as Barker: Edward Gordon Craig.

Group work at the Savoy

In order to achieve his quest to discover the true meaning of Shakespeare's plays and to bring them to life for a contemporary audience, Barker had to remove from the plays the layers of sediment that had built up over the previous decades. This entailed stripping away the conventions of romanticism and illusion in which they and their characters had become entrenched. He was, to all intents and purposes, successful in this quest and helped the audience to look again at Shakespeare's plays. As the critic W.A. Darlington observed: 'It was as if I had been looking at a wax figure in a glass case, when Barker came and whisked away the glass to show me that what I had mistaken for a cleverly moulded dummy was in fact a living and breathing man.'[47] Barker continued this quest in the pages of his influential *Prefaces to Shakespeare* long after he ceased staging productions himself.

The intention was for the Savoy productions to mark the beginning of a sustained experiment in staging Shakespeare, and while the outbreak of the First World War in August 1914 put paid to such plans, they indicate clearly the direction in which Barker was headed. His choice of plays with which to begin this experiment was both deliberate and calculated. Shakespeare's own break with realism in *The Winter's Tale* – complete with appearing and disappearing bears, rapid jumps in time, space and genre, and the climactic 'resurrection' of Hermione twenty years after her 'death' – afforded Barker an ideal opportunity to push the boundaries of stage Naturalism and verisimilitude. *Twelfth Night* and *A Midsummer Night's Dream*, on the other hand, were staples of the actor-managers' repertoires and had become heavily steeped in the Victorian traditions of romantic sentimentalism and overplayed comedy. Barker used the plays to demonstrate clearly his challenge to such conventions and to the expectations of the audience, calling for a total re-appreciation of Shakespeare's plays and, in particular, his comedies.

This desired break from illusion and spectacle was, of course, signified in the visual aesthetics and design of each production. In labelling Barker's *The Winter's Tale* 'Post-Impressionist Shakespeare', Walkley identified accurately the director's alignment with the modernist experiments and his predilection for creating an impression or atmosphere over the reproduction of the minutiae of a particular scene.[48] While Colin Chambers has already discussed the innovative aesthetics of these productions in the preceding chapter, it is useful to draw brief attention to one example that has particular pertinence for the present subject matter. In his reform of stage lighting, Barker replaced the conventional footlights with spotlights that hung from the dress circle in full view of the audience below. He was not, of course, the first to use such an approach, but, as Kennedy explains, it allowed him to challenge the priority placed on the individual 'star' performer by creating a lighting scheme that was more egalitarian and 'made supers seem as visually important as stars'.[49]

A commitment to truth also underpinned how Barker's actors delivered Shakespeare's text. He stressed the centrality of verse and argued that Shakespeare used it as the primary means of emotional expression. However, he rejected the common practice of speaking the verse in a slow, overstretched and rhetorical manner as if it were a piece of literature, where soliloquies became little more than displays of the 'star' actor's elocutionary prowess. Barker taught his actors to treat the texts as pieces of living theatre and perform the dialogue truthfully. When rehearsing Nesbitt in the role of Perdita, for example, Barker warned her repeatedly: 'Remember – be not poetical. Be *honest*, always. Don't ever let yourself sing.' His final piece of advice to her, which took the form of a note on her dressing-room mirror, echoed the sentiment: 'Be swift, be swift, be not poetical.'[50]

The centrality given to the verse indicates the teachings of William Poel, who was a major influence on Barker during his formative years and whose Elizabethan Stage Society was a fellow combatant in the fights against the Victorian approach to Shakespeare playing. However, where Poel drilled his actors to ensure that they mastered the precise elocution, rhythm and melody of the verse – in keeping with his objective to recreate as closely as possible the Elizabethan methods of staging Shakespeare – Barker believed it was more important to communicate the emotion of the lines than the exact meaning of each word. He identified in the speeches of Leontes, for example, a certain confusion of thought and intricacy of language that was dramatically justified given the character's emotional state. 'Shakespeare is picturing a genuinely jealous man ... in the grip of mental epilepsy', he argued. 'We parse the passage and dispute its sense; spoken, as it was meant to be, in a choking torrent of passion, probably a modicum of sense slipped through, and its first hearers did not find it a mere rigmarole.'[51] Bearing this reading of Shakespeare in mind, it is not surprising that he advised Henry Ainley in the role of Leontes: '[The audience] don't have to understand you with their ears, just with their guts. You are really just babbling in a rage and anguish, it's a primitive emotion. You can accelerate and accelerate, just sounding vowels.'[52] Such instructions restored a sense of pace and 'liveness' to the plays and made clear their relevance for contemporary audiences.

Barker's close attention to the actors' vocal performances was also to ensure that they achieved the required vocal unity and harmony, where the individual voices came together as a symphony. In his preface to *A*

Midsummer Night's Dream, Barker discussed at length the need to be mindful of the different voices, notes and harmonies that Shakespeare weaves into his text, where, for example, the cheerful 'chirping' of Hermia is offset perfectly by the 'wistful, troubled' and 'defeated silence' of Helena, acting as an antiphony. 'If the scene is sung to the wrong tunes,' Barker warned, 'if the time is not adjusted, if the discords and harmonies are not valued, its essential character will be obscured and lost.'[53] This marks another point of departure from Poel's more dogmatic approach. He, too, believed in the need to achieve a vocal harmony but allowed it to determine his casting choices, where he placed more weight on the vocal quality of the actor than on her or his performance ability. Barker warned of any attempt to push the analogy of music too far, and focused on bringing the voices together organically through rehearsal as opposed to forcing the actors to follow a predetermined score.[54]

The need for each voice to contribute to the overriding harmony of the play was indicative of Barker's approach to acting and characterization in his Shakespeare productions in general. Nesbitt's account of *The Winter's Tale* rehearsals confirms Barker's commitment to working with all the actors and involving them in the process, as opposed to focusing his attention on the 'star' roles. Having introduced all the actors to each other in the first rehearsal, he encouraged them to work together, which took the form of long rehearsals with the entire company on the Savoy stage, often until the early hours of the morning.[55] Such practices encouraged the actors to see themselves as a group working together towards the same goal.

The group rehearsals also helped to instil in the actors the understanding that each made a vital contribution to the production regardless of the size of her or his role. Barker used such tactics to restore a sense of balance to plays that had long been performed as top-heavy 'star' vehicles. He similarly engaged established actors to play small roles that were often overlooked, in direct contrast to the 'star' system. Nigel Playfair, for example, played Paulina's Steward in *The Winter's Tale*, having been assured by Barker that 'you will find the part worth it'.[56] Such actors were given the space and opportunity to create three-dimensional characters and to bring new significance to scenes that were usually ignored entirely. Christine Dymkowski discusses the way in which Barker used the actors' physical performances in *Twelfth Night* – including their positions on the stage, gestures, entrances and exits, and so on – to the same end. Such seemingly small gestures as a nudge or exchanged glances between Sir Toby, Sir Andrew and Fabian in Act 3, Scene 2 not only established a more complex relationship between the three characters, but also showed them to be more lifelike and human, in contrast to the practice of playing them as one-dimensional caricatures.[57] The cohesive ensemble pictures that Barker created on the stage were thus given nuance and inflection by a collective of individual characters developed in relation to each other.

The fairy chorus

The quest for unity in Shakespeare manifested itself most clearly in Barker's production of *A Midsummer Night's Dream*. He dispensed with several of the conventions traditionally associated with the play, including the tendency to present the three main groups of characters – Theseus, Hippolyta and the lovers; the fairies; and the mechanics – as reduced caricatures that were distinct from each other. The result of such an approach was something of a hotchpotch of styles that was far from the harmony Barker desired. He instead focused on drawing links between the three groups, acknowledging and celebrating their differences, but encouraging his spectators to see the parallels between them.

There are countless instances that could be quoted from the production's prompt book to illustrate his handling of the acting group and the central position afforded to it. The positioning of the mechanics in Act 1, Scene 2, for example, is indicative of the group dynamic that Barker was trying to relay, placing Bottom deliberately between Quince and the majority of the company so as to increase the efficacy of his interjections. Small movements were also used to indicate the relations between characters and bring the dialogue to life in much the same way as in *Twelfth Night*. Thus, when Quince tells Bottom, 'You can play no part but Pyramus' in response to his request to play the Lion, Barker gave the following direction: 'All look at Bottom except Quince who has turned towards Snug; he sees Snug's expression and turns back to placate Bottom.'[58] Not only did this direction provide motivation for Quince's subsequent dialogue, but it also provided the audience with an insight into the inner workings of this group and the diplomatic 'handling' of Bottom that was clearly a ubiquitous feature of life.

The arrival of the fairies at the beginning of Act 2, Scene 1 is a moment of particular interest, and brings me back to the point on which this chapter began. This meeting of Oberon and Titania mirrored closely the arrival on stage of Theseus and Hippolyta at the beginning of the play, and thus physicalized the parallel Barker drew between the mortal and the fairy world. The first scene's emphasis on rigid formality and courtly procession was echoed in its fairy counterpart both aurally and visually: the same trumpet call marked the beginning of each scene, while the actors adopted similar positions on the stage, creating clean, straight and uniform lines. The formality of these two stage pictures was further reinforced by the informality of the mechanics' scene that sat between them. There were, of course, no trumpets to herald the arrival of Quince and company, and their grouping on the stage embodied their lower-class status in much the same way as their use of prose did. The clean, straight and formal lines of the respective courts were replaced by figures huddled in a loose semi-circle, with Snout sitting casually on the steps and looking out to the audience.

With the exception of the mechanics' scenes, Barker adhered closely to the rules of symmetry when directing his actors. This was, in part, to create a sense of order, but, more importantly, it allowed him to tease out and explore Shakespeare's own preoccupation with binary oppositions in the play – man and woman; love and hate; the fairy and mortal world; and so on – and the consequences that arise when they are challenged, blurred and confused. Theseus' court, for example, was organized on strict symmetrical lines: Theseus and Hippolyta occupied thrones in the centre of the stage facing the audience and were flanked by four Amazonian women, positioned downstage right of Hippolyta and facing left, and four male courtiers, positioned downstage left of Theseus and facing right. The picture was completed by two pairs of stewards, standing on either side of the stage, and Philostrate, who took his place to the left of Theseus' throne.[59]

This symmetry was echoed in Oberon's meeting with Titania. Entering from stage left, Oberon took his position at the centre of the stage, followed by six male trainbearers and other members of his court. Titania did the same from the right, positioning herself face-to-face with Oberon, with her six female trainbearers lined neatly behind her in pairs, creating another spatial gender binary. Each had a further entourage of six fairies, who took largely corresponding positions in the appropriate half of the stage. Puck, for example, stood on a seat on the far left of the stage, while a member of Titania's court, whom Barker named Old Man Fairy, sat in the seat on the far right of the stage. The four smallest fairies – Peaseblossom, Cobweb, Mustard and Moth – positioned themselves democratically on the floor in the middle of the stage, directly in front of Oberon and Titania. As well as highlighting the oppositional relations at the heart of the play – creating what John Palmer called 'a battlefield' – this staging allowed Barker to utilize every area of the stage space.[60] It also served to make clear the significance of every single figure in the final cohesive and coordinated stage picture. The surviving photographs of the production are striking in this respect, capturing the importance placed on the group and Barker's unwillingness to isolate any figure in it. This was particularly true of Titania's bower in Act 2, Scene 2, where her attendants formed a unified chorus, first distributing themselves across the playing area in lines of three and then encircling the mound on which Titania slept and dancing around it (See Figure 6.1 on p. 146).[61]

It is useful to pause here and consider briefly the influence of Reinhardt on the creation of such a stage picture. Critics were quick to draw comparisons between Barker's Shakespeare productions and the work staged by the German director in London during the preceding years.[62] In its review of *The Winter's Tale*, for example, the *Daily Express* claimed that Barker had 'killed Shakespeare as completely as Herr Reinhardt killed Sophocles in the production of *Oedipus Rex* at Covent Garden'.[63] J.T. Grein made similar accusations against Barker's 'Reinhardtised Shakespeare'.[64] While Barker denied any influence, there are certain points of convergence that are worth noting. Reinhardt was, of course, in the process of developing and maintaining his own ensemble company at the time, and, like Stanislavski, provided Barker with a model to emulate.

Likewise, the meticulous precision with which Reinhardt rehearsed his company and his desire to create unified group pictures on the stage resonated with the British director. Walkley made the connection between Barker's *The Winter's Tale* and Reinhardt's work in London in 1911: 'Squads of supers have symmetrical automaton-like movements which show the influence of *Sumurun*.'[65] Such comments were echoed in relation to Barker's fairies, who 'pose themselves in "tableaux vivants" fashion and group themselves in awkward attitudes ... more often [giving] the impression of lifeless automata than of the airy, graceful folk of fairyland'.[66]

Although bringing a similar level of precision to the orchestration of his scenes, Barker had, in fact, worked hard to avoid any sense of the automata or any attempt to replicate Reinhardt's treatment of the group as 'a seething mass that spoke as one'.[67] His aim was, instead, to show the individuality of each member of the group. To return to the arrival of the fairies, Barker orchestrated an elaborate and comic sequence of movements that took each fairy to her or his final stylized position in the procession. These movements served to counterbalance the formality of Oberon and Titania's subsequent exchange, to distinguish the fairy woodland from the rigidity of Theseus' court, highlighting the frivolity of the former, and, as Dymkowski argues, to prevent the action from becoming too uniform or artificial.[68] Barker's stage directions in the prompt book give a sense of the atmosphere created on the stage:

The Major and 3 Small Fairies [Cobweb, Moth and Mustardseed] rush on simultaneously [from left and right, respectively]. They meet at the centre, and the Major frightens them with his sword; they run right and meet Peaseblossom at the Right Prosc[enium] Seat.

The Twins enter together, meet the Major L[eft] C[entre] as he is going down. He twists them round and they continue whirling to the lower entrance left. Major to Left Prosc. Seat above Puck ....

Old Man Fairy to Children at Right Prosc. Seat. He frightens them to Centre lower stage, where they crouch in tiny groups on the steps.[69]

It is important to note first Barker's decision to name the fairies and with it give them a specific character and a purpose in the world of the play. Included in Oberon's party, for example, were The Major, The Professor and the Doctor, while Titania counted Duenna and Old Man Fairy among her followers. Rejecting the usual habit of treating the fairies as a nondescript mass, Barker used the names to assert, again, the individuality of each fairy. Just as the vocal harmony was created through the variation and juxtaposition of notes, so he needed to demonstrate to the audience the variety of personalities within the fairy group in order to make it more lifelike, truthful and harmonious.

These distinct personalities were communicated to the audience by the fairies' movements on the stage and their relation to each other. The Major's threatening movements towards the smaller fairies noted above, for example, indicated his role in Oberon's entourage, where he was something of a protector or guardian. This was further corroborated during the fairies' departure from the stage, which was also choreographed carefully: 'Old Man and Duenna up to Oberon and make a mocking bow; Oberon stamps his foot and motions to the Major who rushes across the stage, left to right, flourishing his sword; Duenna and Old Man hurry off right.'[70] Such small moments and actions succeeded in transforming *A Midsummer Night's Dream* into what the *New York Times* called 'a no-star performance with all its pieces as nicely adjusted as bits in a mosaic'.[71] They also brought the whole fairy world to life, giving it variety and a sense of spontaneity, demonstrating Barker's desire to bring informal, everyday movement to the play.

Although these movements were carefully rehearsed, he wanted to give the impression that they were improvised. Further, the rehearsal of such sequences was far from the rigorous drilling used by Irving and others. As Nesbitt recalled: 'He was not one of those directors who does a lot of homework with a set of puppets, and then says to the actors "I have you standing stage left on that line and moving stage centre on this." He worked *with* his actors.'[72] It is therefore highly likely that Barker choreographed such sequences in response to the discoveries and experiments of the actors in rehearsals.

Much has already been written about Barker's decision to forego the traditional cherubic child fairies in wings and replace them with adults in Eastern-inspired dress, making any further exposition here redundant.[73] It is, however, important to note that the choice of costume was not solely to startle audience members or reinforce the fairies' position as 'otherworldly'. It also served the purpose of unifying the fairies as a group and distinguishing them from both the group of lovers, whose costumes were based loosely on Grecian designs, and the mechanics, in their informal working clothes in which 'it does not seem as if they would be strangers, quite, in Stratford market-place'.[74] Puck's costume, on the other hand, marked him as an anomaly in the fairy group. Dressed in flaming scarlet, he stood out like the veritable sore thumb in a fairy woodland coloured almost exclusively in hues of gold, bronze, copper and mauve. Yet the use of scarlet was not to distinguish Puck as the 'star' character, as it had been with Irving twenty-eight years earlier, but to highlight his liminal position between the fairy and the mortal worlds. 'Puck accounts himself a fairy,' Barker explained, yet his behaviour and style of speech suggested 'that he is at least of another and inferior breed.'[75] Where Barker saw the other fairies to be undoubtedly foreign and exotic, seemingly 'at home in India', he believed Puck to be characteristically English and dressed him accordingly in a doublet and breeches. Kennedy details how Donald Calthorp's performance as Puck corresponded to this costume, playing him as a hobgoblin from English folklore and, above all else, a prankster.[76]

Barker's break with sentimental illusion in the costumes was again mirrored by the actors' performances. In what was perhaps the most acute demonstration of his embrace of the modernist challenge to illusion and Naturalism, he dispensed with any attempt to suspend disbelief and convince the audience of Oberon's invisibility in Act 3, Scene 2. It was enough for Dennis Neilson-Terry to state plainly: 'I am invisible.' This allowed Barker to keep Oberon, Puck and a small group of other fairies on stage and in plain sight for the rest of the scene. Desmond MacCarthy recalled: 'They group themselves motionless about the stage, and the lovers move between them and past them as casually as if they were stocks of stones. It is without effort we believe these quaintly gorgeous metallic creatures are invisible to human eyes.'[77] The presence of the fairies on the stage, and the need for the mortals to move around them, illustrated physically the interpolation of the two worlds, as well as the central role played by the fairies – and, indeed, the group in general – in the play.

The performance of *Pyramus and Thisbe* in Act 5, Scene 1 provided Barker with a final opportunity to use the group to focus and direct the audience's attention. He positioned Theseus, Hippolyta and their guests reclining on sofas at the front of the stage with their backs to the audience, offering a delicate counterpoint to the formality of the production's opening

FIGURE 6.3 *The mechanicals perform in front of the Athenian court,*
A Midsummer Night's Dream, *1914 (ArenaPAL/University of Bristol).*

scene and suggesting a new relaxed intimacy and camaraderie between the survivors of the night in the woods. The actor-mechanics delivered their performance directly to the audience, which served to increase its immediacy and theatricality, and to blur further the lines between the play and the play within the play. The court audience played a crucial role in this: its liminal position between the stage and the auditorium saw it adopt the role of the chorus in much the same way as the crowd in *Votes for Women!*, as noted at the beginning of this chapter. This position again brought the scene to life, and was singled out by Walkley for praise: 'Theseus's courtly lead in the applause, the whispered comments of Demetrius and Lysander, the lively interest of the courtiers. It was all alive, this scene, and the high-watermark of excitement.'[78]

The audience were encouraged to align themselves with the wedding party, who were, incidentally, presented as much more sympathetic and understanding to the mechanics' intentions and whose light-hearted interjections and exclamations could easily represent the audience's own attitudes towards the theatre. Further, the lovers' willingness to laugh at the mechanics, oblivious to the fact that they were themselves the subject of the fairies' mirth a few hours earlier, suggested, albeit gently, the need for the audience to pause and consider their own willingness to laugh at the action on stage. As Dymkowski explains, 'the court laughs at the mechanicals, the fairies at the court, each group blind to its own ridiculousness'.[79] Barker, it seems was asking his audience to start to contemplate their own action and behaviour.

Iphigenia in the United States

A brief examination of Barker's work on Euripides' tragedies provides a useful expansion on – and a coda to – my discussion of his work with groups in Shakespeare. It was, after all, in these plays that Barker first experimented with different ways of presenting the group on the stage, developing many of the techniques and strategies that he used so effectively in *A Midsummer Night's Dream*. At the same time, he brought his experience of staging Shakespeare at the Savoy to bear on his subsequent Greek productions in order to find solutions to the problem posed by the chorus. A particular preoccupation was the question of how to make the chorus appear relevant and alive to a contemporary audience.

His production of *Iphigenia in Tauris* is of particular significance, since it signified something of a breakthrough in Barker's struggles with the chorus. He first staged the play in March 1912 as part of his Kingsway Theatre season with Lillah McCarthy, before presenting a reworked version of it alongside *The Trojan Women* during his tour of the east coast of North America in 1915. Barker had crossed the Atlantic following an invitation from the New York Stage Society to direct a season of work at the Wallack's

Theatre, a move that, as the legend goes, was encouraged by H.H. Asquith as part of the war effort.[80] This season comprised productions of Shaw's *Androcles and the Lion* and *The Doctor's Dilemma*, Anatole France's *The Man Who Married a Dumb Wife*, and his production of *A Midsummer Night's Dream*, for which he had an entirely new and local company, with the exception of McCarthy as Helena. It was during a visit to the Yale Bowl in New Haven that Barker was struck by the opportunity such a space offered for the presentation of Greek plays, and he soon arranged a tour of *Iphigenia* and *The Trojan Women* to the stadia at Yale, Harvard, Princeton, the City College of New York and the University of Pennsylvania.

This tour provided Barker with the chance to realize his long-time ambition of staging Euripides' plays outside. He was himself aware of the artificial limitations that the proscenium arch placed on such plays, having been forced to struggle with it in his earlier productions. 'The mere transference from outdoors in will prove deadening,' he warned, 'and no one who has ever sat in a Greek theatre, and felt how the choric movements, patterned in the circle of the orchestra, both relieve and enhance by contrast the dignity of the individual action uplifted against the proscenium, will easily be reconciled to the disfiguring of all this behind footlights.'[81] The open-air stadium, by contrast, brought a sense of freedom and gave Barker the space to experiment with his chorus, creating elaborate movement patterns in order to make clear their central role in the performance. The larger space also gave him room to have a chorus of twenty individuals plus the leader as opposed to the eight or ten with which he usually had to settle owing to the confines of the proscenium space. It likewise turned the performances into huge community events, bringing an average audience of between 5,000 and 8,000 people comprising a range of ages and professions. Indeed, the size of the audience at each performance was a distinctive feature of the productions, and it was estimated that around 60,000 people saw the plays over the course of the tour.[82]

Barker ensured that the performances were not lost in the mammoth stadia through his use of the stage space and set, which was, again, designed by Norman Wilkinson and reflected Barker's modernist and non-naturalist style. Drawing on the traditional spatial arrangements of Greek theatre, Barker included a *skene*, or stage, at the back of the space, which comprised a large wooden building with three large golden doors and a narrow platform on which the actors performed, which was lifted five steps from the ground. Between the *skene* and the audience lay the *orchestra*, the large circular space in which the chorus danced, sang and spoke to the audience directly. It was 100 feet in diameter with a raised altar in the centre, and was made of white canvas with a series of interlocking geometric squares and circles. This was one of the ways in which Barker ensured audience members could see the staging regardless of where they sat in the stadium.

The geometric design both determined and accentuated the movements of the chorus, as was noted by some of the critics.[83] For their first entrance into the performance space, the chorus, divided into two groups of ten, marched down either side of the *skene* in pairs and crossed in front of it, meeting in the middle with Alma Kruger, the leader of the chorus, in the centre. Symmetry was, again, a guiding principle for Barker. Having delivered the first section of their speech from this position, the group then walked forward before positioning themselves around the largest circle on the ground cloth while delivering the line: 'The wells and the garden / And the seats where our fathers sate.'[84] Kruger maintained her central position, this time at the top of the circle, while the chorus members were placed evenly around its circumference. Later in the play, when Iphigenia entered the temple to prepare for the arrival of the two latest sacrifices, Kruger moved to a standing position directly in front of the altar within the smallest square on the ground cloth, with a chorus member positioned in each corner of the square. The rest of the chorus was positioned around the slightly larger square, which was rotated to form a diamond shape. A chorus member stood at each of the points, while a further three stood along each side.[85]

These examples demonstrate how the ground cloth was used to plot the movements of the chorus as they completed the various formal ceremonial patterns, as well as marking the positions at which each member needed to arrive. However, by following these lines and arranging themselves accordingly, the chorus drew attention to the various shapes and forms woven into the intricate design and, further, brought to life the various geometric possibilities that were on offer. In this sense, Barker used the chorus to explore the dynamics of space and to create coherent pictures where the whole space was used, in much the same way as he did in *A Midsummer Night's Dream*.

The above examples also indicate the intricacy and precision of the choreography. The detailed notes in the chorus prompt book show that each chorus member was given a number from one to twenty so that she could know where she needed to be and at what times. This was particularly important as the production progressed and the patterns became increasingly complex. Indeed, there was a great deal of movement throughout the performance, where the chorus were continually changing positions and creating new formations and new shapes on the stage. As Iphigenia left the stage to make her escape with Orestes and Pylades, for example, the sequence of movements performed by the chorus was as follows:

12, 1, 11, 9   continue reciting

7, 19, 13, 2, 8, 15} walk to centre of circles
18, 6, 17, 5, 8, 5}

7, 19, 13, 2, 8, 15} face right hand inward and form 'star'
18, 6, 17, 5, 8, 5}

7, 19, 13, 2, 8, 15} wheel in 'star' formation[86]
18, 6, 17, 5, 8, 5}

Having held this position for little more than three lines of dialogue, the chorus returned to the larger circle before fragmenting again into different groups and a more complex variation of the star formation.

The precision with which Barker choreographed and rehearsed his chorus once again led critics to draw comparisons between him and Reinhardt. While there is certainly weight to such claims, one can also see traces of the influence of Edward Gordon Craig and, in particular, his work with the Purcell Opera Society. Craig started the amateur society with Martin Fallas Shaw in 1900, and during its two-year existence they staged four productions: *Dido and Aeneas, The Masque of Love, Acis and Galatea* and *Bethlehem*. While the last piece was staged after the demise of the Society, it included a large number of former members in its company. Craig directed the movement for the productions, where he trained the company rigorously to develop their flexibility and coordination and to encourage them to work together as a unified group as opposed to a collection of individuals. His intention was to capture the atmosphere of Purcell's operas as opposed to any precise meaning, and he reduced elements and gestures down to an almost archetypal level. To achieve this, he developed a detailed system of notation from which to rehearse them and choreographed slow movements to be performed in synchrony that were, as Christopher Innes argues, more in line with a Greek chorus than a corps de ballet.[87] It is possible to see this approach reflected in Barker's own method of working with actors, particularly with regard to his Euripidean productions. He was certainly aware of what Craig was doing; he was a subscribed supporter of the Society and no doubt attended the few productions that it staged.[88] He also acknowledged publicly that *Bethlehem* had been a formative influence for him at a time when he was denying that a similar debt was owed to Reinhardt.[89]

However, the motive behind each director's quest for a unified group of actors was very different. In keeping with the ideas outlined in his controversial 1908 essay 'The Actor and the Über-marionette', Craig's aim was to transcend the individual personality of the actor and subordinate her or him to the overall design of the production. This entailed reducing the actors on stage to an indiscernible mass of abstract bodies. In *Acis and Galatea*, for example, he used the same strips of ribbon for the chorus's costumes as those used for the scenery, making it almost impossible to distinguish the performers from each other and from the scenic design. Barker used a similar device in his Greek productions, where he often dressed the chorus in dark colours so he 'could bring them into the prominence when required, but could avoid the awkwardness of eleven unoccupied ladies hindering sightlines when the action resumed'.[90] Yet this was, for Barker, more a question of logistics and an attempt to integrate the chorus in his production more organically than a desire to silence and dominate the actor. As has already been seen, his aim was to embrace the individuality of each performer and character, and to bring them into dialogue with each other as part of a composite whole.

Barker used the same techniques he exercised on *A Midsummer Night's Dream* on *Iphigenia* so as to avoid the indistinct mass put forward by both Reinhardt and Craig, albeit with some necessary adjustments. The stylized nature of Greek tragedy, for instance, precluded him from introducing the spontaneous fun of the fairies, but he found other, more subtle ways to achieve this. He used the voice, for example, to create a sense of aural variety on the stage, dividing the text into sections and distributing it among the group. This meant that Barker could alternate between the group chanting, speaking or singing in unison and solo or duet voices taking up the refrain, and thus avoid too strong a sense of repetition or uniformity. He also varied from where the voices and sounds were coming, having voices singing together from opposite sides of stage, or splitting a particular song between a group downstage left and one upstage right, as he did with the chorus's song that followed *Iphigenia*'s recognition scene.[91] Similarly, his choreographed movements were not necessarily to be performed in union and instead included a range of gestures that suggested variation within the chorus.

Such small and simple strategies helped Barker to achieve with this production something that had evaded him on previous attempts, namely to integrate the chorus into the production and to eradicate from it and the play in general accusations of anachronism. In short, he wanted his chorus to appear realistic and truthful, just as he wanted his fairies to appear alive on the stage. Even when repeating carefully rehearsed movements, they had a sense of being live and responding to the events on stage. Thus the direction for the chorus to 'rush to groups of four' on the arrival of the Messenger bearing news of Iphigenia's escape suggested a real sense of fear among the group and the need to pull together physically to defend the coming onslaught. The effect on the audience was palpable, where

> with a growing and horrifying war as the backdrop, and a pacifist mood at large in America, Euripides may have spoken more directly than at any time since the defeat of Athens. To gather 10,000 people at a single performance of a play in the twentieth century is itself an accomplishment; to have them also feel the power of an ancient poet is almost unheard of.[92]

Once again, Barker's innovative presentation of the group on the stage succeeded in cutting through centuries of conventions and expectations to speak to his audience directly.

NOTES

Introduction to the Series

1 Simon Shepherd, *Direction* (Basingstoke: Palgrave Macmillan, 2012).

2 P.P. Howe, *The Repertory Theatre: A Record & a Criticism* (London: Martin Secker, 1910).

3 Alexander Dean, *Little Theatre Organization and Management: For Community, University and School* (New York: Appleton, 1926), 297–8.

4 Constance D'Arcy Mackay, *The Little Theatre in the United States* (New York: H. Holt, 1917).

5 William Lyon Phelps, *The Twentieth Century Theatre: Observations on the Contemporary English and American Stage* (New York: Macmillan, 1920); Hiram Kelly Moderwell, *Theatre of Today* (New York: Dodd, Mead & Co., 1914, 1923); Dean, *Little Theatre Organization and Management*.

Introduction to Volume 4

1 *Magdeburg Theater-Ausstellung*, Amtlicher Katalog (official catalogue), Mitteldeutsche Ausstellungs-Gesellschaft, Magdeburg, 1927, exhibit nos. 1074–97, 208–9.

2 See p. 43 of this volume.

3 H. Bahr, *New York Times*, 30 December 1923, 10.

4 D. Kennedy, ed., *The Oxford Encyclopedia of Theatre and Performance*, vol. 1 (Oxford: Oxford University Press, 2003), 112.

5 W. Worringer, *Abstraktion und Einfühlung*, 3rd edn (Munich: Piper, 1916), 19–20.

6 W. Kandinsky, *Über das Geistige in der Kunst* (Munich: Piper, 1912), 23.

7 P. Klee, *Tagebücher*, ed. F. Klee (Cologne: Du Mont Schauberg, 1957), entry no. 951, 323.

8 See p. 65–6 of this volume.

9 M. Billington, *The Guardian*, 1 December 1986.

10 B. Brecht, 'Die Not des Theaters', in *Schriften zum Theater I*, ed. W. Hecht (Frankfurt am Main: Suhrkamp, 1963), 116.

11 F. Jameson, *Beyond the Cave: Demystifying the Ideology of Modernism* (Loyola University, Chicago: The Midwest Modern Language Association, 1974), 10.

12   A.S. Jackson, *Theatre Studies* 20 (Columbus, OH: Ohio State University Research Institute, 1973–4), 54.

13   J.L. Styan, *Max Reinhardt* (Cambridge: Cambridge University Press, 1982), 14, 40.

14   H. Granville Barker, *Prefaces to Shakespeare*, 2 vols; vol. 1 (Princeton: Princeton University Press, 1946–7, vol. 1), 5.

Chapter 1

1   H. Ihering, 'Der Volksbühnenverrat', cit. Erwin Piscator, *Schriften*, vol. 1 (Berlin: Henschel, 1968), 50. All translations, unless otherwise indicated, are my own.

2   G. Strehler, *Für ein menschlicheres Theater* (Berlin: Henschel, 1972), 109.

3   In *Grosse Szene* (The Big Scene, 1915), *Komödie der Worte: drei Einakter* (Berlin: S. Fischer, 1918), 119.

4   H. Bahr, 'The Makings of Max Reinhardt', *New York Times*, 30 December 1923, 10.

5   Styan, *Max Reinhardt*, 33.

6   See p. 70–2 of this volume.

7   Ernst Stern, *Bühnenbildner bei Max Reinhardt* (Berlin: Henschel, 1955), 38.

8   Siegfried Jacobsohn, *Max Reinhardt* (Berlin: E. Reiss, 1921), 11.

9   L.M. Fiedler, *Max Reinhardt in Selbstzeugnissen und Bilddokumenten* (Reinbek bei Hamburg: Rowohlt, 1975), 44.

10   P. Kornfeld, 'Nachwort an den Schauspieler', in *Die Verführung* (Berlin: Fischer, 1916), 202; reprinted in Paul Pörtner, ed., *Literatur-Revolution 1910–1925*, vol. 1 (Darmstadt: Luchterhand, 1960), 350.

11   W. Turszinsky, 'Tilla Durieux', in *Bühne und Welt*, vol. 12 (Hamburg: Verlag von Bühne und Welt, 1910), 609.

12   Jacobsohn, *Max Reinhardt*, 77–8.

13   In *Der Zuschauer* (Berlin, 1894), cit. E.S. Shaffer, 'Christian Morgenstern and Max Reinhardt: The Early Years in the Cabaret', in *Max Reinhardt: The Oxford Symposium*, eds Margaret Jacobs and John Warren (Oxford: Oxford Polytechnic, 1986), 131.

14   *Geschehen* (Nendeln: Kraus reprint, 1974), cit. Bernhard Diebold, *Anarchie im Drama* (Frankfurt am Main: Frankfurter Verlags-Anstalt, 1921), 27. I have omitted the stage directions.

15   G. Rühle, *Theater für die Republik 1917–1933. Im Spiegel der Kritik* (Frankfurt am Main: Fischer, 1967), 20.

16   'Notiz zur Bettler-Aufführung', in *Das Junge Deutschland* (Berlin: Deutsches Theater, 1918), vol. 1, no.1, 30; reprinted in Rühle, *Theater für die Republik*, 97.

17   Jacobsohn, *Die Schaubühne* (Berlin, 1918), reprinted in Rühle, *Theater für die Republik*, 304.

18 E. Faktor, *Berliner Börsen-Courier*, 4 March 1918, reprinted in Rühle, *Theater für die Republik*, 115.

19 Jacobsohn, *Die Weltbühne* (Berlin, 1921), reprinted in Rühle, *Theater für die Republik*, 307.

20 Kerr, *Berliner Tageblatt*, 13 April 1921, reprinted in Rühle, *Theater für die Republik*, 304.

21 Erwin Piscator, *Das politsiche Theater, Schriften*, vol. 1 (Berlin: Henschel, 1968), 245.

22 *Max Reinhardt Schriften*, ed. Hugo Fetting (Berlin: Henschel, 1974), 112. It is unclear why Venizelos appears in the list of autocrats, since he was a liberal democrat – perhaps because he was prime minister of Greece during the Balkan Wars of 1912–13.

23 Kraus, *Die Fackel* (Vienna, March 1922), Jg. 23, No. 588–94, 5.

24 Piscator, letter to *Die Weltbühne* (Berlin, 10 November 1928).

25 B. Brecht, *Arbeitsjournal 1938–42/1942–55*, ed. Werner Hecht (Frankfurt am Main: Suhrkamp, 1973), 639.

26 Piscator, *Das politische Theater, Schriften*, 14–15.

27 See H.S. Chamberlain, *The Foundations of the Nineteenth Century* (London: John Lane, 1911).

28 John C.G. Röhl, *The Kaiser and his Court: Wilhelm II and the Government of Germany* (Cambridge: Cambridge University Press, 1994), 210.

29 Bertolt Brecht, *Briefe*, ed. Günter Glaeser (Frankfurt am Main: Suhrkamp, 1981), 240.

30 G. Reinhardt, *The Genius: A Memoir of Max Reinhardt by His Son* (New York: Knopf, 1979), 365.

31 G. Adler, *Max Reinhardt* (Salzburg: Festungsverlag, 1964), 43.

32 *Vossische Zeitung* (Berlin), 15 June 1913.

33 G. Fuchs, *Revolution in the Theatre*, condensed and adapted by Constance Connor Kuhn (Ithaca, NY: Cornell University Press, 1959), 175.

34 Ibid., 146.

35 Ibid., 29.

36 Franz Hadamowsky, *Reinhardt und Salzburg* (Salzburg: Residenzverlag, 1963), 21.

37 A. Kahane, letter to Hofmannsthal, 29 November 1910, cit. H. Von Hofmannsthal, *Jedermann. Das Spiel vom Sterben des Reichen Mannes und Max Reinhardts Inszenierungen. Texte, Dokumente, Bilder*, eds Edda Leisler and Gisela Prossnitz (Frankfurt am Main: Suhrkamp, 1973), 176.

38 P. Hammond, *Herald Tribune*, 8 December 1927.

39 Hadamowsky, *Reinhardt*, 33.

40 Ibid., 37.

41 H. von Hofmannsthal, 'Reinhardt as an International Force', trans. Sidney Howard, in *Max Reinhardt and His Theatre*, ed. Oliver M. Sayler (New York: Brentano, 1924), 25–6.

42   Interview in *Theaterrundschau* (Berlin), 1352 (1911), cit. *Max Reinhardt Schriften*, ed. Fetting, 448.

43   'In search of a living theater', trans. Lucie R. Sayler, in *Max Reinhardt and His Theatre*, ed. Sayler, 189.

44   Ibid., 190.

45   S. Janson, *Hugo von Hofmannsthals Jedermann in der Regiebearbeitung durch Max Reinhardt* (Frankfurt am Main: Lang, 1978), 16.

46   Ibid., 12.

47   Hadamowsky, *Reinhardt und Salzburg*, 36.

48   Cit. *Max Reinhardt and His Theatre*, ed. Sayler, 192.

49   Cit. *Max Reinhardt Schriften*, ed. Fetting, 473.

50   H. Von Hofmannsthal, 'Dritter Brief aus Wien', in *Aufzeichnungen* (Frankfurt am Main: Suhrkamp, 1959), 297.

51   Cit. *Max Reinhardt and His Theatre*, ed. Sayler, 191–2.

52   Janson, *Hugo von Hofmannsthal's Jedermann*, 11.

53   *Das litterarische Echo* (Berlin, 1910–11) 13, cit. *Max Reinhardt Schriften*, ed. Fetting, 446.

54   Janson, *Hugo von Hofmannsthal's Jedermann*, 65–6.

55   I am indebted to Nigel Ward for pointing this out in his unpublished PhD dissertation, 'The Development in European Drama of a Theoretical Framework by Which Directors Approach a Text and Translate It to Performance' (University of Warwick, 1999), 26.

56   Robert Breuer, 'The Dramatic Value of Space and the Masses', in *Max Reinhardt and His Theatre*, ed. Sayler, 26.

57   *Die Fackel*, Jg. 36, No. 890–905, June 1934, 147–8.

58   M. Fortier, *Theory Theatre: An Introduction* (London: Routledge, 1997), 114.

59   Adler, *Max Reinhardt*, 42.

60   H. von Hofmannsthal, 'Reinhardt', cit. *Max Reinhardt and His Theatre*, ed. Sayler, 26.

61   *Max Reinhardt and His Theatre*, ed. Sayler, 64.

Chapter 2

1   Alexander Weigel, *Das deutsche Theater: Eine Geschichte in Bildern* (Berlin: Propyläen, 1999), 54–94.

2   Ibid., 64.

3   I am aware of the fact that the terms 'authenticity' and 'faithfulness' refer to problematic and profoundly discussed concepts in Theatre and Performance Studies and I only use them in this context within the historical confines of the contemporary setting. Brahm's style was perceived by his contemporaries to be particularly true to life and respectful of the literary original.

4   Peter W. Marx, *Max Reinhardt: Vom bürgerlichen Theater zur metropolitanen Kultur* (Tübingen: Francke, 2006), 34.

5   In 1901 with a few of his Deutsches Theater colleagues, Reinhardt started the political cabaret Schall und Rauch (Noise and Smoke), which, from 1902 onwards, produced serious drama in direct competition to the Deutsches Theater under the name Kleines Theater. See Norbert Jaron et al., eds, *Berlin: Theater der Jahrhundertwende. Bühnengeschichte der Reichshauptstadt im Spiegel der Kritik (1889–1914)* (Tübingen: Max Niemeyer, 1986), 467–8.

6   Arthur Kahane, *Tagebuch eines Dramaturgen* (Berlin: Bruno Cassirer, 1928), 116.

7   Ibid., 115.

8   Ibid., 119.

9   Ibid., 116.

10 This theatre building is known today as the Theater am Schiffbauerdamm, which permanently hosts the Berliner Ensemble.

11 Paul Legband, *Bühne und Welt*, 5.14 (1903), cit. Jaron, *Berlin*, 521.

12 F. Stahl, *Berliner Tageblatt*, 4 April 1903, cit. Jaron, *Berlin*, 513.

13 I. Landau, cit. Jaron, *Berlin*, 512.

14 A. Klaar, *Vossische Zeitung*, 4 April 1903, cit. Jaron, *Berlin*, 517–20.

15 The terms 'Theatropolis' and 'Parvenupolis' are both taken from theatre scholar Peter W. Marx. He used the term Theatropolis in a paper he presented on Wilhelmine Berlin (July 2013, unpublished). The term Parvenupolis is central to his monograph: Peter W. Marx, *Ein theatralisches Zeitalter: Bürgerliche Selbstinszenierungen um 1900* (Tübingen: Francke, 2007).

16 H. Ihering, *Begegnungen mit Zeit und Menschen* (Bremen: Carl Schünemann, 1965), 105.

17 Peter Fritzsche, *Reading Berlin 1900* (London: Harvard University Press, 1996), 7.

18 Alexandra Richie, *Faust's Metropolis: A History of Berlin* (London: Harper Collins, 1998), 20.

19 Marx, *Ein theatralisches Zeitalter*, 251–64.

20 Six for opera and operetta, eighteen for legitimate drama and comedies, five for popular theatre forms and farces, six so-called 'Spezialitätentheater' (variety shows and circus acrobats) and the Metropoltheater which specialized in the genre of 'Ausstattungsstück' (shows with a focus on decorations and astonishing stage machinery). In addition to these theatres, Berlin had to offer many more evening entertainments with its popular 'Singspielhallen' (music halls) and more than 300 pubs, restaurants, nightclubs and cabarets which had obtained the licence to entertain. See Annemarie Lange, *Das Wilhelminische Berlin: Zwischen Jahrhundertwende und Novemberrevolution* (Berlin: Dietz, 1984), 520–1.

21 M. Epstein, *Theater als Geschäft* (Berlin: Fannei und Walz, 1996), 13.

22 Ihering, *Begegnungen mit Zeit und Menschen*, 22.

23   Jacobsohn, *Max Reinhardt*, 21.

24   Ibid., 21.

25   Ibid., 21.

26   Marx, *Ein theatralisches Zeitalter*, 263–4.

27   *The Oxford Encyclopedia of Theatre and Performance*, ed. Dennis Kennedy (Oxford: Oxford University Press, 2003), vol. 1, 387.

28   One of the more constant members of the dramaturgical team was Heinz Herald. See Arthur Kahane, 'Die Jahre 1905–1924', in *Max Reinhardt: 25 Jahre Deutsches Theater*, ed. Hans Rothe (Munich: R. Piper, 1930), 32.

29   Kahane, *Tagebuch*, 71–3.

30   Eduard Von Winterstein, *Mein Leben und meine Zeit* (Berlin: Henschel, 1982), 254.

31   Ibid., 255.

32   Ibid., 254.

33   Ibid., 254–6.

34   Kahane, *Tagebuch*, 9–23.

35   The titles of articles dedicated to Kahane's work mostly refer to Kahane in connection to the 'bigger name' Max Reinhardt. See Franz Horch, 'Reinhardts Dramaturg. Zu Arthur Kahanes 60. Geburtstag', *Die Scene* 22, no. 5 (1932): 98–9; Etta Cor, 'Max Reinhardts erster Dramaturg. Zur Position des Dramaturgen am bürgerlichen Theater', *Theater der Zeit* 14, no. 3 (1959): 30–8; Henry Kahane, 'Arthur Kahane, Reinhardt's Dramaturge', *Theatre Research International* 4, no. 1 (1978): 59–65.

36   Anat Feinberg, 'Was Dramaturg? Noch nie gehört, was ist das?', *Aschkenas* 17, no. 1 (2007): 225–71.

37   F. Hollaender and A. Kahane, 'Vorwort', *Blätter des Deutschen Theaters* 1 (1911/12): 1–3.

38   In his theatre journal *Die Schaubühne* in 1911, Siegfried Jacobsohn denounces the harsh critique of Reinhardt's work by the contemporary press whose 'unkind, disdainful and snide tone' might drive Reinhardt out of Berlin. See Siegfried Jacobsohn, 'Reinhardts Zukunft', *Die Schaubühne* 40 (1911): 285–7.

39   In his speech in Mannheim in 1784, Schiller points to the vital function of theatre for the improvement of a humanistic society: 'The jurisdiction of the stage begins where the tribunal of secular law ends … As surely as a visible representation has a more powerful effect than the dead letter and a cold narration, the stage as surely acts more profoundly and more lastingly than morality and the law.' Friedrich Schiller, 'The Stage Considered as a Moral Institution,' abbreviated version in *Theatre in Europe. A Documentary History: German and Dutch Theatre 1600–1848*, ed. George W. Brandt (Cambridge: Cambridge University Press, 1992), 212–17.

40   The term 'arena' refers to the Zirkus Schumann, where Reinhardt staged his production of *Oedipus Rex* in 1910 and his production of *Everyman* in 1911. In 1919, after a fundamental reconstruction and transformation, Reinhardt re-

opened the Circus under the name Grosses Schauspielhaus. The building had the capacity to accommodate up to 3,200 spectators. While at first instance the size of the theatre sounds like an obstacle to the development of a special relationship between the audience and the stage, Reinhardt tried to mirror the masses of spectators in the auditorium with a large number of performers distributed all over the theatre. Thus, he tried to minimize the auditorium–stage divide and introduce the audience to a new spatially immersive experience.

41 Fritzsche, *Reading Berlin 1900*.

42 Kahane in a letter to Rudolf Alexander Schröder 1911, Deutsches Literaturarchiv Marbach, no shelf-mark given.

43 A. Kahane, 'Glossen zum Theater der Fünftausend,' *Blätter des Deutschen Theaters* 2 (1911/12): 9–12.

44 Ibid., 11.

45 Theatre historian Jacky Bratton developed the term intertheatricality in analogy to the term intertextuality, yet 'an intertheatrical reading goes beyond the written. It seeks to articulate the mesh of connections between all kinds of theatre texts and their users.' Jacky Bratton, *New Readings in Theatre History* (Cambridge: Cambridge University Press, 2003), 37.

46 J. Keller, *Berliner Lokal-Anzeiger*, 2 December 1911, cit. Jaron, *Berlin*, 713.

47 G. Eysoldt, 'Penthesilea', *Blätter des Deutschen Theaters* 3 (1911/12): 5.

48 Alfred Klaar, *Vossische Zeitung*, 24 September 1911.

49 Leonhard M. Fiedler, ed., *Der Sturm Elektra. Gertrud Eysoldt, Hugo von Hofmannsthal, Briefe* (Salzburg: Residenz, 1996), 9.

50 S. McMullen, 'From the Armchair to the Stage: Hofmannsthal's "Elektra" in its Theatrical Context', *The Modern Language Review* 80, no. 3 (July 1985): 646.

51 A. Kahane and F. Hollaender, 'Der Blätter erstes Jahr', *Blätter des Deutschen Theaters* 20 (1912/13): 305.

52 Max Epstein, *Max Reinhardt* (Berlin: Winckelmann Söhne, 1918), 42–3.

53 Ihering, *Begegnungen mit Zeit und Menschen*, 149.

54 Huntly Carter, *The Theatre of Max Reinhardt* (New York: Benjamin Blom, 1964), 119.

55 Carter, *The Theatre of Max Reinhardt*, 21.

56 Simon Shepherd, *Direction: Readings in Theatre Practice* (Basingstoke: Palgrave Macmillan, 2012), 98.

57 Carter, *The Theatre of Max Reinhardt*, 20.

58 Ibid., 23.

59 From 1925 onwards, Harry Kahn took over the editorship, followed by Hans Rothe in 1928 and Franz Horch from 1930 to 1932. See Alexander Weigel, 'Das Junge Deutschland. Ein Überblick über die Blätter des Deutschen Theaters (II)', *Blätter des Deutschen Theaters* 2 (1985/86): 36–44.

Chapter 3

1 Jacob is generally regarded as a patriarch of the Israelites.

2 L. Jessner, 'Jüdische Politik', *Aufbau*, 1 October 1943.

3 Letter from Jessner to the Ministerium für Wissenschaft, Kunst und Volksbildung, 22 December 1922, Personalakte Jessner, 2.10.6. Nr.2468, Geheimes Staatsarchiv, Preußischer Kulturbesitz.

4 Yoram K. Jacoby, *Jüdisches Leben in Königsberg/Pr. im 20. Jahrhundert* (Würzburg: Holzner, 1983), 8, 57, and 141.

5 Unpublished interview between Prof. Leohnard Fiedler (Frankfurt University) and Alfred Perry, 1 April 1977.

6 Fritz Gause, *Die Geschichte der Stadt Königsberg in Preußen*, vol. 2 (Cologne: Graz Böhlau, 1968), 592.

7 Ibid., 612.

8 O.K., 'Jessners Jugendjahre im Theater', *Theaterdienst*, 10. Jg., Heft 44, October 1955, 5.

9 L. Jessner, *Schriften: Theater der zwanziger Jahre*, ed. Hugo Fetting (Berlin: Henschelverlag, 1979), 197.

10 Ibid., 66.

11 Ibid., 222.

12 Carl Heine, 'Mein Ibsen-Theater', *Velhagen & Klasings Monatshefte*, 40. Jg., Heft 4, 1925, 424.

13 Carl Heine, *Herren und Diener der Schauspielkunst* (Hamburg: Kriebel, 1904), 13.

14 Paul Möhring, *Von Ackermann bis Ziegel: Theater in Hamburg* (Hamburg: Christians, 1970), 112.

15 P. Möhring, 'Erinnerungen an Leopold Jessner', *Der Freihafen*, Heft 10, 1952/53, 104.

16 M. Hatry, 'Das Thalia-Theater in Hamburg 1894–1915' (Phil. Diss., Berlin, 1966) and M. Giesing, 'Die Norddeutsche Burg', in *Thalia Theater, Sonderheft Merian* (Hamburg: Merian, 1993).

17 Hatry, 'Das Thalia-Theater in Hamburg 1894–1915', 24–6.

18 Ibid., 66–70.

19 Jessner, *Schriften*, 66.

20 Günther Rühle, *Theater in unserer Zeit* (Frankfurt am Main: Suhrkamp, 1976), 66.

21 F. Wedekind, *Gesammelte Briefe*, ed. Fritz Strich, vol. 2 (Munich: Georg Müller, 1924), 198–315.

22 Günter Seehaus, *Frank Wedekind und das Theater, 1898–1959* (Munich: Laokoon-Verlag, 1964), 290.

23 F. Wedekind, *Werke*, ed. Erhard Weidl, vol. 1 (Munich: Winkler, 1990), 639–44. Wedekind explains in his Introduction to *Pandora's Box* why Countess Geschwitz becomes the central figure of the second part of the *Lulu* tragedy.

24 Jessner, *Schriften*, 167.

25 Ibid., 146.

26 Hatry, 'Das Thalia-Theater in Hamburg 1894–1915', 163.

27 Jessner, *Schriften*, 200.

28 Rühle, *Theater in unserer Zeit*, 52.

29 Herbert Ihering, 'Zwischen Reinhardt und Jessner', *Sinn und Form*, 2. Jg., Heft 2, 1950, 61–4.

30 Jessner, *Schriften*, 13–16.

31 Ludwig Goldstein, *Das neue Schauspielhaus, Königsberg Pr: ein Stück ostmärkischer Theatergeschichte anlässlich der Eröffnung des neuen Hauses am 29. Sept. 1927* (Königsberg: Gräfe & Unzer, 1927), 24.

32 G. Rühle, *Theater für die Republik im Spiegel der Kritik*, vol. 1 (Frankfurt am Main: S. Fischer, 1988), 28.

33 Jessner, *Schriften*, 271.

34 Julius Bab, *Das Theater der Gegenwart: Geschichte der dramatischen Bühne seit 1870* (Leipzig: J. J. Weber, 1928), 78.

35 Ludwig Marcuse, *Mein zwanzigstes Jahrhundert: auf dem Weg zu einer Autobiographie* (Frankfurt am Main: Fischer 1968), 46.

36 L. Marcuse, 'Erinnerungen an Leopold Jessner', *Die Zeit*, Ausgabe 11, 13 March 1958.

37 Jessner, *Schriften*, 52–3.

38 Ihering, 'Zwischen Reinhardt und Jessner', 61.

39 See Rudolf Bernauer, *Das Theater meines Lebens: Erinnerungen* (Berlin: Lothar Blanvalet, 1955), 367, and Bernhard Reich, *Im Wettlauf mit der Zeit: Erinnerungen aus fünf Jahrzehnten deutscher Theatergeschichte* (Berlin: Henschelverlag, 1970), 179.

40 Wolfgang Drews, *Theater: Schauspieler, Regisseure, Dramaturgen, Intendanten, Dramatiker, Kritiker, Publikum* (Vienna: K. Desch, 1961), 135.

41 Jessner, *Schriften*, 92 and 95–7.

42 Eckart Von Naso, *Ich liebe das Leben: Erinnerungen aus fünf Jahrzehnten* (Hamburg: Krüger, 1953), 437.

43 See F. Kortner, *Aller Tage Abend* (Munich: Deutscher Taschenbuch Verlag, 1976), 222–31.

44 Rühle, *Theater für die Republik*, 13–21, and Carl Zuckmayer, *Als wär's ein Stück von mir* (Frankfurt am Main: S. Fischer, 1966), 267.

45 Naso, *Ich liebe das Leben*, 443.

46 Jessner, *Schriften*, 293.

47 Ibid., 236.

48 Reich, *Im Wettlauf mit der Zeit*, 182.

49 Rühle, *Theater für die Republik*, 338.

50 Klaus Völker, *Fritz Kortner: Schauspieler und Regisseur* (Berlin: Hentrich, 1987), 109. Völker's book contains a complete list of Kortner's films.

51 In an unpublished letter from Jessner to Herbert Ihering dated 12 December
    1922 he explains in detail how he failed in all his attempts to keep hold of
    Kortner. Nachlaß-Nr. 002160, Herbert-Ihering-Archiv, Akademie der Künste
    Berlin.

52 Bab, *Theater der Gegenwart*, 183.

53 Erika Fischer-Lichte, *Kurze Geschichte des deutschen Theaters* (Tübingen:
    Francke, 1993), 380–4.

54 Kortner, *Aller Tage Abend*, 230.

55 Rühle, *Theater in unserer Zeit*, 65.

56 B. Brecht, *Schriften zum Theater*, vol. 1 (Frankfurt am Main: Suhrkamp,1963),
    83.

57 The archives of the Staatliche Schauspielschule (State Academy for Acting)
    is, unlike those of the Staatstheater (State Theatre), stored in totality in the
    archive of the Hochschule der Künste (Academy for the Arts).

58 L. Marcuse, 'Leopold Jessners Stil', *Süddeutsche Zeitung*, 22–23 January 1966.

59 Sitzungsprotokoll des Preußischen Landtages (Minutes of the Prussian
    Parliament), 1. Wahlperiode, Akte 2405, Rep. 90, 166, Geheimes Staatsarchiv,
    Preußischer Kulturbesitz.

60 H. Ihering, *Theater in Aktion: Kritiken aus drei Jahrzehnten, 1913–1933*, eds
    Edith Krull and Hugo Fetting (Berlin: Argon-Verlag, 1987), 167–8.

61 H. Ihering, *Das Tagebuch*, Heft 21, 24 May 1925.

62 A. Bronnen, *Arnolt Bronnen gibt zu Protokoll* (Kronberg/Ts.: Athenäum
    Verlag, 1978), 174.

63 Zuckmayer, *Als wär's ein Stück von mir*, 458.

64 Bronnen, *Arnolt Bronnen gibt zu Protokoll*, 134.

65 Rühle, *Theater für die Republik*, 678.

66 Jessner, *Schriften*, 192.

67 Rühle, Theater für die Republik, 721–7.

68 Große Anfrage der Fraktion der Deutschnationalen Volkspartei (interpellation
    by the German National Party), Sitzungsprotokoll des Preußischen Landtages
    (minutes of the Prussian Parliament), 2. Wahlperiode, Akte 2406, Rep. 90, 294.

69 Jessner, *Schriften*, 192. The article appeared originally in the *Vossische
    Zeitung*, where Jessner was challenged to respond to the objections of the
    public.

70 See Walther Karsch, *Walter Franck* (Berlin-Zehlendorf: Rembrandt Verlag,
    1962), 9, and Rühle, *Theater für die Republik*, 821–2.

71 Rühle, *Theater in unserer Zeit*, 74, and Rühle, *Theater für die Republik*, 850.

72 Felix Ziege, *Leopold Jessner und das Zeit-Theater* (Berlin: Eigenbrödler-
    Verlag, 1928), 51. On Jessner's fiftieth birthday two Festschriften were
    published. One was the book by Ziege containing articles by those who had
    worked with Jessner, the other was a book by Carl Theodor Bluth on Jessner's
    principles of directing. The March edition of the journal *Die Scene* was also
    devoted exclusively to the Director of the Staatstheater.

73 Brecht, *Shriften zum Theater*, 220.

74 H. Ihering, 'Der Fall Jessner', *Berliner Börsen-Courier*, no. 154 (3 April 1929).

75 A. Kerr, *Mit Schleuder und Harfe*, ed. Hugo Fetting (Berlin: Henschel, 1981), 455.

76 Marcuse, 'Leopold Jessners Stil'.

77 B. Minetti, *Erinnerungen eines Schauspielers*, ed. Günther Rühle, 2nd edn (Stuttgart: Deutsche Verlags-Anstalt, 1986), 64.

78 Rühle, *Theater für die Republik*, 1108.

79 A copy of Jessner's diary from the last year of his life is in the possession of Prof. Fiedler (Frankfurt University).

80 R. Forster, 'Wie war Jessner?', *Theater heute*, Heft 8, 1967, 23.

81 Leopold Lindtberg, *Reden und Aufsätze* (Zürich: Atlantis-Verlag, 1972), 202.

82 Albert Klein and Raya Kruk, *Alexander Granach. Fast verwehte Spuren* (Berlin: Hentrich, 1994), 137.

83 Marcuse, 'Erinnerungen an Leopold Jessner', 4.

84 Marcuse, 'Leopold Jessners Stil'.

85 Berthold Viertel, *Schriften zum Theater*, ed. Gert Heidenreich (Berlin: Henschelverlag, 1970), 379.

86 F. Kortner, 'Symbol der revolutionären Theaterkunst', *Aufbau* 11, no. 51 (December 1945): 21.

87 F. Kortner, cit. Völker, *Fritz Kortner*, 180.

88 G. Rühle, *Theater in unserer Zeit*, vol. 2: *Anarchie in der Regie?* (Frankfurt am Main: Suhrkamp, 1982), 100.

89 Ibid., 101.

90 Jessner, *Schriften*, 94.

91 Rühle, *Theater in unserer Zeit*, vol. 2, 100.

Chapter 4

1 Ernst Legal: no title, *Die Scene* (Berlin: Oesterheld, 1928), 78. All translations, unless otherwise indicated, are my own.

2 Alfred Kerr, 'Wilhelm Tell auf der Freitreppe', *Berliner Tageblatt*, 12 December 1919.

3 N, 'Wilhelm Tell. Neueinstudierung des Schauspielhauses', *Der Reichsbote*, 13 December 1919.

4 I am here using the translation by Patrick Maxwell, published by Walter Scott, London (1893?).

5 I follow the way Paul Fechter described the anecdote: Paul Fechter, '"Wilhelm Tell" mit Hindernissen', *Deutsche Allgemeine Zeitung*, 13 December 1918. Others, like Jessner's dramaturg Eckart von Naso and critic Jakob Scherek, remember the moment slightly differently and view the line 'I'll set me down

upon this rocky bench' as the uproar's cause. The latter line is part of the same monologue. Most of the reviews, however, mention the 'hollow way' line as the starting point for the riot. Theatre history has mainly remembered the second variation of the anecdote.

6   Peter M. Boenisch, *Directing Scenes and Senses: The Thinking of Regie* (Manchester: Manchester University Press, 2015), 73.

7   Felix Ziege, 'Leopold Jeßner und das Zeit-Theater', in *Leopold Jeßner und das Zeit-Theater*, ed. Felix Ziege (Berlin: Eigenbrödler, 1928), 9.

8   Rühle, *Theater in unserer Zeit*, 51.

9   Matthias Heilmann, *Leopold Jessner – Intendant der Republik. Der Weg eines deutsch-jüdischen Regisseurs aus Ostpreußen* (Tübingen: Max Niemeyer, 2005), 89.

10   David Román, *Performance in America. Contemporary U.S. Culture and the Performing Arts* (Durham, NC: Duke University Press, 2005), 1.

11   Jessner, *Schriften*, 95.

12   Ibid., 43.

13   Rühle, *Theater in unserer Zeit*, 10.

14   Jessner, *Schriften*, 164.

15   Ibid., 18.

16   Ibid., 172.

17   Lothar Müthel, 'Jeßner als Regisseur', in *Leopold Jeßner und das Zeit-Theater*, ed. Ziege, 53.

18   Jessner, *Schriften*, 214.

19   Ibid., 104.

20   Ibid., 175.

21   Ibid., 146.

22   Ziege, 'Leopold Jeßner und das Zeit-Theater', 21.

23   See Jessner, *Schriften*, 103.

24   Ibid., 146.

25   Ibid., 146.

26   Ibid., 155.

27   Ibid., 155.

28   Ibid., 155.

29   Cf. ibid., 154.

30   Ibid., 138.

31   Ibid., 96.

32   Ibid., 91.

33   Cf. ibid., 126.

34   Ibid., 75.

35   Cf. Walter Laqueur, *Weimar. Die Kultur der Republik* (Frankfurt: Ullstein, 1974), 250.

36   Jessner, *Schriften*, 128.

37   Cf. ibid., 169–70.

38   Cf. Jens Roselt, 'Der Regisseur als souveräner Interpret – Leopold Jessner', in *Regie im Theater. Geschichte – Theorie – Praxis*, ed. Jens Roselt (Berlin: Alexander, 2015), 254–5.

39   Jessner, *Schriften*, 24.

40   Cf. ibid., 34.

41   Ibid., 66.

42   Boenisch, *Directing Scenes and Senses*, 76.

43   Ziege, 'Leopold Jeßner und das Zeit-Theater', 9.

44   Stefan Großmann, 'Wilhelm Tell in der Volksbühne', *Vossische Zeitung*, 25 December 1918.

45   o.A., '"Tell" at the Schauspielhaus', 19 December 1919 [?], Review Archive, Theatre Museum Vienna.

46   H. Th., 'Theater und Musik. Neue Skandalszenen im Schauspielhaus', *Deutsche Warte*, 14 December 1919.

47   P.C. 'Aus den Theatern. Wilhelm Tell', *Neue Preussische (Kreuz-)Zeitung*, 13 December 1919.

48   Konrad Elert, 'Staatstheater: "Wilhelm Tell" in Leopold Jeßners Inszenierung', *Königsberger Allgemeine Zeitung*, 16 December 1919.

49   Scott Palmer, *Light: Readings in Theatre Practice* (Basingstoke: Palgrave Macmillan, 2014), 75.

50   Cf. Karl Theodor Bluth, *Leopold Jessner* (Berlin: Oesterheld & Co, 1928), 18.

51   Thyssen, 'Wilhelm Tell im Schauspielhaus', *Germania*, 16 December 1919.

52   Josef Adolf Bondy, '"Wilhelm Tell" mit Hindernissen', *National-Zeitung*, 14 December 1919.

53   Heilmann, *Leopold Jessner*, 89.

54   Boenisch, *Directing Scenes and Senses*, 87.

55   H. Th., 'Theater und Musik. Neue Skandalszenen im Schauspielhaus'.

56   N, 'Wilhelm Tell. Neueinstudierung des Schauspielhauses'.

57   Eckart von Naso, *Ich liebe das Leben. Erinnerungen aus fünf Jahrzehnten* (Hamburg: Wolfgang Grüger, 1953), 490–1.

58   For an overview of the appropriation of *Hamlet* as a German see Peter W. Marx, 'Challenging the Ghosts: Leopold Jessner's Hamlet', *Theatre Research International*, no. 1 (2005): 72–87.

59   Rühle, *Theater in unserer Zeit*, 31.

60   Leopold Jessner, 'Hamlet, der Republikaner', *Vossische Zeitung*, 15 December 1926.

61   Emil Faktor, 'Hamlet', Review Archive, Theaterwissenschaftliche Sammlung, University of Cologne.

62   Gerhard Müller, Dieter Götze and Ariane Handrock, *Apollos Tempel in Berlin. Vom Nationaltheater zum Konzerthaus am Gendarmenmarkt*, eds Berger Bergmann and Gerhard Müller (Munich: Prestel, 2008), 172.

63 Marx, 'Challenging the Ghosts', 76.

64 Alice Rayner, *Ghosts. Death's Double and the Performance of Theatre* (Minneapolis and London: University of Minnesota Press, 2006), 130.

65 Faktor, 'Hamlet'.

66 Ernst Heilborn, 'Gruß dem Zeitgerechten', in *Leopold Jeßner und das Zeit-Theater*, ed. Ziege, 36.

67 Alfred Klaar, 'Hamlet', *Vossische Zeitung*, 4 December 1926.

68 Bluth, *Leopold Jessner*, 65.

69 Marx, 'Challenging the Ghosts', 84.

70 Felix Hollaender, 'Der moderne Hamlet', 4 December 1926, Review Archive, Theaterwissenschaftliche Sammlung, University of Cologne.

71 Curt Hotzel, 'Staatstheater. "Hamlet"', 15 December 1926, Review Archive, Theaterwissenschaftliche Sammlung, University of Cologne.

72 Rühle, *Theater in unserer Zeit*, 74.

73 Cartoon in *Leopold Jeßner und das Zeit-Theater*, 4.

Chapter 5

1 'A theatre that might be', *The Use of the Drama*, based on a lecture given in 1944, published 1946, in *Granville Barker on Theatre*, eds Colin Chambers and Richard Nelson (London: Bloomsbury Methuen Drama, 2017), 217. Barker was of his time in using the male pronoun to stand for both men and women. This usage has been retained for ease of reading.

2 In Barker's day, the term producer was regularly used instead of director. In order to avoid confusion, director has been used instead of producer throughout this chapter, including quotations in which producer appears in the original.

3 *Quality*, a lecture delivered and published in 1938, in *Granville Barker on Theatre*, 122.

4 Introduction to Leo Tolstoy's *Plays*, 1928, in *Granville Barker on Theatre*, 161.

5 Introduction to *The Players' Shakespeare*, 1923, in Barker, *Prefaces to Shakespeare*, vol. 6 (London: B.T. Batsford, 1974), 43.

6 'The Heritage of the Actor', 1923, in *Granville Barker on Theatre*, 67.

7 Introduction to first series of *Prefaces*, 1927, in Barker, *Prefaces to Shakespeare*, vol. 1 (London: B.T. Batsford, 1963), 8.

8 'The Heritage of the Actor', 67–8.

9 *The Exemplary Theatre*, 1922, in *Granville Barker on Theatre*, 50.

10 Harley Granville Barker, *The Exemplary Theatre* (London: Chatto & Windus, 1922), 46.

11 'Notes on Rehearsing a Play', 1919, in *Granville Barker on Theatre*, 19.

12 Harley Granville Barker, *A National Theatre* (London: Sidgwick & Jackson, 1930), 8.

13 'Repertory Theatres', 1909, in *Granville Barker on Theatre*, 5.

14 Introduction to *The Players' Shakespeare*, 43.

15 *The Exemplary Theatre*, in *Granville Barker on Theatre*, 50.

16 Ibid., 50.

17 'Repertory Theatres', 3.

18 Letter to Helen Huntington, whom he was about to marry, undated but June 1918, in *Granville Barker and His Correspondents*, ed. Eric Salmon (Detroit: Wayne State University Press, 1986), 341.

19 Barker, *The Exemplary Theatre*, 46.

20 'The Heritage of the Actor', 53.

21 Introduction to Barker's translation of Sacha Guitry's *Deburau* (London: William Heinemann, 1921), 5. Barker was aware that a play was more than performance, and he elaborated this when devoting much of his later life to scholarship. Writing in 1923 ('Some Tasks for Dramatic Scholarship') of the value of the 'realisation of the drama as a living thing, of the integrity of a play as acted in a theatre, never fully alive till then', he said: 'Its larger life – for I admit it has one – is the extension of that, but never to be attained by leaving that out of account.'

22 *The Exemplary Theatre*, in *Granville Barker on Theatre*, 50.

23 'On Translating Plays', 1925, in *Granville Barker on Theatre*, 75.

24 Ibid., 75–6.

25 Introduction to first series of *Prefaces*, 1927, 7.

26 'Notes on Rehearsing a Play', 14.

27 'The Heritage of the Actor', 56.

28 Harley Granville Barker, *The Use of the Drama* (London: Sidgwick & Jackson, 1946), 34.

29 *The Exemplary Theatre*, in *Granville Barker on Theatre*, 49.

30 'Notes on Rehearsing a Play', 14. Barker was known to use musical terminology while directing (for example: 'You deliver your lines as if you were the trombone, whereas you really are the oboe in this *ensemble*.')

31 *The Exemplary Theatre*, in *Granville Barker on Theatre*, 42.

32 H. Granville Barker, *Prefaces to Shakespeare*, 2 vols; vol. 1 (Princeton: Princeton University Press, 1946–7), 5. Barker uses the drill sergeant metaphor in several of his essays.

33 *The Exemplary Theatre*, in *Granville Barker on Theatre*, 42.

34 See for example Harcourt Williams, *Old Vic Saga* (London: Winchester Publications, 1949), 164.

35 Introduction to *The Players' Shakespeare*, 54.

36 Although Barker presented full versions of Shakespeare, he did make cuts, e.g. some fifteen lines in *The Winter's Tale* and some twenty in *Twelfth Night*, removing obscure and sexual references. His revolution had its limits. It also differed from that of Poel: 'I don't go as far as Mr Poel,' wrote Barker. 'I think his method is somewhat archaeological; there is somewhat too much of the

Elizabethan letter, as contrasted with the Elizabethan spirit.' (Letter to the *Evening News*, 3 December 1912.)

37 Letter to Thomas Hardy, 6 July 1923, in *Granville Barker and His Correspondents*, 374.

38 'Some Tasks for Dramatic Scholarship', in *Essays by Divers Hands*, vol. 3, ed. F.S. Boas (London: H. Milford, Oxford University Press, 1923), 37.

39 *The Exemplary Theatre*, in *Granville Barker on Theatre*, 102.

40 'Notes on Rehearsing a Play', 15.

41 'The Heritage of the Actor', 68.

42 Ibid., 64.

43 *The Exemplary Theatre*, in *Granville Barker on Theatre*, 105.

44 'The Heritage of the Actor', 64.

45 *The Exemplary Theatre*, in *Granville Barker on Theatre*, 102.

46 Ibid., 223.

47 For production details, see Dennis Kennedy, *Granville Barker and the Dream of Theatre* (Cambridge: Cambridge University Press, 1985), 118–21.

48 Ibid., 186.

49 He had wanted to take John Masefield's *The Witch*, his own *The Madras House* and possibly Masefield's *Philip the King* and Molière's *Le Mariage Forcé*, but the tour was proving more expensive than expected and the box office was not strong enough to merit trying them.

50 Quoted in J.L. Styan, *The Shakespeare Revolution* (Cambridge: Cambridge University Press, 1983), 84.

51 Quoted in Kennedy, *Granville Barker and the Dream of Theatre*, 126. Rothenstein changed his name during the First World War to Rutherston.

52 Quoted in Arthur Scott Craven, 'Modern Scenic Art', in *The Stage Year Book 1914* (London: The Stage, 1914), 20.

53 Introduction to *The Players' Shakespeare*, 50.

54 The Craig acknowledgement comes in a letter to the *Daily Mail*, 26 September 1912, in *Granville Barker and His Correspondents*, 527–8. The quotation comes from a letter to *Play Pictorial*, November 1912, ibid., 531–2.

55 *Harper's Weekly*, 30 January 1915, 115.

56 Letter to the *Daily Mail*, 26 September 1912, in *Granville Barker and His Correspondents*, 528.

57 Cathleen Nesbitt, *A Little Love and Good Company* (London: Faber & Faber, 1975), 65.

58 Letter to Harcourt Williams, quoted in his book *Four Years at the Old Vic* (London: Putnam, 1935), 43.

59 'On Translating Plays', 75.

60 'Hints on Rehearsing a Play', in *Granville Barker on Theatre*, 91.

61 Introduction to *The Players' Shakespeare*, 53.

62 Barker, *The Exemplary Theatre*, 43.

63 Ibid., 17.

64 'Repertory Theatres', in *Granville Barker on Theatre*, 6.

65 Ibid., 6–7.

66 'Hints on Rehearsing a Play', 91.

67 Barker, *The Exemplary Theatre*, 45.

68 Ibid., 45–6.

69 Ibid., 46.

70 Ibid., 47.

71 'Hints on Rehearsing a Play', 90.

72 Barker, *The Exemplary Theatre*, 43.

73 'Hints on Rehearsing a Play,' 90.

74 Ibid., 15.

75 Barker, *The Exemplary Theatre*, 41.

76 Ibid., 42.

77 'Notes on Rehearsing a Play', 16.

78 Ibid., 8.

79 Ibid., 17.

80 'Hints on Rehearsing a Play,' 87.

81 'Notes on Rehearsing a Play', 17–8.

82 Letter to Harcourt Williams, 15 June 1934, quoted in C.B. Purdom, *Harley Granville Barker* (London: Barrie & Rockliff, 1955), 242–3; emphasis in original.

83 *From the Wings* (London: W. Collins Sons & Co., 1922) by 'The Stage Cat', ed. Elisabeth Fagan, 163.

84 Lewis Casson, 'Harley Granville-Barker', in *The Dictionary of National Biography, 1941–1950* (Oxford: Oxford University Press, 1959). He became Granville-Barker after his second marriage, in 1918. For discussion of the hyphen, see Postscript in *Granville Barker on Theatre*.

85 Williams, *Old Vic Saga*, 163.

86 Lewis Casson, Foreword to Purdom, *Harley Granville Barker*, vii.

87 Quoted in Russell Thorndike, *Sybil Thorndike* (London: Rockliff, 1950), 230. A critical article, 'Mr Granville Barker's gramophones', credited to an anonymous actor claiming to be a member of Barker's *The Winter's Tale* cast, appeared in 1913 (*New Age*, 9 January). It said: 'The actor for Mr Barker is nothing more than a gramophone record made during rehearsals by Mr Barker himself.' The author has never been identified.

88 Richard Eyre, *Talking Theatre: Interviews with Theatre People* (London: Nick Hern Books, 2009), 4.

89 P.G. Konody, *Observer*, 29 September 1912.

90 P.P. Howe, *Dramatic Portraits* (New York: H. Kennerley, 1913), 186. Howe's description (197) of Barker's dramaturgical method could also stand for his directorial method: 'This building of a play cell by living cell, as it were, goes a

good way to achieve a living organism, and it is the fact that Mr Barker's plays have extraordinary life.'

91 Quoted in Norman Marshall, *The Producer and the Play* (London: Macdonald, 1962), 281.

92 Richard Eyre, Foreword to Barker's *Prefaces to Shakespeare* (London: Nick Hern Books, 1993), x.

93 *Love's Labour's Lost*, in *Prefaces to Shakespeare*, 1.

94 See, for example, *Shakespeare, Theory and Performance*, ed. James C. Bulman (London: Routledge, 1995).

95 'The Heritage of the Actor', 68.

96 *A National Theatre*, 17–18. In Barker's scheme, the most important person is the Director, what would now be called the Artistic Director, and s/he is not concerned with directing. This would be undertaken by directors brought in for the purpose, and the Literary Manager, another role pioneered by Barker, wields more institutional power than these directors.

97 'Notes on Rehearsing a Play', 17.

Chapter 6

1 *A Midsummer Night's Dream* opened on 6 February 1914 and followed Barker's production of *The Winter's Tale* in September 1912 and *Twelfth Night* in November 1912.

2 An Ordinary Playgoer, 'Gilt Faces: The Pit and Shakespeare Lovers', *Daily Mail*, 10 February 1914.

3 'The Theatre: "A Midsummer Night's Dream" at the Savoy', *The People*, 8 February 1914.

4 '"A Midsummer Night's Dream" at the Savoy', *The Athenaeum*, 14 February 1914.

5 J.T. Grein, 'At the Sign of the "Rose": Granville Barker Produces "A Midsummer Night's Dream" at the Savoy', *Financial News*, 7 February 1914.

6 A.B. Walkley, '"A Midsummer Night's Dream": Mr Barker's Production', *The Times*, 7 February 1914.

7 Lewis Casson provides a detailed account of Barker's approach to rehearsals at the Court Theatre in Anthony Jackson, 'Harley Granville Barker as Director at the Royal Court Theatre, 1904–1907', *Theatre Research* 12, no. 2 (1972): 132–3.

8 H. Granville Barker, 'Hints on Rehearsing a Play', unpublished article, Harley Granville Barker Collection, Victoria and Albert Archive, London (no date), 12.

9 Archibald Henderson, *George Bernard Shaw: His Life and Works* (London: Hurst and Blackett, 1911), 368.

10 Elizabeth Robins, *Votes for Women!* (London: Mills and Boon, 1909), 51.

11 E.A.B., '"Votes for Women!" A Suffragette Tract. Trafalgar Square on the Stage', *London Daily News*, 10 April 1907.

12 '"Votes for Women!" A Dramatic Tract in Three Acts', *The Times*, 10 April 1907.

13 E.A.B., 'Votes for Women!'

14 Kennedy, *Granville Barker and the Dream of Theatre*, 59.

15 Christine Dymkowski gives the example of Henry Irving's *Romeo and Juliet*, where he removed scenes that established the Capulet–Montague feud and important crowd scenes in order to centralize the two titular characters. Dymkowski, *Harley Granville Barker: A Preface to Modern Shakespeare* (London and Toronto: Associated University Press, 1986), 20.

16 As part of his Court Theatre seasons, Barker staged *Hippolytus* (1904), *The Trojan Women* (1905), *Electra* (1906) and *Hippolytus*, again (also 1906). He then staged *Medea* in 1907 at the Savoy Theatre, *Iphigenia in Tauris* at the Kingsway in 1912, and then *Iphigenia* and *The Trojan Women* in the United States in 1915.

17 Noel K. Thomas, 'Harley Granville-Barker and the Greek Drama', *Educational Theatre Journal* 7, no. 4 (December 1955): 294. The notable exception is Kennedy's *Granville Barker and the Dream of Theatre*, which includes detailed discussion of Barker's work with Attic tragedy. See also Niall W. Slater, 'Touring the Ivies with Iphigenia', *Comparative Drama* 44, no. 4 (Winter 2010): 441–55, and '"The Greatest Anti-War Poem Imaginable": Granville Barker's Trojan Women in America', *Illinois Classical Studies* 40, no. 2 (Fall 2015): 347–71.

18 H. Granville Barker, 'On Translating Greek Tragedy', in *Essays in Honour of Gilbert Murray*, ed. J.A.K. Thomson (London: George Allen & Unwin, 1936), 243.

19 H. Granville Barker, Handwritten programme note for William Poel's production of *The Bacchae* at the Court Theatre in November 1908, Harley Granville-Barker Collection, Harry Ransom Center, University of Texas at Austin, n.p.

20 Dennis Kennedy, 'The New Drama and the New Audience', in *The Edwardian Theatre: Essays on Performance and the Stage*, eds Michael R. Booth and Joel H. Kaplan (Cambridge: Cambridge University Press, 1996), 132.

21 Programme of the Provisional Committee for the New Century Theatre, cit. James Woodfield, *English Theatre in Transition, 1881–1914* (London and Sydney: Croom Helm, 1984), 56.

22 Philippa Burt, 'Granville Barker's Ensemble as a Model of Fabian Theatre', *New Theatre Quarterly* 28, no. 4 (November 2012): 307–24.

23 Stanley Jones [Leonard Merrick], *The Actor and His Art: Some Considerations on the Present State of the Stage* (London: Downey and Company, 1899), 20.

24 George Moore, *Impressions and Opinions* (London: David Nutt, 1913), 175.

25 For a detailed account of common rehearsal practices throughout the Victorian period, see Michael R. Booth, *Theatre in the Victorian Age* (Cambridge: Cambridge University Press, 1991), 104–9.

26 Madeline Bingham, *Henry Irving and the Victorian Theatre* (London: George Allen & Unwin, 1978), 159.

27 Irving cit. Russell Jackson, 'Henry Irving', in *The Routledge Companion to Director's Shakespeare*, ed. John Russell Brown (London and New York: Routledge, 2008), 175.

28 Michael Baker, *The Rise of the Victorian Actor* (London: Rowman & Littlefield, 1978), 30.

29 Barker, *The Exemplary Theatre*, 223.

30 Max Beerbohm, *Around Theatres* (New York: Greenwood Press, [1924] 1968), 159.

31 George Bernard Shaw, *Our Theatre in the Nineties*, vol. 2 (London: Constable and Company, 1932), 198.

32 Christopher Innes, *Edward Gordon Craig: A Vision of Theatre* (London and New York: Routledge, 2004), 12.

33 Booth, *Theatre in the Victorian Age*, 124.

34 Nesbitt, *A Little Love and Good Company*, 59.

35 Moore, *Impressions and Opinions*, 175; original emphasis.

36 Beerbohm, *Around Theatres*, 403–4.

37 Desmond MacCarthy, *The Court Theatre, 1904–1907* (London: A. H. Bullen, 1907), 7.

38 '"Bad Drama as Bad as Typhoid" – Granville Barker', *New York Times*, 31 January 1915.

39 Barker, *The Exemplary Theatre*, 121.

40 Ibid., 182.

41 Edith Wynne Matthison cited in Harley Granville Barker and John Eugene Vedrenne, *Dinner in Honour of H. Granville Barker and J. E. Vedrenne, 7 July 1907, Criterion Restaurant, London*, Unpublished Programme, British Library, London, 20.

42 Lillah McCarthy, *Myself and My Friends* (London: Thornton Butterworth, 1934), 90.

43 See, for example, 'Granville Barker Talks on Acting', *New York Times*, 20 March 1915; H. Granville Barker, 'At the Moscow Art Theatre', *The Seven Arts* 2 (October 1917): 659–61; Barker, 'Notes on Rehearsing a Play', *Drama* 1, no. 1 (July 1919): 2–5; Barker, *The Exemplary Theatre*, 230.

44 Barker, 'At the Moscow Art Theatre', 660.

45 Ibid., 661.

46 Ibid., 659.

47 W.A. Darlington, cit. Kennedy, *Granville Barker and the Dream of Theatre*, 134.

48 A.B. Walkley, 'Post-Impressionist Shakespeare', *The Times*, 23 September 1912.

49 Kennedy, *Granville Barker and the Dream of Theatre*, 129.

50 Nesbitt, *A Little Love and Good Company*, 65. Barker's insistence on a swift delivery has strong similarities with the 'Jessner speed' which Leopold Jessner encouraged his actors to adopt. See p. 79, 110.

51 H. Granville Barker, *Prefaces to Shakespeare: A Midsummer Night's Dream, The Winter's Tale, and Twelfth Night* (London: Nick Hern Books, [1914] 2009), 14–15.

52 Barker cit. Nesbitt, *A Little Love and Good Company*, 65.

53 Barker, *Prefaces to Shakespeare*, 60.

54 Kennedy, *Granville Barker and the Dream of Theatre*, 150–1.

55 Nesbitt, *A Little Love and Good Company*, 61.

56 Barker cit. ibid, 62.

57 Dymkowski, *Harley Granville Barker*, 56–7.

58 *A Midsummer Night's Dream*, Stage Manager's Book, Harley Granville-Barker Collection, Harry Ransom Center, University of Texas at Austin, n.p.

59 These positions were reproduced carefully in the above prompt book.

60 John Palmer cit. Dymkowski, *Harley Granville Barker*, 58.

61 *A Midsummer Night's Dream*, Stage Manager's Book, n.p.

62 For a detailed discussion of Reinhardt's supposed influence on Barker, see Nicholas John Dekker, 'The Modern Catalyst: German Influences on the British Stage, 1890–1918' (Unpublished PhD Thesis, Ohio State University, 2007), 87–138.

63 'Post-Impressionism on the Stage. Mr Granville Barker's Latest', *Daily Express*, 16 November 1912.

64 J.T. Grein, 'The Winter's Tale', *The Sunday Times*, 22 September 1912.

65 A.B. Walkley, 'The Winter's Tale', *The Times*, 23 September 1912.

66 'Shakespeare and Mr Barker's Fairies', *The People*, 8 February 1914.

67 Dekker, *The Modern Catalyst*, 121.

68 Dymkowski, *Harley Granville Barker*, 58.

69 *A Midsummer Night's Dream*, Stage Manager's Book, n.p.

70 Ibid.

71 'A Glimpse of Mr Barker from Behind the Scenes', *New York Times*, 21 February 1915.

72 Nesbitt, *A Little Love and Good Company*, 62; original emphasis.

73 See Barker, *Prefaces to Shakespeare*, 55–6; Dymkowski, *Harley Granville Barker*, 60–5; Christopher McCullough, 'Harley Granville Barker', in *The Routledge Companion to Director's Shakespeare*, 105–22.

74 Barker, *Prefaces to Shakespeare*, 56.

75 Ibid., 67.

76 Kennedy, *Granville Barker and the Dream of Theatre*, 160.

77 Desmond MacCarthy, 'A Midsummer Night's Dream', *New Statesman*, 21 February 1914.

78   Walkley, 'A Midsummer Night's Dream'.

79   Dymkowski, *Harley Granville Barker*, 74.

80   Purdom, *Harley Granville Barker*, 170.

81   Barker, 'On Translating Greek Tragedy', 240.

82   Nearly all of the national and regional newspapers reporting on the productions centred their attention on the size of the audience. See, for example, 'Greek Play Delights a Big Audience at Harvard Stadium', *Boston Post*, 19 May 1915; 'Euripides' Work at the Stadium. "The Trojan Women" Effectively Produced – Large Audience Enjoys Play', *Boston Herald*, 20 May 1915; 'Lewisohn Stadium, Modelled on the Coliseum, is Opened with Greek Play', *The Sun*, 30 May 1915.

83   'At the Stadium. "Iphigenia in Tauris" Acted by Granville Barker's Players', *Boston Evening Transcript*, 19 May 1915.

84   *Iphigenia in Tauris*, Chorus Promptbook, Harley Granville-Barker Collection, Harry Ransom Center, University of Texas at Austin, 9.

85   Ibid., 19.

86   Ibid., 78.

87   Innes, *Edward Gordon Craig*, 63.

88   Barker is included on Shaw's 1902 list of subscribers, which is held at Eton College Library, Berkshire.

89   Barker in *The Daily Mail*, 26 September 1912.

90   Kennedy, *Granville Barker and the Dream of Theatre*, 121.

91   *Iphigenia,* Chorus Promptbook, 65.

92   Kennedy, *Granville Barker and the Dream of Theatre*, 185.

BIBLIOGRAPHY

General

Banham, Martin, ed. *The Cambridge Guide to World Theatre*. Cambridge: Cambridge University Press, 1988.

Beerbohm, Max. *Around Theatres*. New York: Greenwood Press, [1924]1968.

Boenisch, Peter M. *Directing Scenes and Senses: The Thinking of Regie*. Manchester: Manchester University Press, 2015.

Brown, John Russell, ed. *The Routledge Companion to Director's Shakespeare*. London: Routledge, 2008.

Chambers, Colin, ed. *Continuum Companion to Twentieth-Century Theatre*. London: Continuum International Publishing, 2006.

Ihering, Herbert. *Von Reinhardt bis Brecht*. Edited by Rolf Badenhausen. Reinbek bei Hamburg: Rowohlt, 1967.

Kennedy, Dennis, ed. *The Oxford Enyclopedia of Theatre and Performance*. 2 vols. Oxford: Oxford University Press, 2003.

Patterson, Michael. *The Revolution in German Theatre 1900–1933*. London: Routledge, 1981.

Peter, John. V*ladimir's Carrot: Modern Drama and the Modern Imagination*. London: Andre Deutsch, 1987.

Roselt, Jens, ed. *Regie im Theater. Geschichte – Theorie – Praxis*. Berlin: Alexander, 2015.

Rühle, Günther. *Theater für die Republik im Spiegel der Kritik*. 2nd edn. Frankfurt: S. Fischer, 1988.

Rühle, Günther. *Theater in Deutschland 1887–1945*. Frankfurt am Main: Fischer, 2007.

Rühle, Günther. *Theater in unserer Zeit*. Frankfurt: Suhrkamp, 1976.

Rühle, Jürgen. *Theater und Revolution*. Munich: Deutscher Taschenbuch Verlag, 1963.

Shepherd, Simon. *Direction: Readings in Theatre Practice*. Basingstoke: Palgrave Macmillan, 2012.

Styan, J.L. *The Shakespeare Revolution*. Cambridge: Cambridge University Press, 1983.

Max Reinhardt

Adler, Gusti. *Max Reinhardt*. Salzburg: Festungsverlag, 1964.

Epstein, Max. *Max Reinhardt*. Berlin: Winckelmann Söhne, 1918.

Fetting, Hugo, ed. *Max Reinhardt Schriften*. Berlin: Henschel, 1974.

Fiedler, L.M. *Max Reinhardt in Selbstzeugnissen und Bilddokumenten*. Reinbek bei
    Hamburg: Rowohlt, 1975.
Fuhrich, Edda, and Gisela Prossnitz, eds. *Max Reinhardt in Europa*. Salzburg: Otto
    Müller, 1973.
Fuhrich, Edda, and Gisela Prossnitz, eds. *Max Reinhardt: The Magician's Dreams*.
    Salzburg: Residenz, 1993.
Hadamowsky, Franz. *Reinhardt und Salzburg*. Salzburg: Residenzverlag, 1963.
Jacobs, Margaret, and John Warren, eds. *Max Reinhardt: The Oxford Symposium*.
    Oxford: Oxford Polytechnic, 1986.
Jacobsohn, Siegfried. *Max Reinhardt*. Berlin: E. Reiss, 1921.
Janson, Stefan. *Hugo von Hofmannsthals* Jedermann *in der Regiebearbeitung
    durch Max Reinhardt*. Frankfurt: Lang, 1978.
Jaron, Norbert, et al., eds. *Berlin: Theater der Jahrhundertwende. Bühnengeschichte
    der Reichshauptstadt im Spiegel der Kritik (1889–1914)*. Tübingen: Max
    Niemeyer, 1986.
Kahane, Arthur. *Tagebuch eines Dramaturgen*. Berlin: Bruno Cassirer, 1928.
Leisler, Edda, and Gisela Prossnitz, eds. *Jedermann: Das Spiel vom Sterben des
    Reichen Mannes und Max Reinhardts Inszenierungen. Texte, Dokumente,
    Bilder*. Frankfurt: Suhrkamp, 1973.
Luckhurst, Mary. *Dramaturgy: A Revolution in Theatre*. Cambridge: Cambridge
    University Press, 2006.
Marx, Peter W. *Max Reinhardt. Vom bürgerlichen Theater zur metropolitanen
    Kultur*. Tübingen: Francke, 2006.
Reinhardt, Gottfried. *The Genius: A Memoir of Max Reinhardt by His Son*. New
    York: Knopf, 1979.
Sayler, Oliver M., ed. *Max Reinhardt and His Theatre*. New York: Brentano, 1924.
Stern, Ernst. *Bühnenbildner bei Max Reinhardt*. Berlin: Henschel, 1955.
Styan, J.L. *Max Reinhardt*. Cambridge: Cambridge University Press, 1982.

Leopold Jessner

Bluth, Karl Theodor. *Leopold Jessner*. Berlin: Oesterheld & Co, 1928.
Heilmann, Matthias. *Leopold Jessner – Intendant der Republik: Der Weg eines
    deutsch-jüdischen Regisseurs aus Ostpreußen*. Tübingen: Max Niemeyer, 2005.
Jessner, Leopold. *Schriften. Theater der Zwanziger Jahre*. Edited by Hugo Fetting.
    Berlin: Henschel, 1979.
Marx, Peter W. 'Challenging the Ghosts: Leopold Jessner's *Hamlet*'. *Theatre
    Research International* 30, no. 1 (2005): 72–87.
Naso, Eckart von. *Ich liebe das Leben. Erinnerungen aus fünf Jahrzehnten*.
    Hamburg: Wolfgang Grüger, 1953.
Ziege, Felix, ed. *Leopold Jeßner und das Zeit-Theater*. Berlin: Eigenbrödler Verlag,
    1928.

Harley Granville Barker

Barker, Harley Granville. 'At the Moscow Art Theatre'. *The Seven Arts* 2 (October
    1917): 659–61.

Barker, Harley Granville. *The Exemplary Theatre*. London: Chatto and Windus, 1922.

Barker, Harley Granville. 'Notes on Rehearsing a Play'. *Drama* 1, no. 1 (July 1919): 2–5.

Barker, Harley Granville. 'On Translating Greek Tragedy'. In *Essays in Honour of Gilbert Murray*, edited by J.A.K. Thomson, 237–47. London: George Allen & Unwin, 1936.

Barker, Harley Granville. *Prefaces to Shakespeare*, vols 1–6. London: B. T. Batsford, 1963–74; 2 vols, Princeton: Princeton University Press, 1946–7.

Burt, Philippa. 'Granville Barker's Ensemble as a Model of Fabian Theatre'. *New Theatre Quarterly* 28, no. 4 (November 2012): 307–24.

Chambers, Colin, and Richard Nelson, eds. *Granville Barker on Theatre*. London: Bloomsbury Methuen Drama, 2017.

Dymkowski, Christine. *Harley Granville Barker: A Preface to Modern Shakespeare*. Washington: Associated University Presses, 1986.

Jackson, Anthony. 'Harley Granville Barker as Director at the Royal Court Theatre, 1904–1907'. *Theatre Research* 12, no. 2 (1972): 126–38.

Kennedy, Dennis. *Granville Barker and the Dream of Theatre*. Cambridge: Cambridge University Press, 1985.

Kennedy, Dennis. 'The New Drama and the New Audience'. In *The Edwardian Theatre: Essays on Performance and the Stage*, edited by Michael R. Booth and Joel H. Kaplan, 130–47. Cambridge: Cambridge University Press, 1996.

MacCarthy, Desmond. *The Court Theatre, 1904–1907*. London: A. H. Bullen, 1907.

McCarthy, Lillah. *Myself and My Friends*. London: Thornton Butterworth, 1934.

Mazer, Cary M. 'H. Granville Barker'. In *Great Shakespeareans, Vol.15: Poel, Granville Barker, Guthrie, Wanamaker*, edited by Cary M. Mazer. London: Bloomsbury, 2013.

Moore, George. *Impressions and Opinions*. London: David Nutt, 1913.

Morgan, Margery M. *A Drama of Political Man*. London: Sidgwick & Jackson, 1961.

Nesbitt, Cathleen. *A Little Love and Good Company*. London: Faber & Faber, 1975.

Purdom, Charles B. *Harley Granville Barker: Man of Theatre, Dramatist and Scholar*. London: Rockliff, 1955.

Salmon, Eric, ed. *Granville Barker and His Correspondents*. Detroit: Wayne State University Press, 1986.

Salmon, Eric. *Granville Barker: A Secret Life*. London: Heinemann Educational Books, 1983.

INDEX

Note: Page numbers in *italics* refer to illustrations and the letter 'n' followed by locators denote note numbers.